SKIFFY AND MIMESIS

Borgo Press Books by DAMIEN BRODERICK

Chained to the Alien: The Best of ASFR: Australian SF Review (Second Series) [Editor]
Climbing Mount Implausible: The Evolution of a Science Fiction Writer
Ferocious Minds: Polymathy and the New Enlightenment
I'm Dying Here (with Rory Barnes)
Skiffy and Mimesis: More Best of ASFR: Australian SF Review (Second Series) [Editor]
Unleashing the Strange: Twenty-First Century Science Fiction Literature
Warriors of the Tao [Editor with Van Ikin]
Wild Science
x, y, z, t: Dimensions of Science Fiction

SKIFFY AND MIMESIS

MORE BEST OF *ASFR*, *AUSTRALIAN SF REVIEW* (SECOND SERIES)

Edited by

Damien Broderick

THE BORGO PRESS

An Imprint of Wildside Press LLC

MMX

*I.O. Evans Studies In the Philosophy
and Criticism of Literature*
ISSN 0271-9061

Number Fifty-Three

Copyright © 2010 by Damien Broderick
[p. 9-10 shall be regarded as an extension of this copyright page]

All rights reserved.
No part of this book may be reproduced in any form without the expressed written consent of the publisher.

www.wildsidebooks.com

FIRST EDITION

CONTENTS

Acknowledgments   10
Introduction, by Damien Broderick   11

Countries of the Mind

The Planet on the Table, by Jenny Blackford   18
How Cordwainer Smith Came Back from Nothing-at-All!
   by Norman Talbot   22
Always Coming Home, by Yvonne Rousseau   33
Mythago Wood, by Jenny Blackford   37

Philip K. Dick Begins

The Collected Stories of Philip K. Dick, Vols. 1 and 2, by
   Michael J. Tolley   41

Serious Changes

Unwinding the Watchmen, by Zoran Bekric   84
Everything Not Forbidden Is Compulsory, by Janeen Webb   109
Occasional Thoughts on Frank Herbert's *Dune* Sequence,
   by Douglas Barbour   118

The Ambiguities of Utopia

Three Utopias, by Yvonne Rousseau   128
Reactionary Utopias, by Gregory Benford   143
Response by John Foyster   154

Guilt and the Unimaginative UnAmerican Feminist, by
    Yvonne Rousseau   160
The Ambiguities of Utopia, by Norman Talbot   171
Afterword 2010, by Gregory Benford   192

Skiffy and Mimesis

The Role of the Science Fiction Reader: Cyberpunk and the
    Kids in Costume, by John Foyster   194
Sci-Fi and Psi-Fi: How Point of View Influences Reviewing,
    by George Turner   202
Response by Lucius Shepard   209
Desperately Seeking Lucius, by John Foyster   215
Skiffy and Mimesis; or, Critics in Costume, by Russell
    Blackford   219
Such Heat in the Kitchen! by George Turner   232
Letter from George Turner   237
Letter from Lucius Shepard   239
A Comment from John Foyster   244
Letter from Peter Nicholls   249
An Editorial Comment from Russell Blackford   253
Letter from Douglas Barbour   255

Directions

New Directions in Science Fiction, by George Turner   258

Selected Bibliography   267
About the Authors   270
Index   273

For Lord Pringle,

Paul DiFi,

And the Chums
at fictionmags,

a fine watering hole
for us pulpsters

ACKNOWLEDGMENTS

These essays were previously published in the following issues of *Australian SF Review (Second Series)*:

"The Planet on the Table," by Jenny Blackford, issue 12, January 1988, 52-4. Copyright © 1988, 2010 by Jenny Blackford.
"How Cordwainer Smith Came Back from Nothing-at-All!" by Norman Talbot, issue 21, Spring 1989, 22-6. Copyright © 1989, 2010 by the estate of Norman Talbot.
"Always Coming Home," by Yvonne Rousseau, issue 6, January 1987, 50-4. Copyright © 1987, 2010 by Yvonne Rousseau.
"Mythago Wood," by Jenny Blackford issue 1, March 1986, 34-6. Copyright © 1986, 2010 by Jenny Blackford.
"*The Collected Stories of Philip K. Dick*, Vols. 1 and 2," by Michael J. Tolley, issue 16, September 1988, 24-30 and issue 24, Winter 1990, 6-17. Copyright © 1988, 1990, 2010 by Michael J. Tolley.
"Unwinding the Watchmen," by Zoran Bekric, issue 26, Summer 1991, 12-22. Copyright © 1991, 2010 by Zoran Bekric.
"Everything Not Forbidden Is Compulsory," by Janeen Webb, issue 16, September 1988, 20. Copyright © 1988, 2010 by Janeen Webb.
"Occasional Thoughts on Frank Herbert's *Dune* Sequence," by Douglas Barbour, issue 17/18, November 1988/January 1989, 10-13. Copyright © 1988, 2010 by Douglas Barbour.
"Austin Tappan Wright, Catherine Helen Spence," by Yvonne Rousseau, issue 26, Summer 1991, 38-44. Copyright © 1991, 2010 by Yvonne Rousseau.
"Reactionary Utopias," by Gregory Benford, issue 14, May 1988, 11-20. Copyright © 1986, 2010 by Gregory Benford.
Response by John Foyster, issue 16, September 1988, 5-6. Copyright © 1988, 1989, 2010 by the estate of John Foyster.

"Guilt and the Unimaginative UnAmerican Feminist," by Yvonne Rousseau, issue 16, September 1988, 7-10, 19. Copyright © 1988, 2010 by Yvonne Rousseau.

"The Ambiguities of Utopia," by Norman Talbot, issue 16, September 1988, 11-18. Copyright © 1988, 2010 by Norman Talbot.

Afterword, Copyright © 2010 by Gregory Benford.

"The Role of the Science Fiction Reader: Cyberpunk and the Kids in Costume," by John Foyster, issue 20, June 1989, 12-14. Copyright © 1989, 2010 by the estate of John Foyster.

"Sci-Fi and Psi-Fi: How Point of View Influences Reviewing," by George Turner, issue 20, June 1989, 15-17. Copyright © 1989, 2010 by the estate of George Turner.

Response by Lucius Shepard, issue 21, Spring 1989, 27-9. Copyright © 1989, 2010 by Lucius Shepard.

"Desperately Seeking Lucius," by John Foyster, issue 21, Spring 1989, 29-30. Copyright © 1989, 2010 by the estate of John Foyster.

"Skiffy and Mimesis: Or Critics in Costume," by Russell Blackford, issue 22, Summer 1989, 26-30. Copyright © 1989, 2010 by Russell Blackford.

"Such Heat in the Kitchen!" by George Turner, issue 22, Summer 1989, 31-2. Copyright © 1989, 2010 by the estate of George Turner.

Response by George Turner, issue 23, Autumn 1990, 21. Copyright © 1990, 2010 by the estate of George Turner.

Response by Lucius Shepard, issue 23, Autumn 1990, 21-3. Copyright © 1990, 2010 by Lucius Shepard.

Response by John Foyster, issue 23, Autumn 1990, 23, 31-32. Copyright © 1990, 1989, 2010 by the estate of John Foyster.

Response by Peter Nicholls, issue 24, Winter 1990, 28-30, Copyright © 1990, 2010 by Peter Nicholls.

Response by Russell Blackford, issue 24, Winter 1990, 30-31. Copyright © 1990, 2010 by Russell Blackford.

Response by Douglas Barbour, issue 25, Spring 1990, 25-27. Copyright © 1990, 2010 by Douglas Barbour.

"New Directions in Science Fiction," by George Turner, issue 17/18, November 1988/January 1989, 6-9. Copyright © 1988, 2010 by the estate of George Turner.

INTRODUCTION

So what is "skiffy"? And—for those readers not drenched in literary theory—what is "mimesis"?

Skiffy is science fiction as seen through the eyes of its whimsical and sophisticated enthusiasts.

And *mimesis*? Well, it's a handy term for art that imitates or emulates the world we experience every day, the hard-knocks, nuanced world sometimes known as "reality."

§

Skiffy is shorthand, like the British "telly" for television, or the Australian "footy" for football. Don't for a moment think that this indicates supercilious mockery; it's a friendly insiders' term shared lightly by readers who know and love the pleasures that science fiction provides against our workaday world of endless global crises. Consider the gruesome twenty-first-century reality where (according to a 2006 news report) a biology teacher in a London sixth-form college reported that

> most of the next generation of medical and science students could well be creationists..."The vast majority of my students now believe in creationism," she said, "and these are thinking young people who are able and articulate and not at the dim end at all...it's a bit like the southern states of America." Many of them came from Muslim, Pentecostal or Baptist family backgrounds, she said, and were intending to become pharmacists, doctors, geneticists and neuroscientists. (Douglas Campbell, *The Guardian*)

An increasing proportion of kids born well after humans last visited the Moon believe that the lunar landings were a hoax. This is not the world of the radiant future many people expected in the 1940s or even the 1970s. It is a sci-fi world, in the sense that "sci-fi" indexes brainless, ill-considered, conspiracy-clotted blockbuster movies or comic books where science is not just indistinguishable from magic but actually *replaced* by magic, where ancient dogmas get a gaudy refit, where ever more spectacular explosions and car chases at the speed of light splatter any last vestige of disciplined imagination. In a future like this, maybe the best we can hope for is wry skiffy, the amused streetwise cousin of both sci-fi and traditional sf. It's the world of *Watchmen* and cyberpunk, of Philip K. Dick (examined at length in this book), Ursula Le Guin, Kim Stanley Robinson and Lucius Shepard.

How did this funny, silly word "skiffy" come about? Nearly two decades ago, *Australian Science Fiction Review* co-editor Russell Blackford explained:

> The expression "sci-fi" connotes gosh-wow futuristic heroics and space battles. It's used by people who know nothing about sf (that is, science fiction) and have only a reductive concept of the genre. To those of us who are serious about sf, it evidences ignorant dismissal. But it can also be used to distinguish from the rest of sf those works that really *are* full of space battles and gosh-wow futuristic heroics.
>
> By contrast, "skiffy" is a word used only by people who know almost *too much* about the genre and need to remind themselves and their equally sercon audiences that science fiction *is fun*.

"Sercon" means "serious and constructive," and is another whimsy that sf insiders use in an amused, self-mocking way. One of his *ASFR* co-editors, Janeen Webb, added:

> I happened to mention this lexical discussion to Melbourne's resident SF Encyclopedist, Peter Nicholls, who delighted me by faxing the following explanatory historical notes to my brand-new fax machine: "It was the now elderly Californian fan and literary agent, Forrest J. Ackerman (b. 1916), 1 believe, who coined the term 'sci-fi' as a shortening for 'science fiction.' The term was loathed by almost everyone within the field, but became popular with jour-

nalists and media people, first in the USA and now in the UK and Australia—to the point where it is now the term most commonly used.

The late Terry Carr, anthologist, publisher and fan, especially loathed the term, and along with others began to use it ironically, in a derogatory sense, to refer to that form of science fiction which is lurid, predictable and silly: pulp sf adventures, badly written, in short. The real stuff for Terry remained science fiction, the junk was sci-fi.

Terry's friend, the late Susan Wood, Canadian, feminist critic and fan, may have been the person who coined 'skiffy.' It was certainly she whom I first heard use it, c. 1978. She meant by it exactly what Carr meant by 'sci fi,' but she thought making it into one silly word allowed it to trip more readily from the tongue. 'Skiffy' means colorful, silly, junk sf.

I hope, gentle readers, that these contradictory clarifications are helpful. My own dislike for cute terminology inclines me towards the "dismissive" definition, but "skiffy" may well turn out to be a critical term in transition.

That didn't quite happen. There are university departments of Queer Theory but so far as I know not yet any of Skiffy Studies. Perhaps that's a point in its favor.

§

On to mimesis, the process that copies or restages reality. Of course, even people who don't regard themselves as cynics now admit that reality isn't as watertight as prosperous burghers and earthy peasants once supposed. The reality of experience is to some degree, maybe a large degree, a construct, a fabrication we collude in. This insight can go crazy, it's true; the rise of postmodern philosophy and art some decades ago often aroused suspicions that pomo thinkers imagined they could leap from a high window and float to the ground if only they chose, you know, to subvert the dominant paradigm. A parody, admittedly, but there was a notable evasion of grim reality in the rhetoric, at least, of much postmodern and poststructural discourse. That faddish moment is passing, but for a time there was at least one benefit to sf fans: critics were allowed to embrace science fiction's endless questioning of convention, of the hidebound, the dreary limits or smothering comforts of faithful mimesis.

In *Chained to the Alien: The Best of Australian Science Fiction Review (Second Series)*, I described the rise in the later 1980s of that splendidly cantankerous sf critical journal. *ASFR,* as it was known well beyond its native shores, became one of the hallmark magazines seriously yet goadingly investigating the links and contrasts of both skiffy and mimesis. I mentioned in my Introduction to that book, to which this is a companion rather than a sequel, that

> The only element scanted here is the vigorous cut and thrust of the magazine's extensive letters pages and its many shorter pieces and reviews. I hope to showcase some of these in a subsequent volume.

Here you will read a sampling of that cut and thrust, often surprisingly venomous. It is rare these days for a journal of ideas and art to present such vicious slashing at the foe (well, except in small poetry magazines, where it is often mandatory). Still, I haven't chosen these pieces for their scandal, but because I think they display the vigor and passion of science fiction writers and expert readers, something often lost in the *fin de siècle* languor and ingenuity of more traditional fare—and certainly absent from the meat-and-potatoes reviewing of most newspaper reviews of sf and fantasy, where it is taken for granted that these forms of imaginative creation are aimed at children or dullards who move their lips as they read. No such condescension here; the two books drawn from *ASFR (Second Series)* comprise some 180,000 word of smart conversation at the intersection of skiffy and mimesis, playful games with time, space and ruptured identify in a universe where trying to copy the real can leave you staring at the gaps in the void, or trying to clamber through them.

And where those parallel worlds meet—whether in a renovated, newly-observed quotidian, or a star-spangled galaxy—is, as Russell Blackford noted above, a carnival site made for *fun*. Away with solemnity! As that famous sf hero, Gully Foyle, cried as he remade reality in Alfred Bester's sparkling novel *The Stars My Destination* (1956): "Millions for nonsense, not one cent for entropy!"

§

As with *Chained to the Alien,* I thank Yvonne Rousseau and Jenny and Russell Blackford especially for help in locating and scanning certain articles from *ASFR* and aid in proofreading, and my contributors for permitting their work to be reprinted. Thanks to my wife Barbara Lamar, with heartfelt love, for her company, wit and endless help, to the School of Culture and Communication at the University of Melbourne where I am delighted to remain a Senior Fellow even at this planetary distance, and to Rob Reginald and John Betancourt at Borgo/Wildside for bringing these volumes of sf criticism to press.

—Damien Broderick

COUNTRIES OF THE MIND

THE PLANET ON THE TABLE

by Jenny Blackford

I have been faithful to thee, Samuel R. Delany, in my fashion. Long, long ago, in an *ASFR* meeting far, far away, I promised to review Delany's *The Complete Nebula Award-Winning Fiction*. The deadline slipped, and slipped, and slipped. And now, suddenly, I review Kim Stanley Robinson's *The Planet on the Table*. Why?

First, because the Delany collection is just too seductive. Whenever I pick it up to start the review, I start reading from wherever I open the book. In the timeless waking dream of reading Delany, reviewing is just not possible.

Second, I think I'm in love.

It all happened on a business trip to Singapore. My employer sent me there for a week in November to teach a network tuning course. How exciting! How elegant! you cry. How strangely unenjoyable even exotic and luxurious places can be without someone to share them with, I counter. Still, the experience wasn't wasted. I have now watched as in-house movies, huddled in my room with a glass of Laphroaig single malt whisky, *Back to the Future*, *Ferris Bueller's Day Off*, *Weird Science*, *Heartburn*, and *Sweet Liberty*. I know more about American culture, and in particular the sanitized version that the very polite, very repressed state of Singapore allowed, than I ever wanted to know.

But meanwhile, I fell in love. I bought the tape (no CD available yet) of Sting's new album, *Nothing Like the Sun*, after hearing it on the BBC World Service. Sighs of adoration. Call me a woman obsessed, if you will, but I think Sting is moving from wonderful to irresistible as he gets older. And I read *The Planet on the Table*. Love!

My sudden infatuation with—nay, captivation by—Kim Stanley Robinson rather surprised me. I had read *The Wild Shore* (aka The

Wild Snore) on the long, long flight from Melbourne to London. I had been so dismayed by the obviousness of the set-up for the old innocent-adolescent-learns-wisdom (losing his virginity and defeating a few evildoers in the process) story, that even the eventual, rather neat side-stepping of each expected cliché didn't redeem it. And reading *Icehenge*, excellent though I found it, was an intellectual, not an emotional, experience.

I can even pinpoint the exact time I fell in love. It was on the last page of "Ridge Running," one of those essentially American stories where friends who have drifted apart meet and have an Emotional Experience, preferably in the company of Nature. In this case, three old friends are hiking through snow. The story is only contingently sf. The Holy Fool figure in the story gains his specialness and sanctity from having had most of his brain re-grown after an accident; he is re-inventing language and (possibly) the world. Almost nothing happens in the story. The viewpoint character, less fit than the other, tires; the Holy Fool hallucinates; the strong silent man wants to push on. They squabble. Holy and Strong leave their friend to seek, questingly, for a mountain goat which was probably a collective hallucination. Eventually, they decide it has turned into an eagle. Return, reconciliation, food and (temperate) joy ensue.

The characterization is so clean and brave—the people so odd and real, no information given to the reader except through their speech and actions—and the message (if any) about man's relationship with the world and other people through language so subtle and intelligent—that I sat up in the bath, astonished.

Kim Stanley Robinson's introduction records a conversation with a statue of James Joyce. What a wank, I said to myself. But the first story was Good, the second Great, and the third was "Ridge Running," which I have just described. By now, I understood the significance of the conversation with Joyce. This book is only coincidentally, or contingently, sf. Its true antecedent is Joyce's *Dubliners*. The people, the language, the themes—we're talking High Literature here. And every story different!

We get morbid ethnic symbolic: in "Venice Drowned" a self-destructive sailor, who reluctantly takes rich Japanese scavengers to dive around the eponymous city, has a mysterious experience with an old woman in a half-drowned tower in a storm. "Mercurial" is a future interplanetary art-fraud murder mystery comedy with a charmingly amoral ending. "The Lucky Strike" is the most touching alternative time-stream story of all time, with a hero who is martyred for not bombing Hiroshima; it works as a profound and moving anti-war story with nothing predictable, no contrivance. KSR even gives us a re-entrant story of people acting in a Jacobean tragedy, who themselves are enacting an even stranger revenge tragedy. This story, "The Disguise," is one of your old-fashioned Barth-style intellectual and literary *tours de force*. It must be read twice; the suspicions gained in the first reading about the true identity of the villain, the Hieronomo, are confirmed in the second. Every sentence is carefully ambiguous. Besides that intellectual game, we have murder, sword-fights, genuine sf trappings AND an entire original Jacobean tragedy. What more could you ask for?

As in *Dubliners*, the most ambitious and most moving story is the last. I finished it in rather odd tears, in a complex emotional state. Now, I will confess that it isn't at all odd to see me teary over a book. One of my earliest memories is of running into the bathroom so my mother wouldn't see me crying at the bit where Robin Hood shoots the arrow out of the window from his deathbed, asking to be buried where the arrow lands. But this was complex emotion, not just the sorrow which is so easily induced by mere string-pulling in sooks like me.

The hero of this story, "Black Air," is Manuel, a multiply-uprooted black boy impressed into the Spanish Armada from his last peaceful refuge, a Franciscan monastery. Already devoted to Saint Anne, he is purified by the fire of a long and severe fever, in which he is attended by a rather odd Dominican friar, Lucien, who reads to him:

> I assume the appearance of a refiner's fire, purging the dross of forms outworn....Yet when thou hast been tried as by fire, the gold of thy soul shall be cleansed, and visible as fire.

When Manuel recovers, he gains an interesting reputation for passing unhurt through the battles, through all the horror and waste of the failed attack on England. The sailors and soldiers seek blessing through his touch, though most die anyway. He sees others' souls as flames, at death either ascending to heaven, or diving over the side of the ship and becoming porpoises. An Irishman, fighting on the side of the Spanish against the damned English, may have taken the middle road, flying around the ship like a gull, but the "intensely white" feathers suggest his possible angelhood. This Irishman, Laeghr, though an incorrigible skeptic, nonetheless teaches

Manuel the Celtic phrase that will, by a numinous coincidence, save his life.

Though not (I assume) an alchemical mystic himself, KSR treats the sacred with a respectful delicacy, profundity and wit. The crucial virtues of the story, though, are those of the whole collection: humanity, in the humane sense, and intelligence.

HOW CORDWAINER SMITH CAME BACK FROM NOTHING-AT-ALL!

by Norman Talbot

[This article reviews Cordwainer Smith's *Norstrilia* and *The Instrumentality of Mankind*, both released as VGSF Classics, Gollancz, London, 1988.]

I.

Gollancz is one of the extraordinary successes of British publishing, founded and conducted with enough insight and idealism to buoy up a traditionally cold and pragmatic industry. And along with Victor Gollancz's generous sponsorship of radical, social-justice and mystical works he established hard-cover, high-quality lines in detective fiction and science fiction in bold plain yellow dust-jackets.

In the late 1980s, Gollancz offered an exceptional series of paperback reprints called VGSF. Many are texts the convert will be glad to have, and some are perfectly adapted to lure new readers into the sticky web of sf. Most wonderful of all is the reissue of the Cordwainer Smith books, two of which I review here.

Now *Norstrilia* ought to have been very easy to review, especially in Australia. It is the first sf book in which Australia, in any form, is given a major boost, and this has been acknowledged in the name of that sacred Melbourne sf publisher Norstrilia Press. More important, it is the only full-length novel of one of the undeniably great writers of sf.

And yet this novel is not revered, and in many quarters it is scarcely known. One reason is that it has been shamefully abused by the tactics of magazine publication, for which it was cut in two and each part built up to resemble a novel by other (mildly ingenious) material: I bet someone out there has Pyramid or Sphere editions of those two pseudo-texts, *The Planet Buyer* (1964) and *The Underpeople* (1968). Now I resent those books because I love *Norstrilia*, but don't throw them out: set them beside the full novel, and learn a great deal about the writing of fiction.

II.

What is *Norstrilia* like? Well, Gary K. Wolfe says loftily, in the encyclopedia *Twentieth Century Science Fiction Writers*, that

> One wonders, at times, whether Smith's curious style and unusual way of structuring stories is due to his great sophistication or to his ingenuousness as a writer. *Norstrilia* does not stand up as well as do many of the short stories, partly because the narrative tends to ramble, partly because the style seems to grow self-conscious over such an extended narrative. (507)

Beware of critics who drop in that apologetic "tends to...seems to...." They ramble, or else they dodge self-consciously. Gary K. must have been thinking of some other kind of fiction, not Cordwainer's glorious pretence that his readers are on a dedicated quest for perpetual story built back from a harmonious (though ironic) closure. *Norstrilia* is a series of brilliant, self-contained fables laid end to end, linked by their traditional or understood story-line of how someone bought Old Earth (which nobody should have been able to do) and then actually went there (which would have to have been crutting well impossible)!

How is this story "understood," when you and I never knew a word of it before we started reading Cordwainer? By a technique both very ancient and very sophisticated, in which the expository lump of many thousands of years of history is evoked by frequent, cheerily casual references, but never given us. The cool and purposeful confidence of every page and paragraph reassures us that the exposition is there, there somewhere, so we cease to worry that we don't ourselves have it, or have any chance of finding it outside Cordwainer's neatly parqueted stories. We haven't just suspended our disbelief, we take it for granted that these stories are episodes in galactic history. As if to anecdotes of our global history, we respond not by suspense ("What's going to happen next?") but by receptive wisdom ("So that's how it happened. I see.").

That wouldn't work unless those episodes were themselves gripping, each in its own way as primordial and as elegantly self-conscious as tales in *Kalila and Dimna* or poems in the Alice books. Just as serious story-tellers have always felt free to be indifferent to mimesis in order to capture the expectation of their audience, so Cordwainer presents his stories as stories. *Norstrilia* begins with a one-sentence paragraph, followed by a dazzler of a summary:

> Story, place and time—these are the essentials.
>
> 1
>
> The story is simple. There was a boy who bought the planet Earth. We know that, to our cost. It only happened once, and we have taken pains that it will never happen again. He came to Earth, got what he wanted, and got away alive, in a series of very remarkable adventures. That's the story.

The place is Norstrilia ("What other place could it be?" Cordwainer asks cheerfully) and the time is far enough into the future to produce the place: Old North Australia. The outback traditions (including that odd version of the Protestant Work Ethic so characteristic of rural New South Wales that the Catholics have it too) are alive and well on an unimaginably distant planet settled from white Australian grazier stock. The society is fascinating, the economic system more convincing than most we've been sold in recent years in Australia, the life style slow and thoughtful, yet harnessed to a set of unavoidable survival criteria that are awesome in the extreme. This part of the book is funny, threatening and intriguing, and full of wisdom about outback wisdom, people and institutions. Any fool could tell an Australian why to read *Norstrilia*!

But it's not as simple as that. The author was not Australian, and did not usually write about Australians. Nor are Norstrilians really Australians, but a version of what tough, taciturn pastoral Australians might evolve into on that distant, hot harsh planet where all the sheep are sick—and gigantic, and worth a fortune each. Yes, those sheep exude the santaclara drug, also called stroon, and stroon means immortality! And Norstrilia is the only place where they produce it, so these post-Australians are the richest people in the galaxy.

That trend isn't obvious here and now, or here and yet.... Still, you can imagine a few farmers outback becoming mean and suspicious if they knew for certain that most people in the universe were after their property, their sheep, and the profits of their hard, hard labor. But you can also imagine the lean, parsimonious life they would insist on retaining and breeding into. They aren't like beer barons or stock-exchange sieurs or accountancy counts, you know. Would they drink the profits themselves? Would they let their kids get soft? Would they be nice to sweet-talking strangers? No, not a lot.

III.

Readers who know about the astonishing author who lived behind "Cordwainer Smith" can skip this section. He was Paul Myron Anthony Linebarger (1913-1966), and he didn't earn his crust as an sf writer. He was a translator, Asia-watcher, socio-political analyst and internationally acclaimed authority on psychological warfare, who ended up Professor of Asian Politics at Johns Hopkins University—and was Visiting Professor at the Australian National University, where he picked up his odd but perceptive version of Australians and projected them into his odder and wiser future. His parents were American, but his background was cosmopolitan, complex and complicated. He was born in China, and President Sun Yat Sen was his godfather—president because Linebarger senior, a banker, had bankrolled the revolution, as far as we can guess. He grew up there, and in Japan, Germany and France; at twenty he was fluent in six languages.

If a writer tells exciting stories, he may well have lived a profoundly dull life. Not Linebarger. In the US when World War II started, he was appointed to the War Planning Office in the Pentagon after Pearl Harbor. An early duty was to draw up specifications for an intelligence operative to be dropped into China, and he made them so stringent only he could qualify. Top priority, top secret.

Later, as Lt.-Col. Linebarger, he worked for the UN in the Korean War. A no longer top-secret but brilliant invention was a form of words that allowed Chinese soldiers to surrender without losing face: they could shout, in their language, about "honor" and "duty" in an order that sounded much like "I surrender" in American English.

He had nothing to do with the Viet Nam involvement, which he saw as a major mistake. Also he was able to see past war, through the death of racism, to reconciliation. His sf stories are not about humans like us but about what our distant descendants might become. The man was remarkable, his fiction remains irresistibly intriguing—and don't be surprised if the word "wisdom" pops up again in this article.

IV.

As to our future history, there's good news and there's bad news. Much of both is told in the brilliant short stories in *The Rediscovery of Man* (also a VGSF title) such as "The Dead Lady of Clown Town" or "Alpha Ralpha Boulevard." The more elusive and earlier stages are glimpsed too in *The Instrumentality of Mankind*, of which more later. Still, the finest of the historical climaxes is surely the revolt and the liberation of the Underpeople, and Rod McBan the hundred and fifty-first was the undoubted catalyst of that.

Norstrilia's defense capacity, known colloquially as "Mother Hitton's Littul Kittons," makes the rest of the universe powerless to dominate that gray, dry wilderness. The tax-structure on Norstrilia makes the population powerless to betray their "Commonwealth." The rigid controls on population prevent their degrading it. But Rod McBan is apparently non-telepathic, and thus a handicapped child, and so....

No, I won't tell you the astonishing story. Gollancz has actually produced a blurb that works, so I don't need to. Neatly selecting bits of his page 4, the back cover gives you something of the astringent, casual wit of Cordwainer's unique, lyrical prose style:

> What happens in the story?
> Read it.
> Who's there?
> It starts with Rod McBan. We know his family was distinguished. We know the poor kid was born to troubles. He was due to inherit the Station of Doom.
> And then he gets around.... He crosses all sorts of people. C'Mell, the most beautiful of the girlygirls. Jean-Jacques Vomact, whose family preceded the human race. The wild old man at Adaminaby. The trained spiders of Earthport. The Lord Jestecost whose name is a page in history. Tostig Amaral, about whom the less said the better. Ruth, in pursuit. C'Mell, in flight. The Lady Johanna, laughing.

He gets away. He got away. See, that's the story.
Now you don't have to read it.
Except for the details....

The details include entrancing fables of indignation, comedy, puzzle, pathos, heroism, faith, hypersophisticated manipulation and wild inventiveness. The fables are the very nature of Cordwainer's prose, the inventiveness is in the very furniture of his universe, and everything else comes from the elegant energy of the stories he tells.

V.

Rod is in danger when he is likely to be legally destroyed on Norstrilia, and worse danger when he has triumphed and bought Old Earth (in self-defense). He has to be surgically dismantled and sent secretly to Earth, through a literal galaxy of people who want to own him or kill him. Why, when he comes in to land at Earthport, escorted by the ravishing cat-woman C'Mell (lucky tom!), every other passenger on the shuttle from Mars is an exact double of him, all with papers to prove they are Roderick Frederick Ronald Arnold William McArthur McBan the hundred and fifty-first. Fortunately, *he* doesn't resemble himself at all.

C'Mell? Elsewhere there's another story about her but, as Rod's outback mind puts it, "She made every woman in Old North Australia look like a sack of lard." And she belongs to the Insurgency, a splendid secret movement to overthrow the government of Old Earth. Note, though, that many important members of that government, the Instrumentality, want to help with their overthrow!

Old Earth is a paradise for People: our kind, our stroon-preserved, unchallenged, spoiled, bored, boring descendants. People's slightest wishes are attended to by robots or human-shaped Underpeople like C'Mell (the C' stands for Cat). Underpeople are usually engineered from Apes, Bears, Bison and other cattle, Cats, Dogs, Eagles, Rats, Snakes, Turtles, Wolves (for the cops); they have no civil, political or social rights at all, so it's no wonder C' and D' Underpeople are the most common.

C'Mell explains the race-convention succinctly to Rod (disguised as a cat-acrobat) when they are about to enter a wonderful, thrilling, exotic market where tourist People can play at buying things:

> "We can walk through if we are not too big and not too small and not too dirty and not too smelly. And even if we are all right, we must walk straight through without looking directly at the real people and without touching anything in the market."
>
> "Suppose we do," asked Rod defiantly.
>
> "The robot police are there, with orders to kill on sight when they observe an infraction. Don't you realize, C'Rod," she sobbed at him, "that there are millions of us in tanks, way below in Downdeepdowndeep, ready to be born, to be trained, to be sent up here to serve man? We're not scarce at all, C'Rod, we're not scarce at all!" (185)

Cordwainer's hatred of racism, in whatever country, powers both the comedy and the puzzles of *Norstrilia*. The pathos comes from the human recognitions that must live in, or survive from, societies founded before "Mankind" became itself. Now "Mankind" has to re-become a larger itself. As the martyr D'Joan had put it in "The Dead Lady of Clown Town," "*Whoever looks human is human.*"

What is heroic in the stories comes from the common decency of Rod and many other Norstrilians, as well as from the vivid secret faith held by the Underpeople—their revolt is a Holy Insurgency, and Cordwainer writes like a Christian, though a daring one for the fifties. There is even heroism in the hypersophisticated manipulations I mentioned, those of Lord Jestecost and his allies (knowing or unknowing) in and controlled by the Instrumentality.

This is a book to read with delight and curiosity, spiced with gratitude. Enjoy the gimmicks and places Cordwainer offers you. Then it's a book to read with thoughtful wonder, to enjoy the enchantment of stories that hinge on supposed trivia like names, yet invite us to speculate on what we people are, what we are for, and where the constant, half-aware changes "taking place" in us are taking us. In comic and adventurous form we see how sleekly privilege metamorphoses into cruelty (both the half-unconscious and the deliberate kinds), and smugness into tyranny; how the Instrumentality is a beautiful thing whose time has gone; how the "ruthless benevolence" of utopian government, including the absolute prohibition of "news" and "public opinion," both insults us and frees us from the viciousness of our conventional cowardice.

VI.

The Instrumentality of Mankind is a collection of Cordwainer's stories, misleadingly blurbed as though they were all set in the origins and history of the Instrumentality. Nine of them are, including all the best, and it is good to have all his extant work in print—if this is all there is. Not that I have any evidence that more is lying around anywhere, but we can always hope!

The best of these stories are excellent. It is easy to underestimate the effectiveness of major works like "Think Blue, Count Two" or "Drunkboat" because they seem trivialized in a context of juvenilia like "War No. 81-Q*" and little games like "From Gustible's Planet." In a more positive mood, though, I admit that stories set in the same future history can work together and strengthen the alertness of that history's devotees.

Even the slimmest Instrumentality stories offer something. Yes, even "War No. 81-Q*" is refreshingly contemptuous of patriotism, though lacking in most narrative virtues. "From Gustible's Planet" is genuinely funny, and makes a very pretty interplanetary curtsey to Charles Lamb's fantasy, "A Dissertation upon Roast Pig."

Moving up a grade, "No, No, Not Rogov!" is utterly convincing about the scientific geniuses of the USSR, and the Cold War does not chill for a moment Cordwainer's reverence for Russian love, for Russian exploratory courage. How small our global fears and hatreds become when Cordwainer sets them beside the golden dance that interprets Mankind before the gaze of a thousand worlds, in what might have been called AD 13,582.

The two Vomact stories are pleasant, but "Mark Elf" has a touch of genius, and is not weighted down by the implications of its plot as is "The Queen of the Afternoon." The poignant simplicity of Carlotta Vom Acht's mind, dropped like a fragile Dresden ornament into wild future undergrowth, is exactly as elegant and as forlorn as that perfect machine for purposeless slaughter, the Manshonyagger.

The best-known story in this collection, "Drunkboat," is much like the bunch of non-Instrumentality stories of the terror and loneliness of space travel that end the collection, with a pretty fugue of allusions to Rimbaud's "*Le Bateau Ivre*" to decorate it. It's just pure bad luck that the films about that tedious manshonyagger *Rambo* have made it totally suicidal to call the hero Artyr Rambo!

What isn't a matter of luck is that the spectacularly simple story "The Colonel Came Back from Nothing-at-All," not published in the author's lifetime, begins with the same tableau as "Drunkboat," of the three doctors, Timofeyev, Grosbeak and Vomact, looking helplessly at the naked, flat-out figure of a man inexplicably cast from deep space. This story focuses on the unforgettable young healer from the "Post-Soviet Orthodox Eastern Quakers," Liana, whereas in "Drunkboat" soldiers called in by quasi-paranoid Lords of the Instrumentality shoot up the hospital. Which do you prefer, the lyricism of a hymn or the ironies of futile violence? Alas, so have Cordwainer's readers.

The star story of this collection must be "Think Blue, Count Two." All human crime is past, is even forgotten, but something goes wrong:

> Talatashar's hands were on her, pulling her out of her own sleeping-box.
> She tried to fight but he was remorseless as an engine. (102)

Oh no! The young and tender female hero has been caught by the warped, sadistic, increasingly insane male wielder of absolute power, watched by the helpless good guy tied up with emergency wire! This is in the deeps of space, with no one to appeal to for many years of travel! Think what our orthodox fictioneers would have done with a central scene like that! Ugh.

Well, Cordwainer evokes that sort of plotting quite beautifully. First the mad male gloats:

> "I'm going to do what I have to do. I'm going to do things to you that no one ever did in space before, and then I'm going to throw your body out the disposal door...And now you're going to be cut and burned and choked and brought back with medicines and cut and choked and hurt again, as long as your body can stand it. And when your body stops..." (105)

Nothing can dissuade him, and no one is there to stop him. The helpless girl asks, bewildered as well as afraid,

> "Do you hate me? Why do you want to hurt me? Do you hate girls?"

> "I don't hate girls," he blazed, "I hate *me*. Out here in space I found it out. You're not a person. Girls aren't people. They are soft and pretty and cute and cuddly and warm, but they have no feelings...They're something like robots. They have all the power in the world and none of the worry. Men have to obey, men have to beg, men have to suffer, because they are built to suffer and to be sorry and to obey. All a girl has to do is to smile her pretty smile or to cross her pretty legs, and the man gives up everything he has ever wanted and fought for, just to be her slave...Well, you're going to find out now. You will suffer and then you will die. But you won't die until you know how men feel about women." (106-7)

But this is Cordwainer Smith! That can't be the plot!

And it isn't. All we need do is look past the episode to the story's equipment, where Tiga-Belas and the technicians have prepared the girl Veesey-Koosey for the role of wakeable emergency crew in the 450-year trip. There we find the truth of the matter, dazzling yet lucid, expressed as a good old Cordwainer Smith miracle:

> Space sometimes commands strange tools to its uses—the screams of a beautiful child, the laminated brain of a long-dead mouse, the heart-broken weeping of a computer. Most space offers no respite, no relay, no rescue, no repair. All dangers must be anticipated; otherwise they become mortal. And the greatest of all hazards is the risk of man himself. (86)

Just as entering deep space is like encountering God—an indifferent (or at least incomprehensibly Nothing-at-All and preoccupied) God—so the equipment of human experience is ontologically both more powerful and less legible than we had thought. Veesey-Koosey is not only the perfect emergency crew for the job, without knowing it, but all human imaginations are equipped to respond to possibilities and emergencies in which "existence" can never even seem like a predicate.

Who rescues Veesey-Koosey? Read the story and find out. But I'll give you a clue: the star of *Marcia and the Moon Men* comes along later, and Talatashar challenges her with unreality:

"So you admit you're nothing?"

"I will if you want me to," said Marcia, "but this conversation doesn't make much sense to me. Where were you before you were here?"

"Here? You mean in this boat? I was on Earth," said Talatashar.

"Before you were in this universe, where were you?"

"I wasn't born, so I didn't exist."

"Well," said Marcia, "it's the same with me, only a little bit different. Before I existed, I didn't exist. When I exist, I'm here. I'm an echo out of Veesey's personality and I'm helping her to remember that she is a pretty young girl. I feel as real as you feel. So there!" (113)

Like the girl said, so there. Read Cordwainer Smith and loosen up your expectations about the universe!

ALWAYS COMING HOME

by Yvonne Rousseau

Ursula K. Le Guin, *Always Coming Home* (with composer Todd Barton, artist Margaret Chodos, geomancer George Hersh)

"I never did like smartass utopians. Always so much healthier and saner and sounder and fitter and kinder and tougher and wiser and righter than me and my family and friends." These words are spoken by the author of *Always Coming Home*, calling herself Pandora and grumbling at a member of a community she imagines existing many centuries in the future. To enable this community to be, Pandora has had to let loose on our world all the Promethean evils—"war, plague, famine, holocaust, and Fimbul winter"—combined with earthquakes and shifts along fault lines which have sunk half California, extending the Gulf of California into Arizona and Nevada. In this future, which Pandora accuses of being "utopian," much land is still poisoned, and every species has chromosomal damage, with a high proportion of human stillbirths and monstrous births, and two prevalent degenerative diseases unknown to our civilization. As a result, in the towns of *Always Coming Home*, along the thirty-mile Valley of the Na River (in a transfigured California, with new watercourses and an inland sea), there are "not too many" people. Underneath all the evils, there has lurked an unexpected gift: "some room, some time...A living room."

The future person that Pandora is grumbling at denies that the Valley society is utopia—and she also claims to "have no answers." But, utopia or not, the Valley would obviously define our society as a dystopia; we are categorized as people with our heads on backwards (why else would we have poisoned the world?), and the Valley describes what we call history—all the civilized centuries—as "when they lived outside the world": an aberration.

The Valley is a thought-experiment of the kind that, in 1976 (in "Is Gender Necessary?"), Le Guin described as "one of the essential functions of science fiction...reversals of an habitual way of thinking, metaphors for what our language has no words for as yet, experiments in imagination." She imagines a post-holocaust world where information continues to accumulate, "incredibly sophisticated and destructive weaponry" is being developed, and there is mining not only on Earth but also on the Moon and planets. However, the mining is done by robot extensions; the weaponry is devised in the "pursuit of research as a cognitive end in itself"; and the researchers are not human but cybernetic devices or beings, collectively referred to in the Valley as "the City of Mind." The City, which is engaged in "conscious, self-directed evolution," has become "several light-years larger than the solar system, and immortal."

Human communities worldwide have Exchanges (installed on request by City robots), which are computer terminals giving access to the City of Mind's "entire vast network"—including other Exchanges. The Valley has one Exchange, but could have had eight or nine, had it wanted them. Human beings can obtain from the City whatever information they ask for (whether it is recipes for yogurt or recipes for making armored tanks—the main difficulty is to frame a request that produces a limited amount of data). The City likewise requests information about aspects of human life inaccessible to robot or satellite observation—and it keeps in its Memory any texts it is offered (whereas Valley librarians destroy valuable books every year on the principle that "keeping grows, giving flows"). Valley dwellers are "not disposed to regard human existence either as information or communication," and they classify the City of Mind and the Exchanges themselves as "outside the world"—existing in the same mode as the Backward-Heads time which we call civilization, but which they call the City of Man.

I have described the opportunities the City of Mind offers because *Always Coming Home*'s thought-experiment depends on the Valley people's reasons for choosing to take so little advantage of that wealth. In contrast to the post-holocaust dwellers of many other writers' imaginations, these people are not forced to piece together inaccurately fragments of a wrecked culture's knowledge; they do not reverence and long to resemble their civilized ancestors; and their mutant births do not inspire cruel sacrifices to supposedly offended gods. But they have chosen to own the Valley "very lightly, with easy hands"—like the first-comers there. To them, living well does not mean getting more and moving ever forward; and they are mindful of their interconnection not only with human people but with many other kinds: plants, rocks, stars, dreams and animals, for example, are also people. Their respect for the non-human implies a model of evolution resembling their local scrub-oak—where "the little gray branches and twigs grow every which way"—rather than a ladder or tree where other life-forms belong below *Homo sapiens* (in evolution's past), and where true humanity consists in an upward linear progress away from them.

The linear form that a novel usually takes would not attune readers to the Valley, where time itself is envisaged not as an onward-moving stream or arrow but rather as a house that one lives in. The experimental form of *Always Coming Home* (itself somewhat resembling a house to live in) is more than an anthropologist's mode of presenting an unfamiliar society—with its details of customs, kinship systems, the language, myths, recipes, plays, poems, life-stories, one chapter of a novel, some accounts of disputes being settled, Pandora's questioning of inhabitants and of her own enterprise; all surrounding and intervening in the book's longest narrative, by a Valley woman who has also experienced the lifestyle of her father's war-centered culture, which is based several days' journey northeast of the Valley. The discrete elements of *Always Coming Home* are all being related to one another laterally in the process of reading, so that the reader's experience is a microcosm of the Valley people's mode of perception: their mindfulness of the interconnection of "the innumerable kinds of being in the world."

Our own metaphors tend to place things of most value at a summit or a center—thus endowing them with static isolation. The Valley's pervasive "working metaphor" is the hinged spiral, which involves no summit, and a different kind of center. To form an idea of it (which seems necessary in order to understand what kind of novel this is), hold the left hand above the right hand, palms facing and fingers slightly curved; adjust their positions so that the right thumb, curving downwards, lies about an inch above the left thumb, curving upwards. (The system can then be rotated so that the left hand is at the left; I have placed it above initially only to make the instructions clear in the absence of a drawing.) The curve of the left-hand fingers and thumb is the left arm of the double spiral, representing mortality; the right arm of the spiral (the interlocking right-hand curve) represents eternity; and the curves spring from or return to the center, which is the empty space between the thumbs: a gap or a hinge which both connects and holds apart—a place of "reversal from in to out, from out to in"—a discontinuity which the Valley culture sees as "necessary and significant." A Valley town, which to us would look simply messy, is laid out as a hinged spiral, the dwelling places lying along an invisible left arm (or several left arms, if the town is large), while the right arm consist of five *heyimas* (for these there is no simple English translation; but one of their functions is to be sacred meeting-houses). At the hinge of the town there is always running water or a well.

The notion of reversal, associated with the hinge, is very important in Valley culture, which attempts to provide (in Pandora's words) "a way with no away." Thus, their regular ceremonies include elements which reverse the community's normal behavior and principles. There is room and attention for emotions and experiences which in our culture are glossed over as aberrant. A child, having braved a foggy dawn alone on the mountain where she fears that every sound is the stuttering of the traditional White Clowns (not all of whom may be living people), can fully integrate the realization, on her return home, that "part of me wanted to be cold and terrified and lost in the fog."

In the Valley's vision of how to be human, emphasis falls differently. Their experience seems in some ways richer and in others poorer than ours, where attention is focused on our relation to other human beings. They seem, in part, an alien people on an alien planet, although a poem tells us that they were amongst us, "coming closer to the world," from the beginning: "the sold woman,/ the enslaved enemy." We are told: "You did not know us./ We were the words you had no language for."

This book answers some former criticisms both of Le Guin and of contemporary science fiction by being experimental in form and by choosing a female as its most important narrator (in a society which is matrilocal and matrilineal). The landscape, being no mere setting for a chase of some kind, is intensely real—and evokes, oddly, Australian vegetation I have known and loved in childhood. I have seen favorable reports of the music of *Always Coming Home*'s cassette tape (which is not available with the library edition); and the book's design and illustration have been accomplished with a care and grace that attest the Valley's significance for other people, besides Le Guin. This is a book to own, and to dip into at leisure when it has been read through—whether one takes the Valley view that it is a (momentarily heart-lifting) "piece of pacifist jeanjacquerie" or whether one believes that (as I think Pandora hints) to achieve a complete imagination of the Valley might do "infinite good."

MYTHAGO WOOD

by Jenny Blackford

Robert Holdstock, *Mythago Wood*

Like *Earthwind* (Robert Holdstock's earlier novel from 1977), *Mythago Wood* (1984) is written in the first person. I have never really believed that an author has to be the same sex as his/her narrator to be convincing. I suspect that the gulf between all human beings is so wide, and so narrow, that a difference of sex is the least of our problems of understanding. Nonetheless, Robert Holdstock (sadly) wasn't very convincing as a stunningly beautiful woman born on an exotic planet, with diamonds set into her breasts, yet. In *Mythago Wood* he does a much more convincing male English twit—the narrator and hero, Steven Huxley, is the well-off son of a loony father, living in a spooky house near an even spookier wood (that of the title).

Steven's father, George, has discovered that this wood—"three square miles of original, post-Ice Age forestland"—is inhabited by mythagos. (The emphasis, by the way, is on the second syllable.) George Huxley thinks that he brought the mythagos—manifestations from the collective unconscious—into being by using "a sort of electronic bridge which seems to fuse elements from each half of the brain," but this claim is plausibly disputed by a Neolithic river-guardian skilled in necromancy (a mythago himself, of course). Other mythagos in Ryhope Wood include Robin Hood, several other Jack-of-the-Green types, King Arthur, "the guardian of the Horse Shrine," the terrifying Urscumug, who goes right back to the time when forests were claiming the land left by the retreating glaciers of the Ice Age, and a Celtic Earth-goddess type from Roman times, but whose precursors in legend go back to post-Glacial legends.

This brings us to Robert Holdstock's apparent obsession with Celtic and pre-Celtic mysticism. Ancient European mysticism is all very interesting, and many people have made a reasonable living exploiting the public's deeply-held belief that somewhere beneath their boring Anglo-Saxon surface is a wild, natural, nay, mystical Celt trying to get out, little golden sickle and all; and that England is really an exceptionally mystical and wonderful place, where all the layers of the mystical past can be read by those who have the true eye to see it (*i.e.* the reader). Now, *Mythago Wood* exploits those beliefs rather well. Robert Holdstock gives better-than-average pseudo-scientific reasons why this particular wood is mythago-haunted, and thus much more mystical than most. The narrator's atmospherically spooky childhood memories—always fun—build through his deceptively practical worries about his obviously insane father (obsessed by the wood) and his increasingly erratic elder brother (seduced by the wood), until our hero is The Hero taking part in a legend in the midst of a magic wood almost without our realizing it. This is good fun, for those who like that sort of thing. And, I'm afraid, the Celtic and pre-Celtic blood in me that keeps me short (people from my father's village are built like the pit-ponies that they worked with) makes me a sucker for exactly that sort of thing.

Sucker though I am, I was not in the least enchanted by ancient European mysticism turning up, on the slenderest of pretexts, on a distant planet. *Earthwind* would have us believe in aliens responding to similar conditions to those in early England (to tell you what conditions would ruin the plot for you) by drawing similar pictures. These pictures—of the Earthwind—have a mystical function which must also be concealed from you, gentle reader. Suffice it to say that this function is revealed in a mystical denouement which strikes one as amazingly silly, set as it is on an alien planet amongst the highest of technology and the lowest of galactic politics.

On to another couple of Holdstock's obsessions (I suppose it would be kinder to call them themes...): sex and psychology, intermixed and intermingled. *Mythago Wood* gives us a lovely baroque picture of family life. Our hero's Oedipal feelings for his father swell until his father becomes the appalling Urscumug; his elder brother (and therefore, of course, rival) Christian gradually becomes the villain in the magical story they enact in the wood; hero, father and brother compete bloodily and single-mindedly for the affections of the mythago Guiwenneth.

Guiwenneth is a Celtic Earth goddess from Roman times, who is for the men the embodiment of all things good in woman, and with whom each falls passionately in love. (Possible Freudian note: the name Guiwenneth, as one of the brothers remarks, is pretty close to Guinevere; Steven's mother (who dies of a broken heart, neglected by her husband for the wood, and particularly for Guiwenneth) is called Jennifer; Jennifer is the Welsh form of Guinevere...) At any rate, Guiwenneth loves our hero above all others, and Steven's (heroic) struggles to rescue her from Christian—who has become The Outsider, terrorizing all the mythagos of the wood—makes up much of the book. Guiwenneth is really rather a nice creation. She picks up moderate English and the use of modern plumbing very fast. She has the practicality of some of Doctor Who's more exciting, long-past female companions, and is much better at dealing with either spear or dead deer than Steven.

The ending of the book is masterful. We gradually realize that the protagonists are making legend, not re-enacting it. Fate and the pattern of legend have forced Steven, as The Kinsman, to hunt and try to kill Christian The Outsider, who is blighting The Realm. Their hated father, the Urscumug, pursues them both. Steven's companion Keeton gradually becomes The Companion, and wonders whether, ultimately, he becomes Sir Kay. The mythagos in The Realm know many forms of Guiwenneth's legend so far, but not what happens afterwards. Let it suffice to say that the ending is sufficiently mythically fitting, psychologically satisfying, and poignant.

PHILIP K. DICK BEGINS

THE COLLECTED STORIES OF PHILIP K. DICK

by Michael J. Tolley

[Author's Note, 1988: This is the first fruits of a study of the five-volume Underwood/Miller *Collected Stories* of Philip K. Dick. It should not be assumed that my first word is my last word on the subject.]

In *Comedy High and Low*, Maurice Charney lists six distinct areas which "may conveniently define the comic experience." Comedy, he says, "is discontinuous, accidental, autonomous, self-conscious, histrionic, and ironic" (5-6). All of these terms seem applicable to the work of one of the great American comic writers, Philip K. Dick. Take the first of these terms, the discontinuous, as Charney describes it:

> Comedy depends on the breaking of rational order and causality. We may abruptly shift perspective and juxtapose separate pieces of action as if they belonged with each other. The time sequence is flexible and subject-object relations may be reversed. The overall feeling is one of uneasiness, since the patterns created are crazy quilts and random mosaics.

If those ideas do not ring a few bells for the experienced Dick reader, I will be surprised. One may at the same time wish to raise all sorts of objections to a premise which will appear to straitjacket such a various talent in the comic form. Dick is not merely a comic absurdist and sometimes, as for instance in *A Scanner Darkly*, we may feel that the almost unbearable pathos aroused by the spectacle of a drug-addict's behavior overpowers its superficial ridiculous aspects. Nevertheless, to begin with the observation that Dick's work is essentially comic in form and spirit seems appropriate.

Charney's first principle, *Discontinuity*, is invoked, in effect, by Dick's definition of science fiction in a "Preface" to the *Collected Stories* (which is actually taken from a letter written on 14 May 1981). Dick is talking about the relationship between our world and the scientifictional one that is shaped by the introduction of at least one new idea.

> We have a fictitious world; that is the first step: it is a society that does not in fact exist, but is predicated on our known society. That is, our known society acts as a jumping-off point for it; the society advances out of our own in some way, perhaps orthogonally, as with the alternate world story or novel. It is our world dislocated by some kind of mental effort on the part of the author; our world transformed into that which it is not or not yet. This world must differ from the given in at least one way, and this one way must be sufficient to give rise to events that could not occur in our society—or in any known society present or past. There must be a coherent idea involved in this dislocation; that is, the dislocation must be a conceptual one, not merely a trivial or bizarre one—*this* is the essence of science fiction, the conceptual dislocation within the society so that as a result a new society is generated in the author's mind, transferred to paper, and from paper it occurs as a convulsive shock in the reader's mind, *the shock of dysrecognition*. He knows that it is not his actual world that he is reading about.

Charney's other five areas of comic experience may as well be given their expanded descriptions here:

> 2. *The Accidental*: We need to have faith in the validity and significance of random experience, the fortuitous and the unanticipated. This posits a grand creativity in nature, so that any event, no matter how trivial, may have rich comic possibilities: a walk down the street, browsing among unrelated books, a visit to the town dump. What happens spontaneously

happens rightly and therefore feeds the comic imagination.

3. *The Autonomous*: Things have a life of their own. The distinction between the organic and inorganic worlds is false. Material things can be animated if observed closely enough. Machines suggest comic analogies between the life of things and the life of man. Things can be recombined into new and meaningful relations that comment on each other. Clowns have always tried to imitate the inanimate world.

4. *The Self-Conscious*: The body is a material object, and the intense and minute awareness of the body is a vital source of comedy. The separable parts of the body support the mechanical analogy and raise anxieties about castration, impotence, and loss of mechanical function. To be a human being is inherently comic. Can we be reconciled to our own organic disgust?

5. *The Histrionic*: Man is an actor playing a clownish role.

We are intensely aware of the meaninglessness of our attempts to communicate. Language is a fallible instrument and words float freely in a magic reality. The enormous sea of words represents possibilities of expression that can never be used. Words are gestural and have a life of their own available for comic exploitation. Once words and actions are separated from communicable meaning, they are freed of their utilitarian taint. The clown engages more often in soliloquy than in conversation.

6. *The Ironic*: We are forced back to the basic assumption of dreams and poetry: that everything can also mean its opposite. Comedy trains us to expect the pie in the face. Language is especially rife with ironic possibilities, since this is the medium of rational discourse. The ironist is a sly man who is constantly repeating: the only thing I know is that I know nothing. This kind of openness makes a good beginning for comedy.

Not all of these ideas are equally suggestive of Dick's work but each might be redefined to fit his work quite closely.

The first of the five volumes in *The Collected Stories of Philip K. Dick* (Underwood/Miller, 1987) is titled *Beyond Lies the Wub*. The famous story of this title is actually the fourth in order of printing in the book: it was his first published story (*Planet Stories*, July 1952), but not his first written story ("Stability," c. 1947, first published in this edition) and not his first sale ("Roog," received by Dick's agent November 1951, published *F&SF* February 1953), nor indeed his third written work (which we must presume to be "The Little Movement," published *F&SF* November 1952). These details are given in the Notes at the back of the volume, where it is explained that the stories are arranged as far as possible in chronological order of composition, following research by Gregg Rickman and Paul Williams.

"Beyond Lies the Wub," which strikingly illustrates the idea of comic discontinuity, among others, is in conception a brilliant revision of the Circe myth. What happens to the followers of Odysseus on Circe's magic island is that they drink from her enchanted cup and turn into animals. What happens to Captain Franco is that he eats a porcine animal from a magic planet and the animal becomes Captain Franco, while still retaining its essential wubness. Franco believes that what looks like a pig can be eaten like pork and turned into a more satisfied Captain. He does not take "things" seriously but the comic rule of autonomy disagrees with him and he should have been warned by the fact that this particular thing, the wub, can talk, can read and influence minds, and admits to having a high survival factor.

I have discussed "Beyond Lies the Wub" previously in my *Stellar Gauge* article ["Beyond the Enigma: Dick's Questors" in *The Stellar Gauge: Essays on Science Fiction Writers*, ed. Michael J. Tolley and Kirpal Singh, Norstrilia, Carlton, 1980], where I remarked upon Dick's fairness in giving us, through the wub, a reference to *The Odyssey*, and upon the unsettling nature of the story, in that we have only the wub's word that its ethics are to be preferred to those of Captain Franco, so that Franco essentially becomes more human when he becomes more wub. The wub questions Franco before he kills it and its question is not answered:

> "It is interesting," the wub said, "that you are obsessed with the idea of eating me. I wonder why."

Why, indeed? Here, as elsewhere, Dick is clearly attacking the rampant, greedy consumerism of some of his fellow Americans. In the form his satire takes, I find myself wondering whether the wub is not an allomorph of another product of American humor, Al Capp's Schmoo. Capp invented the Schmoo in about 1948 and it seems unlikely that Dick did not know the *Li'l Abner* comic strip well enough to have been, conceivably, influenced by it. Al Capp talks about the Schmoo and another creature, the Kigmy, in an important article published in *Life* in March 1952 called "It's Hideously True," in which he explains why, under McCarthyism, he has retreated from inventive satire to domestic comedy by allowing Daisy Mae to marry her hero. We have to remember that it was precisely in this repressive epoch that Dick's first stories saw the light. Dick started to laugh at America around the time that Al Capp was beginning to realize that the laughing had to stop:

> Now there are things about America we can't kid.
> I realized it first when four years ago I created the Schmoo. You remember the Schmoo? It was a totally boneless and wildly affectionate little animal which, when broiled, came out steak and, when fried, tasted like chicken. It also laid neatly packaged and bottled eggs and milk, all carefully labeled "Grade A." It multiplied without the slightest effort. It loved to be eaten, and would drop dead, out of sheer joy, when you looked at it hungrily. Having created the animal, I let it run wild in the world of my cartoon strip. It was simply a fairy tale and all I had to say was wouldn't it be wonderful if there were such an animal—and, if there were, how idiotically some people might behave. Mainly, the response to the Schmoo was delight. But there were also some disturbing letters. Some writers wanted to know what was the idea of kidding big business by creating the Schmoo (which had become big business). Other writers wanted to know what was the idea of criticizing labor, by creating the Schmoo, which made labor unnecessary.
> It was disturbing, but I didn't let it bother me too much. Then a year later, I created the Kigmy, an animal that loved to be kicked around, thus making it unnecessary for people to kick each other around. This time a lot more letters came. Their tone was an-

grier, more suspicious. They asked the craziest questions, like: Was I, in creating the Kigmy, trying to create pacifism and thus, secretly, non-resistance to Communism? Were the Kigmy kickers secretly the big bosses kicking the workers around? Were the Kigmy kickers secretly the labor unions kicking capital around?

And finally, what in hell was the idea of creating the Kigmy anyhow, because it implied some criticism of some kinds of Americans and any criticism on anything American was (now) un-American?

It is not surprising, then, that Dick was careful not to give his Captain an American name and was careful too to set his attack on imperialism in outer space, rather than, say, Ceaser Siddy in Lower Slobbovia.

It is interesting to see, by contrast, that his later works were set very closely in contemporary California. It is also not surprising that Dick's wub is conceived as basically a sad creature, not happy to be eaten but sorrowful over the evil that must be done to it if it is to be eaten. Dick was, after all, a notorious animal-lover. The wub is, perhaps, a Schmoo seen by a left-wing liberal pet-owner subject to paranoia who started his work in the McCarthy era.

Beside the Homeric myth, the wub refers to the Ishtar story, which like the Circe story involves at one point the idea that her lovers become animals. However, it may help us to go more deeply into the story if we look at what the wub actually says about Odysseus, when it is discussing myth with the sympathetic Peterson:

> The room was quiet.
> "So you see," the wub said, "we have a common myth. Your mind contains many familiar myth symbols. Ishtar, Odysseus—" [...]
> "I find in your Odysseus a figure common to the mythology of most self-conscious races. As I interpret it, Odysseus wanders as an individual aware of himself as such. This is the idea of separation, of separation from family and country. The process of individuation."
> "But Odysseus returns to his home." Peterson looked out the port window, at the stars, endless stars, burning intently in the empty universe. "Finally

he goes home."

"As must all creatures. The moment of separation is a temporary period, a brief journey of the soul. It begins, it ends. The wanderer returns to land and race..."

The wub is interrupted by Franco at that point and it is not until it becomes Franco that he takes up the thread again, although Dick still leaves it dangling at the end. The Ishtar allusion is also maddeningly vague and there is an even more irritating biblical allusion to "a parable that your Savior related," apparently one about foolish behavior. I note that the Ishtar story is principally about her journey to the underworld to rescue her lover, Thammuz, which results in her being stripped and murdered by her terrible sister Ereshkigal, to be eventually revived with "water of life," so that she is able to return to the upper world with Thammuz and also, in one version, with a great many other underworld beings. The biblical parable might be the one about the unclean spirit in Matthew 12: 43-5:

> 43 When the unclean spirit is gone out of a man, he walketh through dry places, seeking rest and finding none.
> 44 Then he saith, I will return into my house from whence I came out; and when he is come, he findeth it empty, swept, and garnished.
> 45 Then goeth he, and taketh with himself seven other spirits more wicked than himself, and they enter in and dwell there: and the last state of that man is worse than the first. Even so shall it be also unto this wicked generation.

Alternatively, the reference may be so vague as to allude not to a parable at all but to the story in Mark 5 of the devils being freed from the "man with an unclean spirit" whose name is Legion and released into a herd of swine.

Is this story, we wonder, about an ancient exiled race, called "the wub" by the natives among whom they live, though the wub "have their own term," now returning to their home, their "land and race," in the bodies of the Captain and his crew? If so, is this a good thing or a bad thing? After eating the wub, has the Captain become a thing? or has the Captain become more truly human?

With "Beyond Lies the Wub" we are thrust immediately into

the well-known world of Phildickian paranoia, a world which has perhaps become almost cozily familiar to us now but which must have been highly disturbing to some of Dick's more thoughtful early readers. Several of the early stories are based on the premise that we shall go exploring foolishly "out there" and, unlike Odysseus, whose virtue it is to arrive back at Ithaca intact, we shall come back changed. Among these stories in the first volume are "Piper in the Woods" (*Imagination*, February 1953), "The Infinites" (*Planet Stories*, May 1953) and "Colony" (*Galaxy*, June 1953). In 1976, Dick said of "Colony" that

> The ultimate in paranoia is not when everyone is against you but when every*thing* is against you. Instead of "My boss is plotting against me," it would be "My boss's phone is plotting against me." Objects sometimes seem to possess a will of their own anyhow, to the normal mind; they don't do what they're supposed to do, they get in the way, they show an unnatural resistance to change. In this story I tried to figure out a situation which would rationally explain the dire plotting of objects against humans, without reference to any deranged state on the part of the humans. I guess you'd have to go to another planet. The ending on this story is the ultimate victory of a plotting object over innocent people.

In "Colony," everything on Planet Blue looks perfect—until a scientist's microscope tries to strangle him. The local predatory life form can mimic anything perfectly, which makes this a more extreme variant of the life form in John W. Campbell, Jr.'s "Who Goes There?" which could become any person or animal. The ending, in which the creature mimics the rescue ship, thus trapping the entire surviving colony—and leaving the future of the whole universe in jeopardy—is perfect. This is one of those stories which come close to putting the reader in the seat of the kids' movie matinee: while you read it you are silently screaming at the characters not to walk into the trap. "Second Variety" is an even more frightening story of this type—but that's in Volume II. With such stories as these, Dick was tweaking a public nerve recently made sensitive by the great horror movie, *The Thing (from Another World)* based on Campbell's story, which came out in 1951. The British were a bit slower to exploit this theme, if we take *The Quatermass Experiment* (TV serial

1953, film version 1955) as the benchmark for them.

A more low-key approach to this theme is "Piper in the Woods," which is less a story of possession, more one of hypnotic control: the title may suggest the Pied Piper of hamsters, which have become forms of pure energy. The hyperhamsters kill Blake but restore Captain Eller and Silvia Simmons to their normal bodies, much to their relief.

Harrison Blake has a power problem, whether or not to use one's advanced evolutionary status to control the rest of the human race. This kind of theme is also employed in "Mr. Spaceship" (*Imagination*, January 1953), in which the brain of an elderly pacifist professor is put in control of a spaceship, as a means of penetrating the defenses of aliens with whom we are at war: the yuks (Yucconae) of Proxima Centauri use living space mines, so that a machine cannot get past them. The warmongers think that Professor Thomas's brain will be unconscious, which is their mistake. He believes that warriors are made not born and uses his power to trick a former student and his alienated wife into becoming a new Adam and Eve on a neglected planet.

Similar in effect to this story is "The Variable Man" (*Space Science Fiction* (British), July 1953), in the sense that it concerns the attempted manipulation by warmongers of a good-natured hero, who works according to a different agenda. This is a novella-length story and so has room for several thrilling episodes, but the plot may be summarized easily enough. Earth is at war with the Centaurans, and Reinhart, the militarist who controls Earth's Council, wants a decisive weapon. Scientist Peter Sherikov decides that a failed FTL [faster than light] drive can be used as a bomb, directed to explode inside Proxima Centauri. When genius fixer Thomas Cole is accidentally brought in a time bubble from the twentieth century to the future dystopia, he is employed to work on the bomb by Sherikov, but Reinhart wants to kill Cole because he is a variable factor in the data which guide his forecasting machine (Reinhart consults statistics the way Indians consult astrologers): because of "the variable man," the forecasting machine cannot predict the outcome of a preemptive attack. Cole barely survives to fix the bomb so that it will work as originally intended, as an FTL device; since the bomb does not explode, the war effort fails and Reinhart is disgraced, but the way is opened to galactic travel.

Another story which starts with the premise of a space war against another race is "Prize Ship," which was published in *Thrilling Wonder Stories*, Winter 1954. (Dick's original title was "Globe from Ganymede.") The Ganymedeans are hindering Terra from sending a supply ship to the colony planets. The desperate Terrans hope that their salvation may life in a new ship they have captured from the Ganymedeans, which they test-drive without understanding the controls. The crew first travel to a world of midget medieval people and think they have landed in Lilliput, an impression confirmed when, at the other end of the drive scale, they find themselves among giants. However, it is not Brobdingnag but the future: their ship is a time vessel and as the universe is an expanding one, time-travel backwards is to a smaller place, forwards is to a world of giants. The Ganymedeans get their globe back, the war having been settled quietly in their favor. They had decided that the globe was a failure, and could not understand why the humans wanted it. The Gany who comes to collect the globe says they had speculated that it was stolen to reach the colonies in deep-space: "But that would have been *too* amusing. We could not really believe that." The humans had believed something even more incredible, that Swift had seen the nature of time in a vision and written it up as a children's story—but at least the crew members are sensible enough to keep that idea to themselves.

"I knew it was only a child's story," Basset said.
"A social satire," Groves corrected him.

Children's stories which are social satires seems like a good description of "The Little Movement" (*F&SF*, February 1953) and "The King of the Elves" (*Beyond Fantasy Fiction*, September 1953, first titled by Dick "Shadrach Jones and the Elves"). "The Little Movement" is a Bradburyan story about a threat from clockwork soldiers that plan to take over the world by controlling our impressionable children—but they are losing men rapidly and we see why when one of them is suddenly attacked by the boy hero's soft toys. It is Teddo, Bonzo the stuffed rabbit and Fred the rubber pig to the rescue—but we are left wondering about their full agenda.

"We'll do it again," Fred said. "I'm getting so I rather enjoy it."
"Me, too," Bonzo said.

In "The King of the Elves," gas-station owner Shadrach Jones gives shelter to a band of Elves, who are being harassed by Trolls. When the old Elf King dies, he nominates Shadrach for the job, which would be all right, except he finds that his old friend Phineas Judd is a Troll leader.

The idea that we might be in the middle of a war about which we know nothing, fostered perhaps by such zoological textbooks as the brilliant *Backyard Jungle*, which I read in the late '40s, is most impressively handled in "Expendable" (*F&SF*, July 1953, first titled by Dick "He Who Waits"). In 1976 Dick said of this:

> I loved to write short fantasy stories in my early days—for Anthony Boucher—of which this is my favorite. I got the idea when a fly buzzed by my head one day and I imagined (paranoia indeed!) that it was laughing at me.

The war going on is between the insects and their natural enemies, spiders and birds. These creatures define life by the species, not the individual, as an unfortunate human who can understand them discovers when he is condemned to death by the ants and other insects who invade his home in vast numbers and has only three spiders to defend him. As they wait in his study while the hordes gather outside, he is told by his "allies" about the war, forgotten by the humans, going back almost a million years, for which the insect-eaters were bred.

> "I think we can save you," the Cruncher put in cheerfully. "As a matter of fact, we look forward to events like this."
> From under the floorboards came a distant scratching sound, the noise of a multitude of tiny claws and wings, vibrating faintly, remotely. The man heard. His body sagged all over.
> "You're really certain? You think you can do it?" He wiped the perspiration from his lips and picked up the spray gun, still listening.
> The sound was growing, swelling beneath them, under the floor, under their feet. Outside the house bushes rustled and a few moths flew up against the window. Louder and louder the sound grew, beyond and below, everywhere, a rising hum of anger and determination. The man looked from side to side.
> "You're sure you can do it?" he murmured. "You can really save me?"

"Oh," the Stinger [a black widow] said, embarrassed. "I didn't mean *that*. I meant the species, the race...not you as an individual."

The man gaped at him and the three Eaters shifted uneasily. More moths burst against the window. Under them the floor stirred and heaved.

"I see," the man said. "I'm sorry I misunderstood you."

For me a less successful story with a somewhat similar premise is "Roog," Dick's first sale (published *F&SF*, February 1953). Here the guardian figure, from whose viewpoint the story is told, is the household dog, who believes that the garbage men are "roogs," alien invaders. Like Judith Merril, I find the description of the roogs by the crazy dog too obscure, despite Dick's brilliant exposition of the story, which is quoted extensively in the Notes. Dick here explains his technique as a story writer of getting inside the heads of his creatures, every one of which has, he believes, a unique way of looking at the world.

In the Cold War of the early 1950s it would be surprising if there were not numerous anti-war stories flowing from Dick's pen. In this volume we have several prophetic stories, among them "The Gun" (*Planet Stories*, September 1952) and "The Defenders" (*Galaxy*, January 1953). "The Gun" anticipates "Second Variety" in that it concerns a self-restoring weapon. On a planet devastated by nuclear fission, there is still a gun watching the skies—and it shoots down a visiting ship. The crew are able to repair their ship and disable the gun but it manages to send a signal to another base when the ship leaves—and out come the hidden repair units.

"The Defenders" was used in the 1964 novel, *The Penultimate Truth*. Machines ("leadies") rule the surface of the Earth, which the humans who live underground think is devastated, like that of the planet in "The Gun." When survivors begin to emerge they discover the truth but are slow to learn the history lesson which the leadies have articulated: now that there are only two enemy blocs in the world, it is possible to get all mankind together and make a fresh start. This closed-environment story employs Dick's favorite false-evidence motif in an Orwellian manner and it also employs the idea that a machine can be more human than the humans, deceiving people for their own good.

The future prognosis is not always so hopeful. In "The Skull" (*If*, September 1952), a hunter is sent from the future to the past (still

Dick's future) of 1960, in order to murder the non-violent founder of a troublesome church which has banished war and so caused a surplus population of disagreeables. His only clue is a skull, stolen from the church, which has a peculiar incisor. He first lands in 1961, is surprisingly recognized, and hurriedly escapes. As 1960 is a McCarthyist anti-Red hysterical epoch, the assassin, Conger, is soon suspected, when he lands in a small mid-Western town, of being a foreigner and a Communist. Quite early in the piece, Dick signals his denouement that Conger will turn out to be the victim not the killer, but what is unexpected is that Dick allows Conger to recognize the skull as his own and hence to acquiesce in his own death, as he says the right words to complete the circle of a time loop which allows the church to continue.

Dick understood that time travel might be as dangerous as space travel if what we bring back from it is a sinister change. A good example of paranoia applied to time travel is "Meddler" (*Future*, October 1954). Dick also knew that personal time travel might not be feasible and so he sometimes used the idea of a time scoop. Merely observing the future can be dangerous, however, as a trouble-shooter finds out when he is sent to look at it by a worried government. Innocent-looking butterflies turn out to be fatally corrosive—and they come back with the machine. In 1978, Dick's note would relate this story to the philosophy of Heraclitus which he was so fond of quoting. He wrote:

> Within the beautiful lurks the ugly; you can see in this rather crude story the germ of my whole theme that nothing is what it seems. This story should be read as a trial run on my part; I was just beginning to grasp that obvious form and latent form are not the same thing. As Heraclitus said in fragment 54: "Latent structure is master of obvious structure," and out of this comes the more sophisticated Platonic dualism between the phenomenal world and the real but invisible realm of forms lying behind it. I may be reading too much into this simple-minded early story, but at least I was beginning to see in a dim way what I later saw so clearly; in fragment 123, Heraclitus said, "The nature of things is in the habit of concealing itself," and therein lies it all.

The time scoop itself is used not only in "The Variable Man" but also in another thriller called "Paycheck" (*Imagination*, June 1953). A man finds that he has lost two years of his memory as a result of working for a Company against a police state. Instead of money, he has arranged to come out of his period of employment with the objects he needs to get back into the Company, steal information, then blackmail the firm's owner into keeping him, not as the technician he was before, but as an executive. With the additional help of the owner's daughter, a mirror and a time scoop, he does just that. Dick explained in 1976 that the story was inspired by an insight into the variable value of apparently little things: one day the key to a locker might be worth twenty-five cents, the next day thousands of dollars. This kind of interest in the little, neglected things of life, so typical of Dick, would surface again in *Ubik*. However, I myself find the story memorable principally for its final image, which illustrates so well Charney's comic principle of discontinuity: it is also a kind of *deus ex machina* (or rather a *deus* in or behind a *machina*). At the end of the story there is one small thing left which must be removed from the present so that the hero may have it in the past; it must also be removed from the present so that it may not cause a time paradox by duplication. This small thing is a slip of paper, a receipt: the hero, Jennings, has it; so also does his girl friend. As they confront the paradox,

> In the air above them something moved. A dark space formed, a circle. The space stirred. Kelly [the girl] and Rethrick [her father] stared up, frozen.
> From the dark circle a claw appeared, a metal claw, joined to a shimmering rod. The claw dropped, swinging in a wide arc. The claw swept the paper from Kelly's fingers. It hesitated for a second. Then it drew itself up again, disappearing with the paper, into the circle of black. Then, silently, the claw and the rod and the circle blinked out. There was nothing. Nothing at all.

I suppose that the young Philip Dick had played with those fairground machines in which you use a mechanical claw to grab a prize from a glass-enclosed box. It is like him to imagine what it would be like at the other end of the grab. This kind of situation occurs frequently in Dick's stories, for instance in *Galactic Pot Healer*.

You have to be pretty smart to make time travel your servant. The more usual self-image offered the reader is that of the foolish "meddler." Travel to the unknown, whether in time or space, is dangerous, but then doing pretty well anything new is dangerous. The principle of automatism—whereby things become alive—may operate, but this may also be stated in terms of the principle of synergy. George Zebrowski discussed this in the *SFRA* Newsletter (October 1987):

> The late R. Buckminster Fuller, who believed in harnessing the essential creativity of every human being as one might develop natural resources, defined *synergy* as the "behavior of whole systems unpredicted by the behavior of their parts taken separately." The term is applied widely nowadays to describe the arising of new things. A joining of inspiration, information, and practical ability may bring about a new whole that is greater than the mere sum of its parts.

Zebrowski describes synergy as

> natural to the human organism. Without synergy's inventive ways, humankind might not have survived; without a more widespread application of synergy to the task of creating a humane future, our kind will perish. Synergy also accounts for large, complex systems getting out of hand, permitting the unpredictable occurrences of things that no one wants.

It is this last effect of synergy with which Dick most typically deals: what you put in is not the same as what comes out.

To exploit for comic purposes this perverse synergistic effect, Dick uses in two early stories an inventor called Doc Labyrinth. "The Preserving Machine" (*F&SF*, June 1953) is rather a surrealistic concept than a story. The machine changes the scores of fragile musical works into animate creatures better fitted for survival; however, to fit the creatures for survival is to render them subject to the evolutionary forces of natural selection. All of the living musical scores change out of recognition and even become somewhat dangerous (Wagner is the chief villain). When they are retrieved and fed back into the preserving machine, the music even of a Bach becomes hideous. Rather pleasanter effects are produced in the second Doc Labyrinth experiment, narrated in "The Short Happy Life of the

Brown Oxford" (*F&SF*, January 1954). The inventor adapts a Dutch oven to the "Principle of Sufficient Irritation," which is a means of inducing animation. He uses it on a man's brown shoe. However, once the shoe has become alive, it needs as much sex as the next creature, and takes steps (pardon the pun) to use the Animator on a lady's white slipper.

Another delightful comic story involving scientists is "The Indefatigable Frog" (*Fantastic Story Magazine*, July 1953), which notably anticipates Richard Matheson's 1956 novel, *The Shrinking Man* and the 1957 film derived from it. Two scientists find an ingenious way of testing Zeno's theory in the laboratory. As a heat-stimulated frog advances along a tube, it trips successive relays which shrink it each time to half its size. Maliciously, the pro-Zenoist scientist Hardy traps the anti-Zenoist Grote inside the tube, so that he like the frog is forced to advance, shrinking as he goes. The test, however, fails when both frog and man shrink so much that they fall between the molecules of the pipe's floor and thus regain their natural size, spoiling Hardy's triumph.

One grim post-holocaust story featuring a sinister machine is "The Great C" (*Cosmos Science Fiction and Fantasy*, September 1953), which was partly recycled for *Deus Irae*. After "the Smash," a suburban tribe is still sacrificing its young men to a computer god; every year a youth is sent to ask the Great C three questions, hoping to find one the computer cannot answer. The hero of the story is No. 50 and he gets eaten just like all the rest, apparently for fuel to keep the mad computer going.

If "Beyond Lies the Wub" is based on the Circe story and "The Great C" on the Andromeda story, "Stability," Dick's first written story, has overtones of Pandora. A "stable" utopian society is destroyed by an evil city shrunk and preserved in a glass bubble: it ends with a society enslaved to machines as in *Metropolis*. The evil city has an ineffectual guardian, the utopia a wise but ineffectual "Controller" and the Pandora figure is a hero-dupe called Robert Benton. These foolish struggling people may be held to anticipate many of Dick's later heroic and even divine figures.

Another old story is reworked for "The Builder" (*Amazing*, December 1953/January 1954), in which a latter-day Noah, E. J. Elwood, is under the compulsion to build an ark in his garden but cannot explain why, much to the exasperation of his sensible wife and the amusement of his acquaintances. Only his younger son, Toddy, helps him. Elwood is presented as a blind, struggling animal, working by instinct but troubled to the point of despair. Like the dog in

"Roog"—and like so many of Dick's later heroes—Elwood is impressive in his plight. Dick lets the circumstances of the story do the preaching: we form our own impressions from its faithful account of what is recognizably our own society as to why a new Noah may be necessary. In this way, he succeeds in bringing science fiction home from outer space.

Happier in tone is a delightful version of the classical story of Leda and the Swan, which might be called "Peggy and the Duck" but is actually entitled "Out in the Garden" (*Fantasy Fiction*, August 1953). Robert Nye's wife Peggy has a pet white duck called Sir Francis (after the Drake), which seems to have cuckolded him. Robert gets rid of the duck but is still uneasy; is his son Stephen (perhaps named after Stephen Duck, the thresher poet) his own? Stephen seems an agreeable lad, but it is not reassuring when he invites his father to join him in the garden for a picnic of worms and spiders.

The motif of a shrunken city found in "Stability" is used again in "The Crystal Crypt" (*Planet Stories*, January 1954). This story, like *Do Androids Dream of Electric Sheep?*, which formed the basis of the movie, *Blade Runner*, is a detective mystery. During a war against Mars, the last Terrans are leaving the planet when they are suddenly detained on Deimos for a lie-detector test. All the passengers pass the test but the Martians know that a woman and two men among them have been responsible for destroying one of their cities. Being safely away, as they think, the criminals tell their story to another passenger, explaining that they did not actually destroy the city, they stole it, shrunk to the size of a glass paperweight. However, the other passenger is a Martian.

The last story to be included in the first volume is "Nanny" (*Startling Stories*, Spring 1955), which anticipates "Second Variety" in its theme of continuously upgraded quasi-animate machines, sums up much of the paranoia induced by meddling inventiveness and greed, and is a bitter Cold War satire. "Nanny" concerns robot nannies which, thanks to the nexus between capitalism and competitiveness, are altered by their designers in line with sales requirements, so that they move from defending their owners' young to attacking each other, fighting savage secret battles in park and garden. Outmoded models get thrashed to death by new and bigger ones, so their owners have to keep up with the Joneses next door, at whatever cost to themselves, by purchasing the latest, biggest and most brutal Nannies. At first the owners do not know what is going on, but when they find out, they do not vent their anger on the manufacturers and suppliers (as it were, the arms dealers); they just fall in with the universal competitive spirit. This is the way the world might end.

§

Volume Two of the *Collected Stories* comprises twenty-seven stories published between 1952 and 1955 and has a short introduction by Norman Spinrad, which combines well-deserved admiration for Dick's prolificity in these early years and praise for his pioneering use of multiple viewpoint characters, with notes on the characteristic Phildickian concerns which may already be seen emerging in his work. He also gives due homage to Dick for speaking out "loud and clear" against "the prevailing hysterias of the times—against militarism, security obsession, xenophobia, and chauvinism." Those years belonged to "the fever pitch of the Cold War," when the voices of Senator Joseph McCarthy and the House Un-American Activities Committee were heard in the land. (Not surprisingly, the volume also has an epigraph from Dick about paranoia as an atavistic sense, often experienced by his characters.) Spinrad stresses the absence of repetition, of sameness, in these stories, as surprising under the circumstances of their rapid production. He does, however, play down to some degree what sameness there is, especially in regard to the shape of the future which is assumed here. Spinrad's remark that, "Except for some rather tenuous connections between 'Second Variety,' 'Jon's World,' and 'James P. Crow,' there is really no attempt at a consistent future history," requires some qualification. In the present account, I concentrate mainly on the themes being articulated in these stories, although I also refer to some features of narrative effect or of plot construction.

"Some Kinds of Life" was first published under the pseudonym Richard Phillips in *Fantastic Universe*, October-November 1953 (the same issue also had a story under Philip K. Dick's real name in it, "Planet for Transients"). Although it is not the first in order in this Volume, it meshes neatly with the last one I discussed above, which happened to be the last placed in Volume I, "Nanny," about the craziness of sacrificing family life on the altar of bigger and better mechanical nurse-maids. "Some Kinds of Life" is a cautionary tale about the foolish practice of fighting wars away from home, merely in order to maintain the standard of living (read "the American way of life"). First the men are sent up to fight aliens on distant planets, then the boys, then the women and children, all to protect rare metals needed for the wondrous new machines that run the homes.

When some Orionians arrive on Terra they find the homes intact but no people to live in them. Baffled, they observe that the air is "Too thin to breathe. For us. But enough for some kinds of life."

Another story dealing with the human urge to commit global suicide is "Planet for Transients" (*Fantastic Universe*, October-November 1953). Some 350 years after the nuclear wars that have subjected the whole of Earth's surface to hard radiation, a few humans survive, but at the end of their tether. They have lived underground but their equipment is breaking down and they still cannot breathe the atmosphere safely. One of their number goes searching for other survivors but finds only the mutants—known variously as runners, rollers, bugs, worms, toads, porpoise types—who have somehow adapted to life in the new "hot" conditions. He is fortunate to be picked up by Canadians who have managed to move off the planet to Mars and have come back to pick up cultural artifacts and other treasures. The air of the new Earth supports "some kinds of life" but not, any longer, the human form. We may return from time to time as visitors but there is no guarantee that we will be welcome. This story was mined for *Deus Irae*, as was "The Great C" (in Volume I), which in basic outline is somewhat similar, though pessimistic.

The alarming tendency humans have to put artificial things ahead of their own less perfect species is demonstrated in the terrifying story, "Progeny" (first published in *If*, November 1954). Here Dick pursues to its logical conclusion Swift's idea that parents are the very last people who should be allowed to bring up their children. Only robots are allowed to teach Peter Doyle from his birth to the age of eighteen years. His distressed father, Ed, cannot do much about this because he has escaped from the urban life of Earth to be a pioneer plumber on one of the Proxima planets. Ed sees his son twice only, after birth and when Peter is aged nine and already too set upon his course as a biochemist to be at all interested in his father's plea that the two go off-planet together. After Ed's discomfited departure, Peter is mightily relieved: he confides to his teacher, the robot Doctor Bish, that his father smells—like a lab animal. The names reinforce a suggestion that Dick is taking a sideswipe at Jesuit theories of education. However, Gregg Rickman has pointed out in his biography that we should see in Peter Doyle an analogue of Phil Dick, victim (as he believed) of a quite directly comparable upbringing. Peter's mother Janet, who has "cold eyes like little blue rocks," calmly acquiesces in a situation in which the most shocking *faux pas* the hapless Ted commits when he first sees his new-born infant is to express the wish to hold the baby—it is promptly whisked out of his reach. Phil's mother Dorothy stated in a 1975 letter to her son that she had gone along with the pediatric theorists of her day, by whom "Cuddling, rocking, kissing [a baby] were frowned on." Rickman notices that although Ted's name recalls Ed Dick, Phil's largely absent father, his physical description is that of Herb Hollis, who acted as his surrogate father in the 1940s. (On the shocking story of Philip Dick's early infancy, see Rickman, *To the High Castle*, especially 15-17 for "Progeny.")

Another child is in danger in the delightful horror fantasy called "The Cookie Lady" (from *Fantasy Fiction*, June 1953). A small fat boy is enticed to visit an old lady in the neighborhood, who panders to his greed because she discovers that, when close to him, her youth temporarily renews itself. He always comes home from these visits very tired, but on what his anxious parents insist must be his last visit, the vampirical Mrs. Drew yields to the temptation to draw the boy's youth permanently away, leaving an empty shell. Oddly, the story is so structured that one feels more sympathy for the wicked witch figure than one does for the victim, who has the unhappy but apt sobriquet of Bubber. Anthony Wolk relates this name to Dick's later vocabulary of entropy: "gubble," "gabble," "gubbish," "kipple," noting the way Bubber ends up as "something gray and dry...A bundle of weeds, weeds and rags blown by the wind" ("The Sunstruck Forest," 23). This relationship prefigures that postulated between Pat Conley and Joe Chip (and the other shriveled victims) in *Ubik*. Comparable is "Of Withered Apples," published first in *Cosmos Science Fiction & Fantasy*, July 1954, a horror story about a magic apple tree which uses a leaf to summon Bostonian Lori Patterson from the Vermont farmhouse where she now lives with her unimaginative husband Steve and his father Ed, up the hill to the derelict farm where it lives. There she evades its embrace but on her way home makes the mistake of eating a withered apple (like "The Cookie Lady" this is an "eating death" story and so belongs loosely with the "Beyond Lies the Wub"" group and the various satires on drug addiction). She dies that night in agony and an apple tree springs from her grave, its early fruit red as her cheeks had been.

More shriveling goes on in another story that had a curious effect on me while reading it (it is one of the stories in this volume which were previously unfamiliar to me). This disturbing story, "Martians Come in Clouds," was first published in *Fantastic Universe* for June-July 1954. The main human figures in the story are Jimmy Barnes, a schoolboy, and his father Ted. Ted Barnes has a fear and loathing of the Buggies which have been descending for some years now from the sky, individually having the appearance of large dry leaves but floating from Mars in clouds. Several land in Ted's suburban neighborhood and he comes home shaken from seeing one being brought down from a roof with a pole: he warns his son to stay away from any of them and if he sees one to turn and run away from it as fast as he can. Naturally, all the lads at school are busy daring each other to catch one; inevitably, Jimmy is the one who first sees a buggie, stranded in a tree. He does not run away and so becomes exposed to the emanations of the alien's mind. It projects scenes to him:

> Scenes—of another world, its world. The buggie was talking to him, telling him about its world, spinning out scene after scene with anxious haste.
> "Get away," Jimmy muttered thickly.
> But the scenes still came, urgently, insistently, lapping at his mind.
> Plains—a vast desert without limit or end. Dark red, cracked and scored with ravines. A far line of blunted hills, dust-covered, corroded. A great basin off to the right, an endless empty piepan with white-crusted salt riming it, a bitter ash where water had once lapped.
> "Get away!" Jimmy muttered again, moving a step back.
> The scenes grew. Dead sky, particles of sand, whipped along, carried endlessly. Sheets of sand, vast billowing clouds of sand and dust, blowing endlessly across the cracked surface of the planet. A few scrawny plants growing by rocks. In the shadows of the mountains great spiders with old webs, dust-covered, spun centuries ago. Dead spiders, lodged in cracks.
> A scene expanded. Some sort of artificial pipe, jutting up from the red-baked ground. A vent—underground quarters. The view changed. He was seeing below, down into the core of the planet—layer after layer of crumpled rock. A withered wrinkled planet without fire or life or moisture of any kind. Its skin cracking, its pulp drying out and blowing up in clouds of dust. Far down in the core a tank of some

sort—a chamber sunk in the heart of the planet.
He was inside the tank. Buggies were everywhere, sliding and moving.

"Get away," I muttered, coming to the end of the page and not wanting to turn over, and I literally stopped reading for some time because I was so oppressed by what I took to be another of Dick's evocations of the "gubble world" of Mars, the vertiginous entropic state he so well, or so horribly, portrays in *Martian Time-Slip*.

When I got back to the story, it was with mixed relief and disgust that I read about Jimmy's escape from the buggie and its subsequent destruction—it is burnt, along with most of the tree in which it has lodged. Philip K. Dick had caught me yet again—and I was disgusted about that, too.

All the Martian had wanted to do was to show the Terran its plight and its hopes: the dying race has come to Earth because of the abundant water here. All they want is to settle somewhere in mid-ocean and live there on big water discs. The individual Martian takes control of Jimmy's mind only in order to beg for his human permission.

Jimmy is only a schoolboy. He watches the cops kill the creature and then he hurries home "as if the buggie were chasing him." Next day his father Ted is seen bragging to his mates in the cafeteria about his son's courage, "all aglow with reflected glory":

> "Not a bit afraid," he murmured, full of pride, a deep glowing pride. "Not one damn bit!"

Philip K. Dick keeps asking the same question: "Is there a human in the house?" and he keeps coming up with the same answer: "Not yet, not here." No wonder he made his American readers uneasy. Like myself, they kept falling prey to the same superstitious fears of the unknown, fears of the strange, of the alien, that have haunted the so-called human race for ever, probably. I could feel the same fear and loathing that Ted and Jimmy felt, even when I could clearly understand, as I was reading, what Dick was actually communicating, in rational terms, that the Martian was merely a polite beggar in desperate need of easily affordable charity. The peculiar horror I associated with the scenes of Martian desiccation was, of course, achieved by notably stark, simple means: the idea of claustrophobic entrapment, underground, among spiders and creatures which, merely by being called "buggies," must be loathsome, whether imagined crawling about a dried-out planet or on the surface of one of "our" oceans. The gratuitous revulsion I experienced as one long-familiar with the Phildickian canon was a bonus for the writer; his story was addressed not to me but to the readers of *Fantastic Universe* in 1954 and I knew more about the gubble world than Dick did, but we sense that Dick progressed as a writer not merely by obsessively exploiting the irrational fears of his readers but also by cultivating and intensifying his own obsessional fears.

In relation to "Martians Come in Clouds," I may mention briefly one of the weaker stories in the volume, "Survey Team," which rather too obviously has the first men from Earth to arrive on Mars discover that it has been totally used up and that the Martians have travelled off-planet many thousands of years ago—to Earth. Earth is now itself uninhabitable, after thirty years of nuclear war, so the originally Martian race has come full circle—as it deserves. One of the survey team, at least, is less than happy with the thought that it may be possible to find a third planet:

> "It's wrong!" Mason shouted. "Two are enough! Let's not destroy a third world!"
>
> Nobody listened to him. Judde and Young and Halloway gazed up, faces eager, hands clenching and unclenching. As if they were already there. As if they were already holding onto the new world, clutching it with all their strength. Tearing it apart, atom by atom...

Banal as the story is, one does have sadly to note that the dilemma it poses for the human race is still completely unresolved. Whether Earth goes the way of Mars or takes the path of nuclear destruction, the chances are that we shall still hope to colonize a third planet, sooner or later.

The "What's in a name" theme, evident in a minor way in "Martians Come in Clouds," is also significant in another too-little known story, "A Surface Raid," first published in *Fantastic Universe* for July 1955. In this case the name of "saps" is given to the surface-dwellers of a future earth that has been ravaged by nuclear wars. The basic situation reverses that of "The Defenders" (used in *The Penultimate Truth* and reprinted in Volume I). *Homo sapiens* has been reduced to a race of savages, supposedly near extinction, but their successors, mutant humans who were produced in order to make the weapons for the wars and were called "technos," still flourish below the earth's surface and most of the story is presented from the point of view of one of them, young Harl, who blackmails his father into allowing him to join a clandestine raiding party for the purpose of capturing some saps to be used for "the basic-industry factory units," in other words, as slave labor. Harl is presented as a typical young gung-ho type, already expert at balancing himself, when he bounds agilely from the tube car into the receiving strip, and his blast gun when he "cradles" it. He is told he will not need the gun but he does require his screen, a portable device which makes him invisible at the press of a switch. On the surface with the adult raiders, Harl is allowed to enter a primitive village and soon loses contact with the others. He naturally has trouble with the light, finding it painful even though he wears goggles. Being invisible, he spends some time examining the strange humans closely. They wear little clothing and have very dark skin from the intense radiation on the surface, whereas his own skin is colorless. He cannot understand their language but after wandering amongst them for some time he makes an independent assessment of them:

> So these were the saps. The race that was dying out—the dying race, soon to be extinct. Remnants.
> But they did not appear to be a dying race. They were working hard, tirelessly chipping at the hydro-slag [the fused surface of the earth which they have gradually broken down], fixing their arrows, hunting, plowing, pounding grain, weaving, combing—

He comes upon a young couple sitting by themselves in the woods. The man is making pots, the woman, who is beautiful, paints a simple design on each pot as it dries. Harl studies her intently, fascinated by the way she uses the same simple pictorial elements each time but always produces a slightly different design. "No two bowls came out exactly the same." Dick does not say so, but it is obvious that the technos never produce works that vary in this way.

These scenes in "A Surface Raid" are recorded with obsessive intensity as if by Wells's own Invisible Man or the hero in "The New Accelerator." Another echo which might be traced is from the eavesdropping monster in *Frankenstein*; indeed, the event suggests that this is a deliberate effect. The young man leaves Harl alone with the woman and Harl feels an overwhelming urge to communicate with her. Standing directly in front of her, he impulsively presses his belt switch and exposes himself. Much to his surprise, she screams and flees, alarming the villagers, who start scattering white powder in the air, which would render the invaders visible if they did not themselves retreat. Harl is able to rejoin his father and go back underground, where we do not follow him. Instead, we are given the sap's eye-view of Harl.

After she has recovered from the shock, Julie the painter is talking to her brother Ken the potter, trying to describe the horror of what she has just seen:

> "What did it look like?" Ken demanded.
> "It was—it was like a man. But it couldn't have been a man. It was metallic all over, from head to foot, and it had huge hands and feet. Its face was all pasty white like—like meal. It was—sickly. Hideously sickly. White and metallic, and sickly. Like some kind of root dug up out of the soil."

To add to the horror, Julie recalls that "It was blind. It had something instead of eyes. Two black spaces. Darkness." They ask a wise old man called Mr. Stebbins what the creature was. This savage tribe has not encountered the technos for some 200 years or more. Mr. Stebbins has to probe in his memory of old books and legends he has heard about "Things that lived under the ground... Like men but not men... Things that dug tunnels, that mined metals... Things that were blind and had great hands and feet and pasty white skin."

It is upon the answer to this question that the wit of the story turns. It seems at first to be an odd way to end the story, to drop the issue of what Harl has learnt from his experience and to concentrate purely on the thought of what the savage humans make of him, what they think that Harl is. You see, we know the answer. We know that Harl was called a techno by the humans who made him—a knowledge new, incidentally, to Harl who has learned this only that day, from an obligingly knowledgeable friend. We also have another answer up our sleeve, if we happen to be smart enough to think of it. Thus the answer the story gives us is a complete surprise.

> "Goblins," Mr. Stebbins stated. "What you saw was a goblin."

Philip K. Dick must have known we, his readers, would think of the Morlocks but his neo-savages reach farther back in time not farther forward and this is absolutely correct for them. They are no

Eloi, they are saps: they have the wisdom of the ages still, the collective unconscious, if you like, and they need to locate the creatures that they fear in the time, the past time, that belongs, now, to both of them. Morlocks—and technos—are only a new form of goblin, after all and the knowledge of this puts both Wells and Dick in their place. The goblins, too, once named, can be put back where they belong. The last words of the story are:

> Julie nodded, gazing down wide-eyed at the ground, her arms clasped around her knees. "Yes," she said. "That sounds like what it was. It frightened me. I was so afraid. I turned and ran. It seemed so horrible." She looked up at her brother, smiling a little. "But I'm better now..."
> Ken rubbed his big dark hands together, nodding with relief. "Fine," he said. "Now we can get back to work. There's a lot to do. A lot of things to get done."

It is a notable feature of "A Surface Raid" that, whereas Harl begins with no doubts about his status as superior to the "saps," his experience casts doubt upon the whole nature of the relationship between himself and what his father assures him are "animals...Savage animals." He cannot understand why the woman had "recoiled from him in blind terror" or why she should seem important. "It did not make sense. He had gone out of his mind and then she had gone out of her mind. There had to be some meaning to it—if he could only grasp it." On the other hand, Julie and the others have no residual doubts about who they are: they are assured of their normalcy. Their question is: "What was it?" and when they are given an answer, they are content. Harl clearly feels attracted to Julie; Julie does not recognize Harl as anything other than a thing: "It was—it was like a man. But it couldn't have been a man."

Blake has a saying, "Attempting to be more than Man We become less" (Luvah in *The Four Zoas*, IX, 135). Harl's race has lost compassion, it seems, and original creativity, by gaining technological skill. The experiment described in "Project: Earth" (from *Imagination*, December 1953), is doomed to failure. Project A was a winged race but proud; they became internecine. The creatures in Project B (ourselves) were, according to the original plan, to have less individualism and a stronger group instinct, but they were contaminated by the Project A types. Project C, a tiny naked race of humanoids with antennae, will also fail to be satisfactory, because of the interference at their birth by an eleven-year-old boy called Tommy. "Project: Earth" is not a convincing story, partly because the project's supervisor, an ancient man called Billings, who is presented as just about to complete a massive typewritten report on Project B, is too accessible, living as he does in an ordinary suburban lodging, and too easily hoodwinked (though the domestication of the supernatural, which makes Billings only a little strange, is a characteristic Phildickian swoop). The conclusion is too pat: Tommy has the nine representatives of Project C, four of whom are female, five male, in his possession for a while and is persuaded to clothe them; Billings recovers them but they all escape from him; however, he knows as soon as he sees their clothes that Project C has gone the same way as the others, through "Rebellion and independence."

Dick himself was all for "rebellion and independence"; his hero James Cutter in "The Hood Maker" (from *Imagination*, June 1955), a characteristic outlaw working on behalf of the human race against a totalitarian self-styled *Homo superior*, asserts that "Nobody should lead mankind. It should lead itself." Cutter makes hoods to protect humans from the probes of the "teeps," telepathic offspring of Malagasians who were victims of a hydrogen bomb accident back in 2004. Now the teeps are being used to solve the Government of the Free Union's most pressing problem: "the detection and punishment of disloyalty." This gives the teeps, the only ones whose disloyalty cannot be tested (except by other teeps), the opportunity to seize power. They systematically frame leading citizens and government leaders but Cutter recruits as many as possible by distributing hoods to those who are threatened; they join him in his secret factory. Unfortunately, the evidence to frame one such man, old Walter Franklin, is prepared by the teeps before they move to arrest and scan him; no sooner does he decide to wear his hood than a mob is stirred up against him and, although he is rescued by Cutter's agents, the teeps can track his course. The showdown comes when Cutter takes Franklin to the robot-guarded home of Senator Waldo (this name inevitably recalls Robert A. Heinlein's story, which appeared in 1942), who is about to bring in a bill to outlaw the wearing of hoods. Franklin knows Waldo and Cutter believes he may persuade him that the Anti-Immunity Bill inherently endangers the human race. They come too late and Franklin is melted by a teep leader, Abbud. However, Cutter destroys Abbud by telling him that none of the teeps has any future; they are not true mutants as they cannot breed. Thus Dick avoids the dilemma of taking sides with *Homo superior* against his own beloved, if fallible species. It is noteworthy that the weapon used by the teeps is called a Slem-gun: this seems too close to the name of van Vogt's genuinely mutant telepaths, the slans, to be a coincidence. (In this story one of the bureaucratic authorities is Clearance Director Ross; in "Adjustment Team" there is a "Clearance Director Douglas.")

That element in the human make-up which persuades us to emulate the machine is pitted against our artistic side in "Souvenir" (*Fantastic Universe*, October 1954), but the choice the reader is implicitly invited to make between the two is not rendered easy by the association of the latter with atavistic principles. The first explorers to colonize beyond the solar system have been lost for 300 years and the idea of Williamson's World has become a kind of holy grail (a carefully chosen metaphor) for contemporary members of the Galactic community. A representative of the Galactic Relay Center, Edward Rogers, is excited when the world is discovered and he goes there to invite the lost colony to join the rest of the Galaxy. Williamson's World looks idyllic at first to the reader, though shocking to Rogers, as its cities are small and its natural surroundings unspoilt. He is taken to a country home by a descendant of Williamson, where he is served simple food from wooden cups and bowls, although young Gene Williamson explains that the colonists are well aware of the new technology, as they have tapped into the Relay transmissions: they simply don't wish to be up to date. Unfortunately, it is a case of join or be killed, because the Galactic union works by having every world march forward together: there is no deviation. The Relay Center transmits new information universally, so that no time is wasted performing the same experiment twice. Williamson's World is in headlong retreat from all of this progress; feudal now, it is becoming progressively more tribal; there are limited wars but there are also many signs of creativity: handcrafting, painting, dancing, drama. Significantly, Rogers's clinical term for creativity is "psychological release." It is also noteworthy that Rogers's model for the planetary union is the Roman Empire, against which the deviant world appears all the more "barbaric." In this "cold equations" story, the colonists elect not to join the Galaxy and they go down the tubes. The intention is that not even the memory of Williamson's World shall remain. However, one trooper brings back a souvenir for his small boy, a wooden cup (thus we see that the grail reference at the start of the story was cunningly placed), which bodes trouble for the more or less distant future of the federated worlds.

In "Second Variety" (*Space Science Fiction*, May 1954), which I suppose will be acknowledged by most readers of Dick to be a classic war story and one of the best non-metaphysical horror stories, there is no suggestion that the reader should prefer the alien, the mechanical, or the mutant to the human species: the problem is one of identification. After Russians and Americans have blown each other to bits, "our side" seems to have the edge with the newly-invented "claws," robot killers that destroy anything that moves—if it does not have an identifying button. However, the claws develop the power to modify themselves into new varieties and soon, especially by the use of mimic humans, become a menace to everybody, even to the humans (if that is what they are) who have escaped to the moon. The only bonus in the situation is that they are also a menace to themselves. In relation to this story, the author commented in 1976 (in a note for *The Best of Philip K. Dick*, published 1977) that here:

> My grand theme—who is human and who only appears (masquerades) as human?—emerges most fully. Unless we can individually and collectively be certain of the answer to this question, we face what is, in my view, the most serious problem possible. Without answering it adequately, we cannot even be certain of our own selves. I cannot even know myself, let alone you. So I keep working on this theme; to me nothing is as important a question. And the answer comes very hard.

It does indeed. We have bred monsters who cannot recognize the human in themselves, to whom others are as unreal as figures on the screen projecting a violent video movie. To extirpate these "second variety" humanoids will make us too uncomfortably monstrous like them, offering us no guarantee that our future lives will be any less nasty, brutish and short than were those of our not-too-remote forefathers.

Although part of the skill of this kind of story must be to mislead the reader (as with Agatha Christie's *And Then There Were None*—originally *Ten Little Niggers*—which in basic outline it somewhat resembles), Dick does offer some pointers to the non-human life forms. The David disguise would be relatively easy for the hero Hendricks to penetrate—if only he were sufficiently alert to be suspicious: he has no use for food, his answers to questions are vague; it is also notable that "His face showed no expression." The Second Variety, too, is "expressionless"; its voice is "like iron" and it admires the beauty of a gun's construction. (That it enjoys smoking cigarettes may be taken as camouflage.) Like Harl, the techno in "A Surface Raid," it moves "expertly"; it does, indeed, anticipate the technos, having been manufactured underground. It may be worth noting that the story does not tell us that Hendricks is killed by the mechanical humanoids that overwhelm him; they may design only to enslave him, having been on an early "surface raid." Although the design of the human inventors was for claws and their descendants to kill all warm-blooded living things, this does not actually mean that the machine-made varieties will do so, indiscriminately. Evolution is accelerated in the world of the story, along Lysenko's lines (his name is invoked when a lizard is seen, "hurrying through the ash. It was exactly the same color as the ash" and Klaus (note the name) notes, "Perfect adaptation....Proves we were right. Lysenko, I mean"—which in context is a slip of the vocal apparatus). Hendricks even speculates along the lines to be developed in the world of the technos:

> "...It makes me wonder if we're not seeing the beginning of a new species. Evolution. The race to come after man."
> Rudi grunted. "There is no race after man."
> "No? Why not? Maybe we're seeing it now, the end of human beings, the beginning of a new society."
> "They're not a race. They're mechanical killers. You made them to destroy. That's all they can do. They're machines with a job."
> "So it seems now. But how about later on? After the war is over. Maybe, when there aren't any humans to destroy, their real potentialities will begin to show."
> "You talk as if they were alive!"
> "Aren't they?"

At the present stage of development, however, each individual of a given variety is identical to its fellows, representing "Perfect socialism....The ideal of the communist state. All citizens interchangeable." Needless to say, this could never be Dick's ideal, though I doubt whether his work has ever held much appeal for readers of the far right.

"Human Is" (from *Startling Stories*, Winter 1955) appears here as another work of central importance in Dick's thought. In 1976, Dick had this to say about it:

> To me, this story states my early conclusions as to what is human. I have not really changed my view since I wrote this story, back in the Fifties. It's not what you look like, or what planet you were born on. It's how kind you are. The quality of kindness, to me, distinguishes us from rocks and sticks and metal, and will forever, whatever shape we take, wherever we go, whatever we become. For me, Human Is is my credo. May it be yours.

The genetic human "man of the future" in this story is represented by Lester Herrick, who is Dick's idea of what "human isn't." Herrick, a machine-like scientist working on toxins for the Military, hates small children and animals, lacks feeling for his wife, is angry, irritable, selfish and is even so anxious to lose no time from his research that he grudges the time spent on eating and would rather everybody were force-fed intravenously. He travels to the planet Rexor IV but the Lester Herrick who returns appears to be an alien life form in his body—the mind of the original Lester is believed to be in suspended animation on the alien planet. The new Lester is a warm, caring courteous man but the authorities decide he should be blasted. However, he must first be testified against by Herrick's wife Jill, who is thus put in the position of having the power of life and death over both her husbands. She makes, we feel sure, the right choice, even though she perjures herself to do so. Note that she could not be absolutely sure before the decision that the "human" who came back from Rexor IV was not the same person as the one who went there. As Wolk notes (op. cit., 30), Rexor IV is "dry and dead," whereas "Terra is a wonderful planet. Moist and full of life"; although the alien's motive for the imposture is self-serving, this does not mean (any more than with the withered aliens of "Martians Come in Clouds") that he is incapable of caring for the members of another species.

A related story, "Impostor" (also, in error, spelt "Imposter" here), which first appeared in *Astounding*, June 1953, is almost devoid of means by which the reader may test the imposition and so appears as a work of pure paranoia: it is certainly one of Dick's most frightening short works. Dick explained in 1976:

Here was my first story on the topic of: Am I a human? Or am I just programmed to believe I am human? When you consider that I wrote this back in 1953, it was, if I may say so, a pretty damn good new idea in sf. Of course, by now I've done it to death. But the theme still preoccupies me. It's an important theme because it forces us to ask: What is a human? And—what isn't?

Spence Olham is about to leave home for his work on "the Project" to develop an offensive weapon against the invading Outspacers when he is arrested and taken to the far side of the moon, for destruction. It is believed that an Outspacer robot, manufactured to mimic him exactly, has taken the real Olham's place after killing him and is undetectable even to the victim because it contains Olham's memories. The robot is known to have a bomb inside it which will be triggered by a particular phrase. Olham believes himself innocent and he manages to evade his capturers and return to his home, where he hopes to prove his innocence through X-ray scanning. His theory is that the alien invader crash-landed and the change-over never occurred. However, when he gets home he finds the military waiting for him. He eludes them and (after working out that this was the cause of a mysterious fire which destroyed a wood) reaches the site of the crashed rocket, where it does indeed appear to the government agents that the robot's "corpse" lies inert. Nevertheless, Spence Olham discovers that he really is the alien impostor and, in making the discovery, utters the words which trigger an explosion that destroys the planet. The question of testing for humanity against a measure of human kindness never gets asked in this story: in a quite believably human way, the robot Spence appears to be activated by the need to survive the immediate crisis and to obtain justice (a fair trial for which the government agents have no time). Only once does Dick allow the mask to slip a little, when "Olham" is surprised to find how much more quickly he can run than his pursuers. It may be observed that in the novel, *Do Androids Dream of Electric Sheep?* (1968), Rick Decard finds no convincing means to test those androids who think they are human, despite the fact that they are supposed to have been made without empathy.

There is a sequel to "Second Variety," "Jon's World" (first published in *Time to Come*, ed. August Derleth). Humans have survived and have discovered time travel. Since the new scientists have lost the secret of the artificial brain used in the "claws" of "Second Variety," two men go back to steal the plans from their inventor, Schonerman. (This scenario is comparable to that in the earlier story, "The Skull.") The world they reach is much greener than the one they leave, it is "Jon's world," seen in a vision by Jon, the son of one of the time travelers, Ryan. This raises interesting speculations (of the kind we have in the alternative history story, *The Man in the High Castle*) and, just to be on the safe side, one of the travelers burns the plans.

Time travel features also in "Breakfast at Twilight" (published in *Amazing*, July 1954). In a remarkable anticipation of Rod Serling's *Twilight Zone* series, which began running some five years later, a suburban family get out of bed one morning to find that outside their house is a foggy "twilight," the name given to the state America is in under rom (robotic operated missiles) attack during World War Three. Heavily armed soldiers charge in from the fog, baffled to find everything intact when all around is rubble. The theory is offered that a rom explosion was so powerful as to suck the house from the past—seven years away (it is now 1980). As is usual in a *Twilight Zone* story, the appalled family group have the opportunity to return to their normal world of 1973, while sheltering from a further rom attack in the basement. Again, as is to be expected after such a weird experience, they are left unable to explain what happened to them, in this case, why the house has been totally devastated. At the end of the story, the residual problem remains of how to obviate the horribly near future, though this is not explored.

A "time loop" idea is employed in "Prominent Author" (from *If*, May 1954). Near-instantaneous matter transmission is being tested by the inventors, Terran Development, and employee Henry Lawrence is delighted when he can use one to beat the traffic to his place of work. However, when he discovers a leak in the floor of the transmitter, called a "Jiffi-scuttler" (a kind of tunnel along which he has only to move five steps), he is so fascinated by what he sees through it that he keeps the information to himself. Below him are tiny figures who move jerkily and rapidly. They attract his attention with a tiny piece of paper which they obviously wish him to read. He has it translated by the Linguistic Machine, finds questions which he uses the Federal Library of Information to answer, retranslates the answers, and gives the results back to the tiny people, who begin to worship him. This exchange takes place every day, although generations seem to pass in the world below: Dick uses the idea of the expanding universe, which was popular in science fiction of the time, and which he had used himself already in "Prize Ship."

The reader has no great difficulty in working out who these people are, but Lawrence, who is no great student of culture (Dick in the early fifties was remarkably prescient in this regard), has no idea what is going on, though he enjoys the adulation and, for the first time in his working career, comes home happy every day. All comes crashing about his ears when his boss discovers what is going on and sacks him, but it is then that Lawrence learns that he has, in effect, written the text of the Holy Bible (a book with which he is utterly unacquainted). Happier than ever, Lawrence basks at home in the glory of being a "prominent author." Perhaps this story was daringly irreverent in 1954.

It is surprising that the remarkable and morally devastating story, "James P. Crow," published in *Planet Stories*, May 1954, was not anthologized in one of the early collections and so remains little known. Possibly the racial implications frightened editors. In the far-future world, perhaps, of "Second Variety" and "Jon's World," or of "A Surface Raid," humans are living as slaves to the robots, on an Earth where history has been so much distorted by the devastation of nuclear wars that it is generally believed that the robots created the humans. (In this light, the already faded knowledge of the true human-techno relationship in "A Surface Raid" appears like a deliberate "plant" to set up this history of the farther future.) Although humans are despised (they smell, as in "Progeny") , the laws provide that they be treated as equals: provided they can pass the "Lists," they may even rise to the top, the Supreme Council. The Lists are set by the robots, for the robots, and it is not surprising that no human has ever passed even the lowest of them—until James P. Crow comes along. The secret of Crow's success is a "Time Window," which enables him to see the answers in advance and so achieve perfect scores. It also enables him to compile evidence of the true history of the robot-human relationship. When he achieves power, Crow (an adopted name which he knows no one but himself can understand) uses his knowledge to persuade all the robots to leave Earth for other planets, thus achieving the sort of goal that the "Hood Maker" would approve, human self-government. So is this utopia? The trouble is, that at the end of the story, James P. Crow looks uncomfortably like the first Lester Herrick. His robot friend, L-87t, asks:

> "Can you give me some idea of the government you'll set up?"
> Crow glanced up impatiently. "What?"

"Your form of government. How will your society be ruled, now that you've maneuvered us off Earth? What sort of government will take place of our Supreme Council and Congress?"

Crow didn't answer. He had already returned to his work. There was a strange granite cast to his face, a peculiar hardness L-87t had never seen.

"Who'll run things?" L-87t asked. "Who'll be the Government now that we're gone? You said yourself humans show no ability to manage a complex modern society. Can you find a human capable of keeping the wheels turning? Is there a human being capable of leading mankind?"

Crow smiled thinly. And continued working.

In the story, Crow has set out firmly the difference between humans and robots, according to which, by definition, the former are not good at government:

"...Humans and robots are completely different. We humans can sing, act, write plays, stories, operas, paint, design sets, flower gardens, buildings, cook delicious meals, make love, scratch sonnets on menus— and robots can't. But robots can build elaborate cities and machines that function perfectly, work for days without rest, think without emotional interruption, gestalt complex data without a time lag.

"Humans excel in some fields, robots in others. Humans have highly developed emotions and feelings. Esthetic awareness. We're sensitive to colors and sounds and textures and soft music mixed with wine. All very fine things. Worthwhile. But realms totally beyond robots. Robots are purely intellectual. Which is fine, too. Both realms are fine. Emotional humans, sensitive to art and music and drama. Robots who think and plan and design machinery...."

Dick is not concerned here, as sf authors often are, with the angst of robots who seek to become more human, more emotional. (See, however, below in the discussion of "A Present for Pat.") He is, instead, very concerned with the human urge to become more and more robotic. It is possible that the Jim Crow allusion has a double meaning. Although the term was used as an insulting reference to American blacks, its original reference (in a song by the original "nigger minstrel," T. J. Rice), was to a renegade or turncoat.

This disturbing implication is considered in a different way in another too-little known story, "Small Town," published in *Amazing*, May 1954, of which Dick had this to say in 1979 (in a note for *The Golden Man*, published in 1980):

> Here the frustrations of a defeated small person—small in terms of power, in particular power over others—gradually become transformed into something sinister: the force of death. In rereading this story (which is of course a fantasy, not science fiction) I am impressed by the subtle change which takes place in the protagonist from Trod-Upon to Treader. Verne Haskel initially appears as the prototype of the impotent human being, but this conceals a drive at his core self which is anything but weak. It is as if I am saying, The put-upon person may be very dangerous. Be careful as to how you misuse him; he may be a mask for thanatos: the antagonist of life; he may not secretly wish to rule; he may wish to *destroy*.

Dick here certainly expresses a truth about Crow and Haskel but what strikes me as surprising is that he suppresses recognition of their creative power. Haskel lives with his adulterous wife Madge in a small town called Woodland, on the outskirts of San Francisco; he is a discontented wage-slave in Jim Larson's Pump and Valve Works. However, in his basement at home, Haskel has an almost perfect model of Woodland set up around a train set, on which he has worked since childhood. Suddenly he surprises himself by an urge to destroy: he rips out the Larson Works and substitutes a mortuary. Soon he is furiously at work changing the whole model into a Woodland that reflects his own desires. Madge notices the change in him, and her lover, Doctor Paul Tyler, investigates the situation in the basement. Tyler is delighted when he is able from Haskel's behavior to make the prognosis that his rival will soon depart this world and become literally merged with his model ideal. This indeed happens, as is consistent with Dick's theory of the "shared reality," which Tyler here articulates:

"The mind constructs reality. Frames it. Creates it. We all have a common reality, a common dream. But Haskel turned his back on our common reality and created his own. And he had a unique capacity—far beyond the ordinary. He devoted his whole life, his whole skill to building it. He's there now."

What Tyler does not realize until too late is that Verne Haskel has not moved into the model Woodtown: rather, he has transformed the "real" Woodtown into his model—where he is the Mayor and where Tyler and Madge are in deep trouble. One may discern in Haskel's coup a larger scale, malign version of the appropriation achieved by the creature in "Beyond Lies the Wub." Several stories in the second volume are related to "Small Town" by theme, among them "The Commuter," "The World She Wanted," "Project: Earth," "The Trouble with Bubbles," "Adjustment Team" and "Prominent Author," but novels such as *The World Jones Made*, *Eye in the Sky* and *Clans of the Alphane Moon*, among others, are also to be associated with it.

Possibly an even larger question than our identity as humans, if the two are not inextricably entangled, as in "Project: Earth," is "Who owns this world?" In "The World She Wanted" (from *Science Fiction Quarterly*, May 1953), the story develops as a battle of individual wills, after Larry Brewster is picked up by a girl who claims that he is living in her world, defined as the best of all possible worlds for her, one in which she is the only real person, whereas Larry, the man she plans to marry, is only partially real. Names such as Plato, Descartes and Herbert Spencer are tossed into their philosophical debates but she fails so radically to convince him—and annoys him so much by her demands upon him—that eventually he calls her bluff and succeeds in banishing her from what he determines shall be his world. The event proves her wrong but does not demonstrate that Larry is in his own best of all possible worlds, solipsistically secure. For all he knows, he could still be merely a partially real being in someone else's reality.

In "The Trouble with Bubbles" (*If*, September 1953), people are able to create their own "bubble" worlds and have Contest Parties to decide who can make the most advanced one. (For the idea of worlds in bubbles, compare the earlier stories, "The Crystal Crypt" and "Stability," although those shrunken worlds are a distinct concept; here the idea is of "sub-atomic worlds, in controlled containers. We start life going on a sub-atomic world, feed it problems to make it evolve, try to raise it higher and higher.") Nathan Hull thinks the bubbles are immoral and hopes to have their sale banned; he sees them as substitutes (the working title was "Plaything") for serious endeavors, in the wake of a failure to discover life on other worlds within the solar system. Frustration mounts to the point where, unable to create worlds answerable to their desires, the contestants at the parties destroy their bubbles, orgiastically. The motif of dependence on substitute life-forms appears not only here but also in the failure experienced by Hull when he tries to plead his cause: the voters are so used to having robots analyze an argument for them that a speech by a mere human has little or even an aversive impact upon them. Hope comes with the contact of other populated worlds from (where else?) Proxima Centauri, so the bubble fad will soon be over, but Hull experiences a deeper unease when a devastating earthquake provokes in him the wild, unanswerable surmise that (though this is not directly stated to us) *if the earth hath bubbles, then ours is of them* (cf. Macbeth, I.iii.79-80).

The experience of being inside Hull's world, however, is more like that of imprisonment in an anthill, where everyone is so busy seeking attention that no one has time to stop and listen. Information is thrust upon the reader but against the current of Hull's impatience, whether it is to rescue his girlfriend Julia from a Contest Party (successively postponed because she wishes to witness the climax of the contest, which Hull is sure will be dangerous) or to drive her home after the failure of his oratory, despite the attempts made by the apparently (if surprisingly) benevolent old inventor of the bubbles, Forrest Packman, to encourage his persistence. The feeling of overload which Dick's technique induces is nightmarish, that of being in a race against time in which everything becomes reduced to the level of irritants. An inability to stop and think allows many of the disasters that occur in Dick's stories to take place. Humans appear creatures of greed and impulse, whether the impulse is to steal, as with Tommy in "Project: Earth," or to fight, as in "Breakfast at Twilight" or "Some Kinds of Life."

§

Destabilization of our fundamental assumptions about the reality of our world is a technique used often by Dick to unsettle the reader. Of "Breakfast at Twilight" he remarked in 1976:

> There you are in your home, and the soldiers

smash down the door and tell you you're in the middle of World War III. Something's gone wrong with time. I like to fiddle with the idea of basic categories of reality, such as space and time, breaking down. It's my love of chaos, I suppose.

"Adjustment Team" (*Orbit Science Fiction*, September-October 1954), is one of the most important stories in the corpus, if only because it provides a relatively healthy, positive resolution to one of Dick's recurring nightmares. It begins with a conversation between a clerk and a family dog (cf. "Roog"). The dog is instructed to summon a man with a car at precisely 8.15 a.m., so that the man of the house, Ed Fletcher, will get early to work. Ed has to be at work then because the sector in which his office is located is to be adjusted. Unfortunately, the dog is old and sleepy and it barks a minute too late, summoning an insurance salesman who makes Ed late for work. Consequently, Ed arrives in the middle of the adjustment. From across the street, the office block looks fine, but within the sector, it is a crumbling ruin—and so are the people inside. As with "Breakfast at Twilight," there you are in your work-place, and the adjustment team charges in and tells you that you have to be de-energized. Ed escapes, finds his wife, Ruth, who also works in town, and tells her all about his experience. Naturally, she thinks he is off his head and tells him to go back to work, to show himself there's nothing to be afraid of. His retort is memorable:

> "The hell with it! After what I saw? Listen, Ruth. I saw the fabric of reality split open. I saw—behind. Underneath. I saw what was really there. And I don't want to go back. I don't want to see dust people again. Ever."

The fear that strikes Hull at the end of "The Trouble with Bubbles," the grotesque terror that pervades *Ubik*, the biblical apprehension that we are, literally, dust, is powerfully evoked in this story. Ed does go back to the office and at first it seems normal, but he realizes that everything has been, more or less subtly, changed. Even the people are different, most noticeably his boss. In panic he flees to a phone kiosk and calls the police but is whisked up to a higher sphere, where an old man (obviously a surrogate for God) explains the mistake that has been made. It is not very reassuring for Ed to be referred to impersonally as a mere "element" in the situation, even though it has been adjusted (principally by making the boss a younger, more open-minded man) so that a future detente between Russians and Americans may take place. He is, all the same, mightily relieved to be allowed to go back as an un-de-energized element, after promising that he will tell no one what he knows (the old man becomes seriously annoyed only when he finds out that Ruth, a woman, has already been told something). When Ed gets home again, however, he is in worse trouble, because Ruth insists on being told where he was all afternoon. Fortunately, or rather, providentially, Ruth is distracted by the visit of a vacuum-cleaner salesman. This story stands as an uneasy positive to set against the equally ambivalent negative of the Death figure in the *Dangerous Visions* novella, "Faith of Our Fathers."

"The Commuter" (*Amazing*, August-September 1953) also describes a world in the process of readjusting to the disruption caused by the initiation of an alternative history. Time and space are disrupted when there is only one vote separating two decisions. Those in World #I assume that a new town proposal did not go ahead; consequently the suburban train does not stop at Macon Heights and the railway staff do not know what to make of a commuter who tries to book a ticket there. In the commuter's World #II, Macon Heights was built and, when he investigates the mystery, Bob Paine finds himself passing from World #I to World #II, all in the course of a day. He starts the day with a girlfriend who is single, Laura; he ends it (very relieved to be home) married to her and with a baby. It is as if it has taken a certain space of time for the reality alteration generated by the change in the vote to catch up and make the due adjustments. This kind of story can never make sense to the reader, but Dick's use of the subjective viewpoint is so skilful that it all seems to be possible while one is immersed in the narrative flow. *Ubik* provides a more extended example of the principle, as indeed does *The Man in the High Castle*. *Counter-Clock World* is perhaps over-ambitious (and was written over-hastily); I do not recall any apologist arguing for its success.

As with biblical miracles, "The Commuter" and "Adjustment Team" seem to present us with the idea of an elastic world in which changes may be relatively local. The alien god in "A Present for Pat" (*Startling Stories*, January 1954) is like a genie from a magic lamp, though the god is activated by an offering of food: its powers are great but restricted within a small range outward from its person. Eric Blake got it as a bargain while working for Terran Metals on Ganymede but it is small and ugly and his wife does not appreciate it. It is not long before she has been turned to stone and an incredulous workmate, Tom Matson, to a toad. When Eric remonstrates with the god, he is told that they got just what they deserved. Eric is summoned to work by his boss, the tyrannical Horace Bradshaw, and carries Tom the toad with him; consequently, Eric loses his job. This delightful comic fable is science fiction and not fantasy and the god explains that his powers are limited but nonetheless great because he comes from an upper plane of existence and has intruded into our inferior plane only because he is a detective in pursuit of a criminal. Needless to say, that criminal is Bradshaw and the two fly off locked in combat: Tom and Pat are restored and Eric has his job back.

In the future world of "A Present for Pat," as often elsewhere in Dick, there are talking machines, here notably a talking door and a talking robot cabdriver. That the latter anticipates Douglas Adams's Marvin the Paranoid Android may be judged from this conversation:

> "What would you do," Eric asked the robot cabdriver, "if your wife had turned to stone, your best friend were a toad, and you had lost your job?"
> "Robots have no wives," the driver said. "They are nonsexual. Robots have no friends, either. They are incapable of emotional relationships."
> "Can robots be fired?"
> "Sometimes." The robot drew his cab up before Eric's modest six-room bungalow. "But consider. Robots are frequently melted down and new robots made from the remains. Recall Ibsen's *Peer Gynt*, the section concerning the Button Molder. The lines clearly anticipate in symbolic form the trauma of robots to come."
> "Yeah." The door opened and Eric got out. "I guess we all have our problems."
> "Robots have worse problems than anybody."
> The door shut and the cab zipped off, back down the hill.

The danger of magpie-like acquisition is illustrated in "The Cosmic Poachers" (*Imagination*, July 1953), a simple story in which, after gung-ho Earthmen have caught arachnoid aliens looting what were thought to be barren planets, they seize the loot for themselves. Little do they know that what appear to be jewels are actually eggs: they will cause trouble back on Terra.

Another horror story is "Beyond the Door" from *Fantastic Universe*, January 1954). Here a man buys his wife a cuckoo clock but finds that the cuckoo dislikes him. After he has caught his wife in the act of adultery and has banished her from the house, the man is left alone with the clock, but the cuckoo now stays behind its little door. He plans to destroy it, but it makes a pre-emptive strike.

Among the minor stories here is "The Impossible Planet" (*Imagination*, October 1953), which deals with a galaxy in which the location of Earth has been forgotten; the planet is thought to have only a mythical existence. Nevertheless, a greedy space captain agrees to take an impossibly old woman there, because she has the money to tempt him. He does some research and picks on the nearest likely target, Emphor III. This pleases the deaf, 320-year-old woman, though the abandoned, pitted planet itself does not. She dies there and her body is rushed into the tainted ocean by her robant (robot servant). The reader is, however, given evidence that the planet was indeed Earth; a coin is picked up idly by Captain Andrews, who does not understand its purpose or the legend upon it, "E PLURIBUS UNUM." This souvenir is thrown away.

My coverage of the stories in Volume II has not invoked a critical field theory, such as that of Maurice Charney's account of comedy, and I noticed relatively few analogues or sources from classical fables (which is perhaps a sign of Dick's growing confidence in his own originality). While we have not surveyed all the short stories published in the first four years of Dick's career, remarkably few of these early stories are so weak as to need apology. We may expect the presence of self-referential intertextuality to loom larger in any survey of the later volumes, because the novels are then in the synchronic background; we have reached the year of the first published novel, *Solar Lottery*.

SERIOUS CHANGES

UNWINDING THE *WATCHMEN*

by Zoran Bekric

Watchmen, by Alan Moore (writer) and Dave Gibbons (artist) aided by John Higgins (colorist), first appeared in the course of fifteen months in 1986-87 as a twelve-issue comic-book serial published by DC Comics, a division of Warner Communications. Since then, DC Comics has collected together and reissued *Watchmen* in a number of different editions as both a hardcover and a trade paperback.

Watchmen originally appeared as twelve separate issues, each of which, although a part of the larger story, seems designed to stand alone. In the collected form of the work, each issue has been transformed into a chapter. Thus, a reference to "issue VIII" is identical to a reference to "chapter VIII." I hope that there will be no confusion.

A STORY-TELLING CATALOGUE

Moore and Gibbons are very talented individuals who tell the story in *Watchmen* superbly. They use some uniquely comic-book effects, but also a variety of devices derived from literature and film.

LITERARY DEVICES

The structure of the work is the most obvious literary device. The twelve issues follow a strict pattern: six contain plot material, while the other six contain background information and biographies of the six major characters. The structure looks like this:

Issue I: "At midnight, all the agents..."

    plot

Issue II: "Absent Friends"

the biography of Edward Blake, the Comedian

Issue III: "The judge of all the earth"

    plot

Issue IV: "Watchmaker"

the biography of Jon Osterman, Doctor Manhattan

Issue V: "Fearful symmetry"

    plot

Issue VI: "The abyss gazes also"

the biography of Rorschach, Walter Joseph Kovacs

Issue VII: "A brother to dragons"

the biography of Daniel Drieberg, the second Nite Owl

Issue VIII: "Old ghosts"

    plot

Issue IX: "The darkness of mere being"

the biography of Laurie Juspeczyk, the second Silk Spectre

Issue X: "Two Riders were approaching..."

    plot

Issue XI: "Look on my works, ye mighty..."

the biography of Adrian Veidt, Ozymandias

Issue XII: "A strong and loving world"

plot and conclusion

Note how the plot-biography pattern reverses itself between issues VI and VII, giving us two biographies back to back and making the final structure a symmetrical one. In literary works this kind of thing dates back to, at least, the geometrical patterns in the narrative of Homer's *Iliad*—but it is rarely seen in a comic book.

The title of each issue is part of a quotation, the full text of which is given at the end of the issue.

Among the sources for these quotations are the Bible, philosophical texts, statements by famous people, English poetry, and pop songs. Within each issue, both the title and the full quotation are referred to again and again, sometimes subtly and sometimes quite obviously. Issue V—"Fearful symmetry"—is perhaps the clearest example, constructed to be completely symmetrical about an axis defined by the double page spread on pages 14 and 15. Each sequence in the first half has its mirror image in the second half, right down to each page and each panel. Pages 10 and 19 use literal mirrors and mirror images in their construction. Furthermore, the narrative itself and the nature of events are also neatly reflected and reversed in the two halves.

In Issue IV, "Watchmaker," the quotation is from Albert Einstein, and the various threads of the issue are tied together by numerous references, scattered throughout the text, to literal watchmaking, physics, clockwork universes, and the flow of time (which is what watches exist to record, after all).

Perhaps the most ironic interplay is found in Issue XI, the biography of Adrian Veidt, Ozymandias, entitled "Look on my works, ye mighty..." The quotation is, of course, from Percy Shelley's poem "Ozymandias." This issue not only presents Adrian Veidt's life story, but also includes Veidt's murder of three million New Yorkers. Look on his works, indeed.

Watchmen—the title of the entire book—works as a multi-layered pun and reference point. Its most obvious reference is to the nickname that the general population of the book's world has given to its costumed crime fighters—"Watchmen" as in "Guardians" or "Custodians," inspired by the famous question asked by the Roman satirist Juvenal: "quis custodiet ipsos Custodes?" ("who watches the Watchmen?"). On other levels, the title plays off the several meanings of the English word "watch" (as opposed to the single meaning of the Latin word "custodio").

"Watch" as a noun can mean a timekeeping device. References include the "watchmaker" analogy used for Doctor Manhattan, and the "Doomsday Clock" (derived from the *Bulletin of the Atomic Scientists*) which appears on the back cover of each issue—the last page of each chapter—and which, from eleven minutes to twelve o'clock, slowly moves to midnight as the story approaches its climax in the mass murder committed by Veidt.

"Watch" as a verb means to look or to observe. All of the characters within the book—even the most active—are observers of some kind. Rorschach keeps a journal in which he records his observations. Veidt, whose actions set the entire plot in motion, sits and views thirty-six television screens simultaneously—literally being a watch-man. Only Edward Blake, the Comedian, never seems reduced to being just an observer of events; he always seems compelled to do something. He's dead from the first page of the story, though—murdered, appropriately enough, while watching television.

Filmatic Devices

In addition to literary devices, *Watchmen* uses filmatic effects for story-telling. Like other comic books, it depends upon art—with the emphasis not on individual pictures, each of them complete unto itself, but on the progression from one picture to the next. In this respect, comics resemble two other visual media: film and television. *Watchmen* employs the filmatic devices of pans, zooms and tracking shots, but it uses them, I believe, in a way that a film could not.

Consider the presentation of Rorschach's life story in issue VI, "The abyss gazes also." Dr. Malcolm Long, the psychoanalyst assigned to Rorschach during his incarceration, is trying to learn why Kovacs became Rorschach. Outlining his early career as a costumed crimefighter, Rorschach explains that he wasn't Rorschach then; he was only Kovacs in a mask. Eventually he gets to the incident which transformed him into Rorschach. He lays the groundwork for his experience on p. 18, and presents the details of the incident on pages 19 through 26. On pages 19 and 20, the voiceover stops and we are presented with a wordless sequence. This is particularly appropriate for Rorschach because he is derived from characters such as the Question and Mr. A. created by Steve Ditko, who often uses wordless sequences in his work. The sequence is also particularly effective in communicating Rorschach's response to his experience.

Following Rorschach into and around the disused dressmakers' premises, we encounter alongside him the various clues that he finds there. As Rorschach assembles the information and realizes what has happened, so do we. Since no one tells us what Rorschach realizes, we have to parallel his thoughts, put the clues together ourselves and reach the same conclusion. The sequence is not a great intellectual puzzle, but the method of presentation makes us get involved with it in a way that simply telling us that Grice killed the six-year-old girl, chopped up her body and fed her to his dogs couldn't. We are drawn into the sequence to such an extent that we understand Rorschach's response much more clearly than we otherwise would; because his response, to an extent, parallels our own. It is a powerful sequence in one of the stronger issues of the book.

This is a very filmatic sequence, but it also employs something which is uniquely comic-bookish. Since the pictures in a comic are static, readers go at their own pace from one to the next. Each reader can look at each picture for as long as he or she needs to, unlike in a film where the length of time the viewer can devote to looking at any image is determined by how long the film editor chooses to let the shot run. Further, a reader can go back and look at previous pictures in the light of information gained from later pictures. This makes working out what has happened to the little girl much easier in the comic than it would be in a similar sequence in a film.

This device is very film-like; the sequence could act as a storyboard for a movie sequence. But it is also very comic-bookish, exploiting features that a film doesn't possess. Ordinarily, when employing such obvious filmatic methods in a comic, the creators are limited by the fact that their images don't move—most filmatic devices are designed to showcase a moving image. Moore and Gibbons exploit the fact that their images don't move.

Another example of a filmatic device being made a particularly comic-bookish one is the rock concert which provides the setting for the initial scene of devastation in issue XII. At no point in the story are we told about the concert. All that refers to it are the various posters announcing "Pale Horse and Krystalnacht in concert" scattered across various features of the background throughout the book. These posters are never brought to our attention in the way that the butcher's tools in the Rorschach sequence were: they just exist—a bit of detail adding verisimilitude to the world of the book. Yet, when issue XII opens at the concert, it comes as no surprise; we have absorbed the knowledge of the coming event subliminally.

A number of film directors are famous for including interesting details in the backgrounds of their shots, but it is only now with the advent of video recorders that one can properly appreciate their efforts. It's much easier to appreciate the effect in *Watchmen*. If you miss it the first time, you can always go back and look for it, taking as long as you need to find it.

UNIQUELY COMIC-BOOK DEVICES

A number of purely comic-book devices are used in *Watchmen*. The most common is the juxtaposition of words and pictures to create specific effects. Moore and Gibbons seem to exploit this device almost playfully, often using it just to create a bit of black humor or dark irony.

A simple example is panel four of p. 9 in issue IX—a large panel showing a huge glass structure (created by Doctor Manhattan) leaving the Martian surface and flying into the air. The panel contains only one bit of copy, a word balloon from Doctor Manhattan. What he says is a continuation of his comments from the previous panel, where he said, "Believe me, I fully understand the seriousness of our circumstances..." In panel four he concludes with "...the gravity of the situation." The action and the remark create a nice contrast, light and humorous, which neatly punctuates the seriousness of the situation being portrayed. This is a purely comic-book device, in that it could not be duplicated by a film maker or a novelist.

Since the word balloon continues the statement from the previous panel, it maintains the ongoing dialogue between Osterman and Laurie Juspeczyk which dominates the entire issue. Without that continuity, the dialogue would be interrupted by the levitation of the glass structure and would lose its momentum. A film maker attempting to use the same device would find that the visual of the glass structure rising would overwhelm the comment, thus both losing the humorous effect and breaking the flow of the conversation. Only the equal weight that a comic book gives to both the words and the pictures makes the effect workable.

A novelist has no way of attempting to duplicate this effect. Like all media which use only prose, a novel presents its information in linear form. Either it can continue with the dialogue between Osterman and Juspeczyk or it can describe the levitation of the glass structure. It would have to interrupt one to present the other; it cannot do both simultaneously. Since both the dialogue and the levitation are important to the story, the novelist's predicament is unenviable. An attempt to recreate the humor of the sequence with a throw-away line would interrupt the seriousness of the tone the novelist had established; the humorous tone would replace the serious one rather than briefly existing side by side with it as in the comic book.

Of course, film makers and novelists have entire arsenals of devices which they can use and which wouldn't work in a comic book. But that's not the point here.

A second example of this type of effect occurs on pp. 6 and 7 of issue III. Two parallel sequences are presented on the two pages, one showing an interview with Jane Slater in the offices of *Nova Express* and the other showing Laurie Juspeczyk's journey from the Rockefeller Military Research Center to Daniel Drieberg's apartment. This second sequence is entirely silent except for the last panel, while the interview is, naturally enough, very wordy. Slater's comments spill over into the panels of the second sequence, filling the captions within them, and acting as a voice-over. Through careful arrangement, Slater's comments are always pertinent to the action being shown within the second sequence, and are usually also funny or ironic in this context.

An even more telling juxtaposition is provided in a third example, panel six of p. 19 in issue II. The panel does not use two separate actions in order to make its point, and is only appreciated upon a second reading of the book. The hands of John Osterman and Adrian Veidt are shown clasped in a handshake while the dejected and shadowy figure of Moloch walks away from them towards the cemetery gates. The caption is part of the Lord's Prayer being delivered by the priest at Edward Blake's funeral service: "As we forgive those that trespass against us..."

At first glance the panel seems to be very simple, serving a purely utilitarian function within the story. Only after the reader has finished the book, and learnt what Veidt will ultimately do to

Osterman, can the irony of the caption and the handshake be properly appreciated. But the irony of the juxtaposition doesn't stop there. The third figure in the panel, Moloch, is a former opponent both of Veidt (in his Ozymandias guise—panel two, p. 19, issue XI) and of Osterman (in his Doctor Manhattan identity—panel two, p. 14, issue IV). He is the most obvious trespasser-against present, and is walking away looking very unforgiven. Again, given what Veidt ultimately does to Moloch (giving him cancer and shooting him in the head), the caption and the contrast with Veidt's interaction with Osterman makes this panel a particularly powerful and subtle bit of story-telling.

These are only three of the many examples of interesting uses of juxtaposition scattered throughout the book. Almost all of them are witty, but a great many also provide an insight into a character, an event, or a situation.

REPEATING A MOTIF

The repetition of a particular motif is used throughout *Watchmen* to unify the disparate elements of the story and to link otherwise unconnected incidents. Perhaps the clearest example of this device is the smiley badge with the splash of blood on its right eye which serves as the cover of issue I (or the chapter page). Gibbons puts variations of this image—an "eye" with a smear across it—all through the book. Examples include

—The Buddha poster in panel one, p. 7, issue V

—The Hallowe'en pumpkin being carved by Hollis Mason, particularly in panel six, p. 12, issue VIII

—Doctor Manhattan's smashed glass structure in the crater on Mars, in panel one, p. 27, issue IX

—Less obviously than some other examples, issue VII's cover (or the chapter page): a dust-free streak across the lens of Nite Owl's goggles. Interestingly, the streak is on the left goggle

—The plug of the "spark hydrant" on 6, issue XII

—And, of course, the splash of ketchup on Seymour's T-shirt in panel seven, p. 32, issue XII—the last panel of the story.

Even the actual shape of the splash of blood appears again and again in the book. The cover of issue XI (or the chapter page) is completely white except for a small patch of color showing a butterfly and some tropical plants. The patch of color is the same shape as the splash of blood. Later in issue XI, when Veidt's "alien" arrives, Bernard the newsvendor and Bernie the kid are reduced to an ashy smear, again the same shape as the original splash of blood.

This is an essentially gentle use of the technique. The repetition of the panels showing Blake's murder is a much more significant use. These panels are introduced on pp. 2 and 3 of issue I. They are intercut into a sequence showing Steve Fine and Joe Bourquin, two police detectives, discussing Blake's murder as they examine his apartment. Starting with panel three on p. 2, every second panel is part of the flashback sequence: panels three, five and seven on p. 2; panels one, three, five and seven on p. 3; and panels two, four and six on p. 4. These panels are set apart from the others on their page by being colored in shades of red. The dialogue between the two detectives continues on through the panels of the flashback, as a voice-over contained within captions. This voice-over creates some nice juxtapositions; but what interest us here is the way it maintains the continuity of the sequence, even though the intercutting disrupts it visually.

Of these ten flashback panels, the first seven of the sequence make up a narrational motif which is repeated twice within the story, intercut into other sequences. The three panels on 4 are not repeated. The first repetition is on pp. 26 and 27 of issue II: significantly, the sixth panel of the sequence is left out. The second repetition is on pp. 24, 25 and 26 of issue XI: here the sixth panel of the sequence is replaced with one clearly showing that the previously unseen figure who pummels Blake and throws him to his death is Adrian Veidt.

In its first appearance, the device seems to be simply a narrative hook. It asks "Who killed Edward Blake?" and sets the story in motion in the same way that so many other murder mysteries are set in motion. Through its repetition, however, the sequence is transformed into a touchstone. *Watchmen* is about a lot more than just "Who killed Edward Blake?"; yet the mystery is not an invalid one. By repeating the same murder panels as a motif, Moore and Gibbons emphasize that the mystery is simply a narrative engine for the story, rather than the story itself. The mystery is ultimately solved, but by that time everyone is preoccupied with other concerns.

Watchmen is a superb creation. This section is by no means an exhaustive catalogue of the story-telling methods employed in the book. A dedicated reader should be kept busy for months simply discovering all its clever and carefully applied techniques, devices and artifices—let alone interpreting their significance. If a university's English Department can be convinced that a comic book is a worthy object of study, then *Watchmen* contains enough thesis fodder to supply a generation of doctorates.

The story in *Watchmen* is very, very well told. But was it worth telling? In answering this, I am interested in at least two other questions: the nature of the changes that Moore and Gibbons envisage in an alternative world where superheroes exist, and the ideological implications of the story. In different ways, both these questions are concerned with "Realism."

REALISM ONE: THE BUTTERFLY EFFECT

The title of this section refers to an idea in Chaos Theory which grew out of attempts to model the behavior of the Earth's atmosphere. These models suggested that the variables which determine the weather are so delicately balanced that even a very small change in initial conditions could lead to vastly different consequences—even a change as small as the flapping of a single butterfly's wings. The title can also be interpreted as a reference to Ray Bradbury's short story "A Sound of Thunder." In that story a time traveler accidentally kills a butterfly in the Mesozoic era, which leads to a number of significant and subtle changes in the present.

Among other things, *Watchmen* is a work of speculative fiction which tries to project what the world would be like if comic-book superheroes really existed. Actually, it posits only one true superhero: Doctor Manhattan. All of the other costumed characters are more properly referred to as "mystery men." Still, only one true superhero is necessary and even the existence of mystery men proves to have some interesting effects.

The first of these costumed adventurers, Hooded Justice, appears in 1939. Since nothing in the book suggests anything different in the world before Hooded Justice appeared, I'll assume that the histories of the *Watchmen* world and our own world are identical up until that point.

The most immediate effect of Hooded Justice's debut is the appearance of other costumed crime fighters. We are told that Hooded Justice inspired Hollis Mason to become Nite Owl, and we can infer that all the other costumed adventurers were similarly inspired, even if only indirectly. Dollar Bill, for example, became a masked hero as part of a bank's publicity campaign—a campaign inspired by the fad created by Hooded Justice and Nite Owl. Sally Jupiter became the Silk Spectre for similar reasons. Why the other four characters—the Comedian, Mothman, the Silhouette and Captain Metropolis—decided to don brightly colored outfits is never revealed, but they are all part of the same "fad."

The Butterfly Effect suggests that even so minor a change as the appearance of a masked vigilante would have profound effects upon the nature of reality. This seems to be the case. In addition to inspiring others to join him, Hooded Justice also managed to change the history of physics and at least a part of the practice of psychiatry.

Physics first. In issue IV we are presented with Jon Osterman's life story. We are told how he came to study atomic physics; how he went to work for the United States government research establishment at Gila Flats; and the circumstances of his accident and his transformation into the entity called Doctor Manhattan. The interesting thing in this sequence is panel four on p. 5, which shows Jon Osterman talking to Jane Slater. She is gesturing to a framed board containing the photographs of assorted researchers at Gila Flats. The board is labeled "At play amidst the Strangeness and Charm." In the context of this sequence, the label seems to be a punning reference to the names given to the properties of various quarks. The board is in the researchers' bar, and the label seems to be the sort of thing that physicists with a sense of humor would put up. We are told that this sequence is occurring on the 12th of May 1959.

In our world, the existence of quarks was first suggested by Murray Gell-Mann and George Zweig in 1963. Drawing inspiration from the works of James Joyce, Gell-Mann proposed that these hypothetical particles be called "quarks." (Zweig, who proposed their existence almost simultaneously with Gell-Mann, wanted to call the particles "aces.") Gell-Mann went on to divide quarks up into a number of "flavors," including up-quarks, down-quarks and strange-quarks. The existence of charmed-quarks wasn't proposed until 1964.

Clearly, in the *Watchmen* world the appearance of the Minutemen led to quarks being proposed at least four years earlier than in our world. How this came about is never even alluded to (or, more probably, I'm too dense to have noticed the allusions), but it is an interesting example of world-divergence. Probably this change in the science of physics was responsible for the nature of the accident that befell Jon Osterman and created Doctor Manhattan. Many of the changes in the history of the sixties, seventies and eighties can be traced back to the appearance of Doctor Manhattan, so if Hooded Justice's appearance brought about the changes that led to Doctor Manhattan, then Hooded Justice is also ultimately responsible for everything else as well.

Alternatively, perhaps Moore and Gibbons made a mistake. But that's too cynical an interpretation. It's probably a very subtle example of the Butterfly Effect.

In the field of psychiatry, Hooded Justice's influence is perhaps a little easier to understand. Doubtless, the appearance of a number of costumed adventurers led psychiatrists to re-evaluate their ideas and practices. This means that standard analytic techniques that still exist in our world have been superseded by different (better?) ones in the *Watchmen* world. An example is found in issue VI, which presents us with Kovacs' biography in the form of a series of interviews between him and his psychoanalyst Dr. Malcolm Long. Part of Long's interviewing style is to give Kovacs a series of inkblots to interpret. Long refers to these as "Rorschach Blot Tests."

Hermann Rorschach was a Swiss psychiatrist who, in the early part of this century, created a diagnostic tool to aid in the analysis of personality. This tool, which was named after him, consists of ten symmetrical inkblot designs which are given to a patient, one at a time, to examine and interpret. The patient's responses are carefully recorded and examined. We know that Hermann Rorschach existed in the *Watchmen* world and invented his famous inkblot test because not only does Dr. Long refer to it but also Walter Joseph Kovacs bases his masked identity upon it.

However, the test has undergone some significant changes in this parallel world. In our world, it consists of ten set designs. Each is symmetrical about an axis, and they look what they originally were: inkblots prepared by placing some drops of ink on a piece of paper, then folding the paper in half over the drops and pressing. While a few of the designs consist of just black ink, most of them contain a variety of different colors.

The ten standard designs were selected by Rorschach from a much larger set of possible inkblot designs. Each design has a set of interpretations associated with it; patients suffering from different conditions see different things in the designs, but the majority of patients suffering from a given condition will see similar things in a particular design.

The practice in our world when giving a Rorschach test is to sit behind and to one side of the patient. This is because, since there are established "good" and "bad" responses to the designs, patients will try to give the "good" ones—or at least the ones they think the analyst wants to hear. If the analyst were to sit in front of the patient, then the patient could pick up subliminal clues as to which lines of interpretation are favored and which aren't, and would tailor responses accordingly. This would, of course, severely undermine the test's effectiveness.

Interestingly, in issue VI Dr. Long not only sits opposite Kovacs but also gives him an inkblot which is not one of the standard ten. The actual Rorschach inkblots are copyright and Moore and Gibbons probably couldn't obtain permission to use one of the official designs (if they, in fact, realized that there were official designs.) Thus, we cannot read too much into the design that Dr. Long uses, but we can note that it seems to be part of a set of thirteen cards. Combined with the position Long assumes relative to Kovacs while conducting the test, this suggests that psychiatry has taken some new and unusual directions in this world.

Doubtless, Long sits in front of Kovacs because Kovacs would be uncomfortable with him in any other position. In his Rorschach identity, Kovacs is a streetfighter and he probably doesn't like having people behind him. A number of gunfighters in the American West last century suffered from the same condition. Long uses a different and larger set of designs—probably a new set devised as part of the re-evaluation of established psychiatry inspired by Hooded Justice and the other Minutemen. This new set of Rorschach inkblots seems to be much simpler, and the analysis of a patient's responses is much more limited.

I must admit that when I first read issue VI, I assumed that Dr. Long was a fake psychoanalyst. Reasoning from what I perceived to be his errors in technique, I thought that he was an agent working for the villain of the piece (who I'd worked out, in issue IV, to be Veidt). I kept waiting for him to do something nasty to Kovacs, since this was surely, I felt, his purpose. It wasn't until later that I recognized my error and began to appreciate the subtlety of the Butterfly Effect that Moore and Gibbons were invoking.

Actually, the changes to the Rorschach inkblot test may not have been caused by Hooded Justice and his contemporaries. They may have come later, as a consequence of Doctor Manhattan. Once he appears, the differences between our world and the *Watchmen* world begin to multiply. For example, Jon Osterman wears an old double-breasted suit for his first public appearance in 1960, and it becomes a fashion statement. Twenty-five years later, in 1985 (the story's present), men are still wearing double-breasted suits.

Doctor Manhattan's ability to transmute one element into another has profound effects on industry and economics. His ability to synthesize lithium allows polyacetylene batteries to be mass-produced, leading to electric cars. By 1975 fast and safe airships are announced to be economically viable, presumably partly as a response to the availability of unlimited quantities of helium. Or perhaps not: the principles governing airships seem to be markedly different in the *Watchmen* world. The flying vehicle known as the Owlship is perhaps the most notable of the amazing arsenal of equipment that Daniel Drieberg, the second Nite Owl, uses in his costumed identity. A few times in issue VIII (panel three of p. 1 and panel seven of p. 8) the Owlship is referred to as an airship it is, then the appearance of Hooded Justice (or perhaps of Doctor Manhattan) did stranger things to physics than was at first apparent.

An airship works on the principle of buoyancy, first proposed by the Ancient Greek philosopher and scientist Archimedes. An airship displaces a certain volume of air. If the weight of the airship is less than the weight of the air it has displaced, the airship will be lifted up off the ground. It will continue rising until, as the air gets thinner with altitude, the weight of the airship exactly equals the weight of the volume of air it has displaced. The same principle applies to ships floating in water but, because air is a much lighter medium than water, a great deal more air must be displaced for a given mass. Usually the cells of an airship are filled with a gas lighter than normal air: hydrogen or helium or hot air. Whatever gas is used, however, an airship needs to displace roughly a cubic meter of air for every one and a half kilograms of weight. As near as I can determine, the Owlship as a whole displaces no more than (approximately) eighty-five cubic meters. This estimate includes internal spaces filled with normal air, which don't contribute anything to lift. So: what holds the Owlship up? Beats me. Wishful thinking, perhaps.

Drieberg's nickname for the ship is "Archie," short for "Archimedes," which seems only appropriate, somehow.

One of Moore's stated intentions in *Watchmen* was to portray an atomic-powered superhero in a way that was consistent with the ideas of modem physics. He seems to have been somewhat successful in his characterization and treatment of Doctor Manhattan. I can't help but feel, though, that if Moore had taken the trouble to learn more real physics, his efforts would have been even better.

Doctor Manhattan's influence spreads further than just to revolutionizing industry. His effect as a living nuclear deterrent is amply demonstrated by the immediate consequences of his departure. His personal intervention in the Vietnam War brings about an American victory. His influence is demonstrated in uncountable little details, ranging from the strange tobacco(?)-holders that people seem to use—through the developments in genetic engineering suggested by Veidt's pet Bubastis and the four-legged chicken seen in panel four, p. 25, issue I—to the "Gunga Diners" which appear to be the *Watchmen* world's equivalent of "McDonald's."

The effect which I find most interesting is political. In the *Watchmen* world, Richard M. Nixon is still president in 1985. This would be his fifth term in office: 1969-72, 1973-76, 1977-80, 1981-84, and 1985-88. The Twenty-second Amendment to the Constitution of the United States, proclaimed on the 1st of March 1951, forbids any individual to hold the office of president for more than two terms; or in the case of a successor, two and a half terms (ten years). Nixon had to get a new constitutional amendment (which would be the Twenty-seventh?) in order to extend his stay in office beyond 1976: this amendment is referred to in panel one, p. 21, issue IV. In our world, Nixon won the 1972 presidential election with the largest majority ever, and he lost the 1960 election with the largest minority ever, so he clearly had a large popular following. However, to get a constitutional amendment passed requires more than just a lot of popular support.

In our world, Nixon was brought down by the Watergate break-in and the scandals and investigations that it sparked off. In the *Watchmen* world, these investigations were cut short when (it's implied in panels four and five, p. 20, issue IX) the Comedian killed Woodward and Bernstein, the two Washington Post reporters who led the investigations. Interestingly, Nixon's vice-president is Gerald Ford. Apparently the Comedian couldn't do anything about the corruption charges brought against Spiro Agnew, Nixon's original vice-president. It should be noted, though, that the Comedian appears to have been in Vietnam at the time.

From at least 1973 on, then, Nixon's vice-president is Gerald Ford, and Henry Kissinger and Gordon Liddy are among his cabinet. This degree of political continuity is not completely unknown but it is rare, and quite remarkable—especially in the modern world. I wish Moore and Gibbons had devoted more space and time to outlining the *Watchmen* world's political history, because I think Nixon's career would be at least as interesting as Doctor Manhattan's. That's just a personal bias, though.

The ultimate manifestation of the Butterfly Effect is, of course, Adrian Veidt's plan. Convincing people that an alien being from another dimension (whatever that means) has arrived, and is responsible for killing three million New Yorkers, must be easier in a world which has already accepted the existence of Doctor Manhattan than it would be in ours.

There are, however, two things in the book which—try as I may—I cannot explain in terms of the Butterfly Effect, or anything else.

The first is quite minor: Rorschach's mask. The fact that the flowing patterns on it always remain symmetrical is something I can accept—the material from which the mask is made is a Doctor Manhattan spin-off fabric, after all. What bothers me is the question of how Kovacs can breathe, let alone see, through it. Completely covering one's head with a latex hood seems to me to be a very good way of ending up dead.

The other inexplicable thing is much more important, and quite directly concerns the climax of the story itself. Veidt's plan depends upon an alien creature whose brain was cloned from that of "a human sensitive" (panel four, p. 26, issue XI): the "psychic and clairvoyant Robert Deschaines," first referred to on p. 4 of the back-up in issue VIII. When the alien creature, created by the advanced genetic engineering procedures of the *Watchmen* world, is teleported to New York, it explodes and dies. As it dies, its massive brain broadcasts a psychic signal which kills three million people telepathically.

Now, I'm a comics fan and, as such, am well practiced in the art of believing at least three impossible things each morning before breakfast. Perhaps in your worldview, psychic powers and telepathy are phenomena which really exist. In my worldview they're not and they don't.

Watchmen is a work of fiction set in a parallel world which can be expected to be different from our own world; it isn't unreasonable for psychic powers to exist there, and if Moore and Gibbons had simply declared that they did, I would have accepted it. But the book is designed to make one think that the *Watchmen* world is exactly like ours, except for the existence of costumed adventurers and of Doctor Manhattan. All the other differences, it's implied, are the consequences of these two differences: the results of the Butterfly Effect. But at no point in the narrative are psychic powers explained or justified as a consequence of the appearance of either the costumed crimefighters or of Doctor Manhattan. They are just introduced as part of the climax in issues XI and XII. One of the other things necessary for the climax is teleportation, and this is nicely established as a logical consequence of Doctor Manhattan: once you've accepted him, you have to accept it. Telepathy, though, is never established.

The entire climax of the book hinges upon something introduced at the last minute—upon, in essence, a deus ex machina. But that is a complaint based on artistic considerations: and these (together with ideology) are the subject of the next section.

REALISM TWO: THE SANTA CLAUS SYNDROME

Watchmen is a "realistic" book; or, at least, it has been praised by a number of commentators for its "realism." What exactly this means, I'm not sure.

"Realism" is a term which seems simple enough on the surface, but which implies a great deal upon closer examination. Its derivation from "real" suggests that it has a concern with "facts," with that which is "genuine" and—most significantly—with the "truth." It is a term which, in artistic and critical spheres, suggests a treatment of a subject as it actually is, rather than as it should be or as we would like it to be. As such, it is a very powerful term and, in the critical climate of the 1980s (at least among those who do not find it altogether irrelevant), a very positive one. To say that a book is "realistic" is to give it very high praise indeed.

"Realism" appears to be an ideal which grows out of the aesthetic ideas of the Greek philosopher Aristotle. He maintained that art was, essentially, imitation; a work of art, whether it was a painting, a statue or a narrative, was an imitation of something in the real world. This immediately implied a method for determining the worth or value of any given work: since art is imitation, the closer the work of art approaches the real thing—that is, the better an imitation it is—the more successful it is and the more it is worth. Of course, Aristotle's aesthetic is inadequate for dealing with a medium such as music, but "realism" has never been a term used in the discussion of music.

Aristotle's idea also immediately implies that art is irrelevant. Since art is just an imitation, why should anyone be satisfied when they could have the real thing? No matter how good a piece of art is, ultimately it is only an imitation and, as such, it is inferior to the original. As an illustration of this point, consider the study of history. It is a discipline which involves the perusal of many original documents, ranging from simple lists and surveys to letters, diaries and transcripts. The Second World War is a particularly rich source of such original documents. While I was studying the history of that conflict, particularly the German invasion and conquest of Poland, Norway, France and Crete, I was presented with copies of letters sent home by German soldiers, diaries kept by various involved parties and journals maintained by a variety of officials. The letters and diaries proved to be particularly interesting. They recorded events and experiences on a personal and human level; they described what individual people saw and felt and did with an intensity and clarity rarely encountered in a fictional narrative.

These documents recorded real events that happened to real people in a real place and at a real time. The reactions felt were real reactions, and the experiences were real experiences, in the most literal sense of the word "real." The stories told didn't have "a feeling of authenticity": they *were* authentic. They didn't "seem to be genuine": they *were* genuine. And they didn't possess "the ring of truth": they *were* true. If a work of art is valued to the extent that it is realistic, then these documents are far superior to any work of art that ever existed or which ever could exist.

In literary terms an imitation is called a pastiche and, as Richard A. Lupoff observed in his *Edgar Rice Burroughs: Master of Adventure*, to the extent that a pastiche duplicates an original, it's superfluous; and to the extent that it deviates from the original, it fractures the original form. As an artistic ideal, Realism is ultimately an attempt to pastiche the work of God (for lack of a better name) and, as such, it is doomed to failure. The original is far more subtle and sublime than arty work could ever hope to be. Please note: I didn't say "than any work is," but "than any work could ever hope to be." To that extent, Realism is an artistic dead-end and a redundancy.

As a realistic work, *Watchmen* represents the culmination of a long-time trend in the superhero genre of comics. During the sixties and seventies, Marvel Comics, which was one of the small survivals of the forties comics boom, grew into the dominant force in the industry. Various observers, both within the industry and in fandom, offered a number of different explanations for this sudden success. Since Marvel Comics was a business which wanted to continue enjoying success, its employees were amongst the most prominent and influential of these observers and analysts. They rejected the simple explanation that Marvel was succeeding because it was publishing the work of a number of very good creators at the peak of their form, while other comic publishers were printing the work of sometimes equally competent but less inspired workers. In the comic-book field of the time, individual creators were regarded as essentially interchangeable, so to acknowledge the importance of the people producing the work would have been an uncomfortable admission, no matter what the various analysts thought personally. Instead, the people at Marvel sought for a "secret ingredient" which would explain their success and which could be incorporated into the work of any creator. They found it in the idea of Realism: Marvel Comics were more realistic than any other comics. It followed that the more realistic a comic was, the better that comic would be.

This analysis was promoted and accepted throughout a large part of the comic-fan community—at least as it applied to superhero comics. It is responsible for those favorite topics of fannish speculation: "What if superheroes were real? What would they be like? How would they change the world?" It is also responsible for a number of efforts to produce the most realistic, and therefore the best, superhero comic ever. The fact that a lot of these efforts resulted in spectacular failures is something that doesn't seem to be considered significant.

The problem with producing a realistic superhero comic is that superheroes do not exist. The ultimate way of ensuring realism is to base the characters and actions in the story on real people and events. If creators were trying to produce realistic private-eye stories, for example, they could examine real private investigators.

They could determine why real people become private investigators and they could base their stories upon what real private investigators do. Creators of realistic superhero stories don't have that sort of fallback. If they ask, "Why do real people become superheroes? What do real superheroes do?" they are confronted with the fact that real people don't become superheroes and real superheroes don't do anything; they don't exist. The ultimate realistic superhero story should be one in which superheroes don't exist. This seems to be a very self-defeating goal.

Watchmen represents the closest any effort has come to being the ultimate realistic superhero story. Given the nature of the ultimate goal, it probably will remain the closest attempt for quite some time. The fact that *Watchmen* is successful will be taken as support for the idea that realism, in and of itself, is good.

In the comics world, the basis for analysis that led to this view of realism were the comics put out by Marvel during the 1960s. Although these comics appeared to be realistic, on close examination they proved to be as fantastic as—if not more fantastic than—the work from other publishers. The key word here is "appeared." The quality that the analysts observed wasn't Realism, but Plausibility and Verisimilitude. It was the ability of creators such as Jack Kirby, Steve Ditko, Stan Lee, Roy Thomas and others to make their work look believable. A proper appreciation of plausibility and verisimilitude, as opposed to a narrow concern with mere realism, would have been a much more important contribution by these comics analysts. One of the reasons that they didn't make it was the fact that they weren't working in a vacuum. Realism was, and is, a concept with a strong and wide currency across a number of artistic media, while plausibility and verisimilitude were not.

Realism exists as a very broadly based critical idea and, as I said earlier, it seems on the surface to be a very simple idea, but upon closer examination it proves to be much more complex. If Realism were concerned only with art and imitation, as it superficially appears to be, it would have collapsed many years ago, as various creators and critics realized its inadequacies. But the term Realism also describes an ideological position: a view of the world which emphasizes its darker and nastier aspects.

In its ideological aspect, Realism manifests an almost paranoid suspicion regarding people's motivations: when presented with an action, it prefers for explanatory purposes a lower need to a middle one and a middle need to a higher one. It prefers a purely materialistic motivation to a social one, and a social motivation to an idealistic or ethical or moral one. By so doing it devalues and ignores a large part of human nature, but it doesn't acknowledge or even seem to be aware of that fact. Realism doesn't appear to believe that higher needs or motivations exist.

In narrative terms, Realism is wedded to Murphy's Law in its most absolute sense. Murphy's Law is a dictum which declares that anything that can go wrong, will. In Realistic fiction, any unpleasant outcome that can occur, will.

As an example, consider these two story outlines:

(1) A young girl runs away from her home in a small town to go to the big city where she wants to become a dancer. There she has a number of unpleasant and disappointing experiences but she perseveres in her ambition and eventually joins a small dance company. Within the company she works hard and eventually becomes one of its best dancers. As she improves, so does the reputation of the company, until finally, after many years of effort, she is the best dancer in the most highly regarded dance ensemble in the city.

(2) A young girl runs away from her home in a small town to go to the big city where she wants to become a dancer. Upon her arrival in the city she is adopted by a producer of pornographic movies who exploits her ambition and uses her in his productions. As an escape from her new existence the young girl becomes a heroin addict. Eventually her addiction and lifestyle rob her of her good looks and she is abandoned by the porn producer. She turns to prostitution to support herself and her habit. In the end, she dies as a result of injuries received from the disciplinary actions of her pimp.

Only the second outline would be considered realistic. The first might be regarded as sentimental or inspirational or, perhaps, naturalistic, but it would definitely be labeled "unrealistic." Yet both stories might be true; both conform to reality as people experience it. As an ideology, Realism does not dispute that events such as those depicted in the first outline can happen, have happened, and continue to happen, but it insists upon regarding only the second outline as Realistic.

In this, Realism is distinctly unrealistic. If Realism was, as its name implies, an artistic preoccupation with imitating the real world, then it would have to present the positive aspects of that world as well as the negative ones. In this aspect, it is a particularly insidious ideology because the name it uses implies that its worldview is realistic—that is, true to the nature of the world as it is.

The philosophy underlying this aspect of Realism seems to have been developed by people who have learnt that there is no Santa Claus and are very bitter about it. This invocation of Santa Claus is not simply an idle cliché. A belief in Santa Claus is often part of a childish worldview which considers happiness as a goal: if only Santa Claus brings me such and such for Christmas, I'll be happy. In a more adult version, Santa Claus is no longer named or even acknowledged but the belief structure is the same: if only I get that job, marry the right person, sleep with so-and-so, get that pay-raise, see that concert, etc., then I'll be happy. Of course, what happens to such people is that they get the job, marry the right person, sleep with so-and-so, get the pay-raise and a bonus, see the concert, and so on and so on, but they aren't happy. Eventually they realize this and begin to believe that happiness is impossible; the best that one can achieve is gratification or a short period of contentment. They begin to think that all those people who claim to be happy are lying and that those who say that they are acting for any other reasons than personal gratification are either cynically dishonest or deluded.

Now, in my opinion there is no single magic ingredient for happiness, just as there is no Santa Claus. Happiness is a process rather than a goal; it comes from how one does things rather than from what one does or achieves. Because Realism fails to realize this, it suffers from what I've called the Santa Claus syndrome.

In the aesthetic sense—Realism as imitation—*Watchmen* is far too mannered and artificial a product to be truly Realistic. The fact that it comes the closest of any superhero story yet to Realism in this sense is actually a comment on the artificiality of superhero stories. However, in the ideological sense of the term, *Watchmen* is very Realistic.

Of the six characters who are explored in depth, Rorschach alone has a higher motivation; it's made quite clear, however, that he's "crazier than a snake's armpit" (panel seven, p. 4, issue I). Apparently morality is something possessed only by the mad. Edward Blake is a psychopath, an amoral bastard who enjoys beating people up. Jon Osterman is a space cadet, alienated and detached, acting only because he's told to by the US military or the American government. Daniel Drieberg is acting out adolescent fantasies and, it's implied, wears a costume because, as screen writer Sam Hamm puts it in *Cinefantastique* (volume 20, numbers 1 and 2), he can't get it up when he isn't. Laurie Juspeczyk is limited and defined by her mother who vicariously continues her own career through her. And

Adrian Veidt is a fascist, complete with a personality cult and an obsession with the Fuhrerprinzip.

Of the lesser characters, Hooded Justice is a sadist, Dollar Bill is just an employee and the Silk Spectre is just a publicity gimmick. Only Nite Owl has any idealism, and he's presented as being quaint.

The action of the story is also (ideologically speaking) very Realistic. Edward Blake rapes and murders, ultimately stopped only because he presents a threat to Veidt's plan. Hollis Mason is beaten to death by a group of hooligans. Dr. Malcolm Long's marriage breaks up and he's driven into despair by Rorschach. And, of course, three million New Yorkers die.

The most Realistic aspect of the story is, undoubtedly, Adrian Veidt. He throws Edward Blake to his death; infects at least three people with cancer; shoots Moloch; forces a poison capsule down a gunman's throat; kidnaps a variety of creative individuals and, once he no longer needs them, blows up the ship taking them home; poisons his three servants; and murders three million New Yorkers. Naturally, he not only gets away with it but he probably goes on to make an immense financial profit from his actions as well.

The end of the story presents us with a world that has been saved from thermonuclear devastation (allegedly) and which is dominated by an accord between the Soviet Union and the United States, two of its most powerful nations. Any advantages the Third World countries once enjoyed from playing off one power against the other is thus effectively neutralized.

The world is actually controlled by Veidt, and there is evidence that one of his earliest actions was the suspension, or perhaps annulment, of the First Amendment to the US Constitution and, by implication, of the rest of the Bill of Rights as well. I base this interpretation on Hector Godfrey's words (panel three, p. 32, issue XII): "Yeah, well you thought wrong! Nobody's allowed to say bad things about our good ol' buddies the Russians anymore, so bang goes a two page column!" I maintain that the term "allowed" implies permission; someone has to allow or to disallow. The First Amendment guarantees, among other things, the right of freedom of speech. Historically, this freedom has been particularly applied to the editorials and other opinion-pieces of newspapers and magazines. For a newsmagazine editor to be denied permission to print an opinion column because it disagrees with the current government's actions suggests that the First Amendment is no longer in force. As the editor of a rightwing journal—*New Frontiersman*—Godfrey is probably used to espousing unpopular causes, so simple public approval of the accord does not seem a strong enough reason for his scrapping his column. If it were, he probably would have chosen some other subject for the column in the first place.

A parallel narrative within the book presents a story from the fictional comic book, *Tales of the Black Freighter*. In this story, entitled "Marooned," a sailor is slowly driven to commit greater and greater barbarisms in an attempt to save his family and the other inhabitants of "Davidstown" from the depredations of a group of hellish pirates. In the end it is revealed that the pirates never intended to attack the town, so all of the callous and cruel acts committed by the sailor were in vain, serving only to condemn his own soul. Moore and Gibbons suggest a connection between the sailor's actions and Veidt's (panel one, 27, issue XII). Together the two stories underline the concept that the noblest of intentions lead only to atrocities. Comparing them only serves to emphasize the fact that Veidt gets away with it. Unlike Veidt, the sailor is punished for his actions, no matter how unfair that punishment may be from a broader moral view.

Watchmen is a dark and depressing book. The story is superbly told but, ultimately, it is a celebration of fascism. When all the other characters confront Veidt in issue XII, they agree—with the exception of Rorschach—not to report or otherwise do anything about his crimes; they agree with Veidt (p. 20, issue XII) when he says to them (in the first two panels of p. 17, issue XII), "Failing to prevent Earth's **salvation** is your only **triumph**..."—"...and yet that **failure** overshadows every past success!"; and even Rorschach accepts Veidt's rationalizations and half-truths (first three panels of p. 24, issue XII). The effect is to suggest that all attempts to do good are ultimately futile. Only those who possess power and an absolute willingness to use it, no matter what the cost, ever achieve anything; only those who recognize that the ethics and morality represented by the traditional superhero are simply fetters, designed by the weak to hobble the great, can "save" the world or, at least, reshape it to their specifications. Nothing can stand against the power of pure unhindered will (Veidt): not psychopaths (Blake) nor madmen (Rorschach) nor gods (Doctor Manhattan) nor heroes (Drieberg) nor even simple humanity (Juspeczyk). The strong lead the weak and the best that we can ever hope for is a benign tyranny—unless we get in the way of some tyrant's schemes and plans.

All I can say is: joy and laughter, joy and bloody laughter.

Watchmen is a very Realistic book; or at least it has been praised by a number of commentators for its "Realism." It's every bit as vile and nasty a piece of work as you'd expect, given that.

Conclusion

So—should you rush out and buy a copy of *Watchmen*? If you are interested in a showcase of superb comic book story-telling, yes. If you want to see what all the fuss is about, yes. If you want a well-told story and don't mind that it celebrates fascism, then yes. Otherwise, no. Spend your money on Frank Miller's *Dark Knight Returns* instead. It's an equally interesting showcase of comic-book story-telling devices, has generated its own degree of controversy, and is a well-told story. It has its own (not inconsiderable) problems but will eventually, I believe, prove to be the more significant work.

EVERYTHING NOT FORBIDDEN IS COMPULSORY

by Janeen Webb

Margaret Atwood's *The Handmaid's Tale* is a cautionary tale of gender politics, taking the form of a dystopia in which the public state has invaded the private domain to the extent that the free family unit no longer exists, and even one's body cannot be said to be one's own—particularly if one is female. The state of Gilead is a rigid patriarchal society, which is to say a feminist vision of hell-on-earth in which women are wholly owned by men, and grouped according to traditionally female functions: they are wives, handmaids, servants, or whores—there are no other available roles.

The Handmaids of the tale are fertile women who have been captured by the state and systematically reduced to the position of breeding cattle, defined only by their viable ovaries, and living under sentence of death if they fail to produce. (This is an interesting variation on earlier British justice, which allowed convicted women to "plead the belly" to effect a stay of execution until the birth of the child. Needless to say, pregnancy was popular in Newgate.) The Handmaids are denied even the dignity of a personal name, being designated only by the possessive "of" coupled with the first name of their owners: thus the narrator is Offred, her acquaintances Ofwarren, Ofglen and so on. This reinforces both their dependency and their expendability—powerful males have an endless supply of "of" women, and don't even have to learn new names in the process. Does this sound extreme? Married women are still in the habit of adopting the surnames of their husbands, changing names when they change partners; and many cheerfully assent to being addressed as Mrs, despite the male ownership implicit in the term. So when does social convenience become threatening? Such naming is a good example of the way in which Atwood operates in this novel to look at the small complicities that might lead to larger capitulations.

In many respects *The Handmaid's Tale* is an examination of the ways in which well meaning people have allowed their good intentions to pave a path to hell. This book is a chilling extrapolation from the "public good" demands of the many pressure groups advocating various reforms. The biblically-named Gilead is a North American state described in the closing frame story, "Historical Notes," as a monotheocracy not unlike contemporary Iran. The social structure is the kind of nightmare that results when moral platitudes are put into practice, so that the moralists get literally what they asked for—the letter rather than the spirit of the slogan—and are trapped by it. This is certainly the fate of the "wife" of this story, Serena Joy, who was formerly a TV bible hour star turned advocate of patriarchal ideology. Serena Joy (whose real name was Pam) had given up singing in favor of making speeches.

> She was good at it. Her speeches were about the sanctity of the home, about how women should stay home. Serena Joy didn't do this herself, she made speeches instead, but she presented this failure of hers as a sacrifice she was making for the good of all. (55)

> She doesn't make speeches any more. She has become speechless. She stays in her home, but it doesn't seem to agree with her. How furious she must be, now that she's been taken at her word. (56)

The irony of this situation is a bitter warning to those who would use their freedom of speech to advocate the repression of others. In Gilead, sin has become synonymous with crime—the public world has entered the private. The religious fundamentalism advocated by the Serena Joys of the 1980s has clearly operated in society as a negative, reductive force, illustrated in the text by the motif of an appallingly literal interpretation of the Biblical situation of Jacob and Rachel's maid Bilah. The childless Rachel suggested to Jacob that he should "go in unto her [Bilah]; and she shall bear upon my knees, that I may also have children by her" (Gen. 30:1-3). In *The Handmaid's Tale*, the role of the Handmaids is to be impregnated by Commanders whose wives have been unable to conceive (it is an article of patriarchal faith that this is the fault of the female, despite "common knowledge" that most of the Commanders are sterile). In an excess of fundamentalist literalism, the protocol-making state has decreed that handmaids will be impregnated between the legs of the wives. Here is Offred's account:

> Above me...Serena Joy is arranged, outspread. Her legs are apart, I lie between them, my head on her stomach, her pubic bone under the base of my skull, her thighs on either side of me...she holds my hands, each of mine in each of hers. This is supposed to signify that we are one flesh, one being. What it really means is that she is in control, of the process and thus of the product. If any....
> My red skirt is hitched up to my waist, though no higher. Below it the Commander is fucking. What he is fucking is the lower part of my body. (104)

Births are arranged in the same way, using a double birthing stool, the wife straddling behind (and slightly above) the laboring handmaid, and claiming the delivered infant as "hers," much like receiving a bouquet of flowers. The Old Testament, of course, provides endless examples of just how far patriarchal owners were prepared to use and abuse their women, and in this context I must admit that it occurs to me that the Handmaids might have been moved to emulate Jael (Judges) rather than Rachel and Leah—but perhaps such precedents are one of the reasons that women of Gilead are no longer permitted to read even the Bible.

Such a society is explicitly what might be expected from extreme groups such as the female apologists for Islam, who have somehow internalized a repressive patriarchal structure, and have decided to live within it presumably on the grounds that decision making is alarming, whereas bondage is predictable, if not exactly safe. The Iranian analogy is made early on in the text, then a group of visiting Japanese come across Offred and Ofglen in the street. The Handmaids, indoctrinated into new ways of thinking, such as "Modesty is invisibility" (39), are fascinated and repelled by the women in short skirts, high heeled shoes, uncovered heads, and lipstick. When the Handmaids decline to permit a photograph, the guide explains their reluctance in terms reminiscent of Islamic culture: "the women here have different customs...to stare at them through the lens of a camera is, for them, an experience of violation" (39). Once again, this is heavily ironic, given that the only thing between the Handmaids and death in the colonies is their monthly, state endorsed physical violation.

How did twentieth century women become so entrapped? Atwood's description echoes those suggested by Suzanne Hayden Elgin in *Native Tongue* and *The Judas Rose*. This takeover, by an unspecified group using vaguely described fundamentalist troopers called Angels, was swift and simple. Society had become cashless, depending on computer credits for all transactions. This meant that when the President and Congress were gunned down and the constitution "temporarily" suspended, it was relatively easy to block the escape routes. Martial law imposed news censorship, roadblocks, identipasses and the like; all female computer bank accounts were confiscated; laws were passed to forbid females to work or own any form of property (said to be held in trust by the nearest male relative); then all second marriages, de facto relationships, and even marriages not solemnized in church were declared adulterous, and the women confiscated for breeding purposes. Denied identity, social status and finance, the women were effectively trapped, then privatized for exclusive male use within a punitive and inflexible caste system.

One of the things that makes *The Handmaid's Tale* uncomfortable reading is that, unlike most feminist dystopias, such as *Native Tongue* and *The Judas Rose*, which place the blame for repression firmly upon the shoulders of aggressive male politics, this book suggests a disturbing complicity on the part of women: both in the events that produced this misogynist monotheocracy, and in its continued operation (it's always said to be ex-slaves who make the harshest overseers). This female complicity extends beyond groups easily identified as being opposed to feminism, so it is possible to read the text as a critique of potentially destructive elements within the feminist movement. The moral conservatives have won, but although the pressures exerted by reactionary groups such as the moral majority, the women-who-want-to-be-women (however tautologous), the right-to-lifers and so on is clear enough, there is also a great deal of textual evidence indicating that the feminist movement, with its insistence on the rights of women to determine what happens to their bodies, and its anti-pornography stance, has provided many of the dogmatisms of the new regime. Offred, longing to return to the days of arguing with her feminist-activist mother (who has now been transported to the lethal colonies), cries out against the part that the women's movement has played in its own downfall:

"You wanted a women's culture. Well now there is one. It isn't what you meant, but it exists" (137).

The bioethical questions surrounding conception and contraception provide a good example of this process. One of the underlying causes of the repression of women in Gilead is the fact that a series of unspecified biological disasters has rendered most people sterile, and since the ruling males in quasi-feudal Gilead crave the political control implicit in dynastic progeny, female fertility has become the means to maintaining male power. There is a flashback to a 1980s women's rally advocating legal abortion on demand, in which we see placards that carry familiar slogans: "EVERY BABY A WANTED BABY. RECAPTURE OUR BODIES. DO YOU BELIEVE A WOMAN'S PLACE IS ON THE KITCHEN TABLE?" But the literalists have been busily conflating slogans, with the result that the sentiments about wanted children have merged with Mom-and-apple-pie statements about the sanctity of family life to produce a compulsory breeding program that has everything to do with producing babies for the patriarchal state, and no regard whatsoever for the breeding stock. The feminist ideal of the "wanted baby" has been thoroughly warped, but it is still there in the background—the difference lies in who does the wanting. As babies have now acquired political as well as social importance (and remember that church and state are one), anti-abortion sentiment has been transformed into a Draconian code of law. This new community exacts vengeance from the past to the extent that there are public hangings, not only of doctors who may have been involved in the termination of pregnancies, but also of anyone else remotely involved in promoting birth control—such as pharmacists, clinicians, manufacturers and so on. "These men...are like war criminals. It's no excuse that what they did was legal at the time: their crimes are retroactive. They have committed atrocities, and must be made into examples, for the rest" (43). A corollary of this extreme position is that any form of birth control is now illegal: Priests are hanged for secretly advocating abstinence; nuns, if captured alive, are either "converted" (by torture) from celibacy, or sent to the colonies to die as an example to others. There is no longer any tolerance for sexual preference, and "gender treachery" has become a hanging offence.

Indeed, the anti-interference in human life sentiment has outlawed not only in vitro and artificial insemination programs, but also any investigatory procedures to determine the viability of pregnancies. Even though the state has no qualms about disposing of unsatisfactory infants—and the majority of babies born are deformed enough to end up in "the shredder"—its anti-abortion dogma requires that all pregnancies are sacred and must proceed to term. This is carried to its extreme conclusion in the fact that any medical assistance, right down to sterile equipment, is denied to women at childbirth. Biblical precedent has always been useful when more logical explanations won't do: its value as an exercise in doublethink is nicely demonstrated in this area when it is made clear that the reason for this particular denial is Genesis 3:16:

> Unto the woman He said, I will greatly multiply thy sorrow and thy conception, in sorrow shalt thou bring forth children.

Incidentally, there is a lovely lesbian-separatist interpretation of this in John Varley's *Wizard*:

> Christians! Robin...leaped to her feet, making the two-fingered protective sign with one hand.... Christians were the very root and branch of the peckish [patriarchal] power structure...Their terrible rites would soon warp one's mind beyond all hope of redemption; then the convert would be infected with a nameless disease that rotted the womb. She would be forced to bear children in pain to the end of her days. (34)

The banning of doctors from birthings shows the state playing God, with a good deal more of what it is pleased to call justice than mercy. Childbirth is supposed to hurt, and it isn't too bad if you're the wife in this scheme of things: perhaps this is one of the many none-too-subtle forms of revenge of wives against the hapless Handmaids. It is certainly symptomatic of the sinister female complicity that underpins this social structure.

I thought that all of this was rather over the top, until I came upon a recent Melbourne *Age* interview with Margaret Tighe (one of the more rabid local right-to-lifers). Her office was described as sporting a row of plastic fetuses, shown at various stages of development, and said to be emblematic of the "murdered babies" dispatched by abortions. And, just in case we needed reminding of the turgid emotionalism of this particular discourse, the article obliged by reporting that she was unable to see the issues as merely black and white, and insisted on seeing the subject in shades of red—for the innocent blood being spilled. Such thinking would ban any termination of pregnancy, whatever the reason, and suddenly Atwood's extrapolations seemed less implausible.

These same bioethical questions were recently examined by Spider Robinson in his Guest of Honor speech at Conviction '88. As I recall it, his solution to the vexed question of what constitutes "the human," and when human life can properly be said to begin, was the proposition that the soul should be located in the ovum: consequently, not only would abortion be outlawed, but so, of necessity, would menstruation. As a result, every post-pubescent female would have to be kept permanently pregnant. As in *The Handmaid's Tale*, all forms of contraception would be banned, celibacy would be outlawed, and male masturbation would become a felony (there is often claimed to be biblical precedent for this, although Onan's sin was coitus interruptus). The implications for world population are truly horrendous, but honor, at least, would be satisfied.

One interesting side issue here is the way in which the question of who owns the unborn keeps coming up. Given that equality of function in conception appears to be unthinkable, the question of whether ovum or sperm is in the ascendency has always been a vexed one. Spider Robinson opted for the ovum as being the more readily identifiable element, particularly where it is likely that more than one sperm donor has been involved, and the logical truism that maternity is more easily proved than paternity was certainly behind many matrilineal forms of family reckoning. But in patriarchal socicties, where female fidelity is important to maintain patrilineal inheritance, the idea that women were created as empty vessels for the reception of male seed is not new as a justification for repression. The earliest example that springs to mind occurs in the *Oresteia*, when Athena rules for Apollo (defense counsel for Orestes) against the Furies (appearing for Clytemnestra), by declaring that the Man is the true father to the child, and Woman merely a convenient incubator. In fiction, women have been getting the rough end of that particular stick ever since, particularly in dystopias such as *Brave New World* and *Swastika Night*, where forced breeding programs function as an indication of the extremity of institutionalized repressive practices.

In *The Handmaid's Tale*, another instance of a well-meaning pressure group's unwitting contribution to the growth of repression is derived from the movement to outlaw or destroy pornographic material. Again, flashbacks show groups of people, mostly women, demonstrating against pornography by burning magazines, and holding up clichéd placards for the television cameras. In Gilead, there is now a very reductive perception of what constitutes the pornographic: any representation of the human body is forbidden; houses no longer have mirrors; no part of the female body is allowed to escape the prescribed, shapeless clothing. Indeed, clothing, once the outward sign of individuality and symbol of liberation in earlier times, has now been institutionalized to the extent that females wear color coded garments which reflect their functional status. In the training school, old porno films are used by the Aunts to terrify the Handmaids about "what things used to be like"; and, as evidence of the degenerate time-wasting of the previous government, they are also shown occasional, censored documentaries which were made by Unwomen—they had some worthwhile ideas, "But they were Godless, and that can make all the difference..." (129).

I began by labeling this a cautionary tale, and the medieval implications were intentional. The setting is cloistered, and the daily activities of the Handmaids are circumscribed by a routine that is relentlessly claustrophobic. Female accoutrements are quasi-medieval, particularly the habits, which are voluminous, ground length dresses with long sleeves: worn with gloves and veils: for extra security, Handmaids have winged caps that operate as blinkers, obscuring their faces and restricting the visual field of their downcast eyes. Many post-apocalyptic novels assume the loss of complex technology and are set in medieval surroundings because they offer an accessible pre-industrial model, with the added advantage that feudal society had a relatively simple social structure based on raw power and the sale of protection from it. What makes *The Handmaid's Tale* unusual is that the end-of-civilization-as-we-know-it catastrophe has applied only to the women. Although the patriarchal power structure seems to be moving towards feudal dynasties, it is only the women who labor under the medieval lack of technology. Men drive cars, use communications networks, medical sciences and social amenities, while women are forbidden even basic literacy. All household labor saving devices appear to have been eliminated: the Marthas complain about having to heat water for the bath, they are making bread by hand, collecting food on a daily basis and so on. What this novel depicts is a medieval division of roles without the basis in mutual respect for function that colored preindustrial-revolution thinking. Medieval notions of co-operation for mutual benefit have been replaced by a *1984*-ish sense of mutual spying, supported by peer group pressure that augments the overriding politico-religious ideology. The Middle Ages was far more civilized in its approach to women, and one is forced to ask whether this mutual repression of women by women is what one would expect in new monotheocracy, rather than the supportive sisterhood that is posited by other writers of feminist dystopias.

The historical transition revealed in the text might point to a fear that the current role of western women may turn out to be an historical aberration. This theory certainly raises questions about the frame ending, "Historical Notes," in which the ironically presented persona gives a trivializing perspective on the document purportedly recorded by Offred. Professor Pieixoto's commentary is smug and self-congratulatory, and although it confirms the historical accuracy of Offred's depiction of life in Gilead, it dismisses its value in favor of the academic search for biographical information about the author. The reader learns that the Gileadean experiment has failed, and is itself being regarded as an aberration, but it is clear that the conference delegates are cheerfully overlooking the cautionary nature of *The Handmaid's Tale*, with its warnings about complacency and complicity. As the Professor notes, "There was little that was truly original or indigenous to Gilead: its genius was synthesis" (319). For me, the scariest lines in the book are a catch-phrase of that "crack female control agency known as the 'Aunts'" (320)—"Don't worry, you'll get used to it."

OCCASIONAL THOUGHTS ON FRANK HERBERT'S *DUNE* SEQUENCE

by Douglas Barbour

Why "sequence," when the term that springs to mind is "saga"? There is a saga quality to many of Herbert's *Dune* books, but there's much more as well. "Sequence" seems better than "series" because it implies a kind of over-arching narrative throughout; yet it is problematic in so far as it contains at least some implications of closure. One of the things I like about the *Dune* books is that no matter how finished they might have felt after any particular volume, there was always—until Herbert's death—the possibility that he would reenter the stream of that secondary universe-creation and demonstrate once more that nothing can be taken for granted there (or here).

What a basic sf moment! Basher Teg's "awakening" under "the Tprobe" (*Heretics of Dune*, 361-7). But though it depends on conventions built up since at least the appearance of A. E. van Vogt's supermen, this textual moment is both aware of the dangers of its own conventionality, and so much better prepared for than most such moments of sudden awareness and superheroics. As well, it's clearly as much an amplification of already impressive intellect as of physical prowess, and, in fact, it occurs through a form of intellection (albeit, pain-induced)—as does so much in this series (another reason to differentiate it from conventional "sagas").

But the moment (and it's not the only one in the sequence) raises an interesting question: why do we—readers in general of this kind of sf—so enjoy reading about this kind of personal superior power in action?

§

Some critics protested that Herbert wasn't playing fair when he introduced the Tleilaxu Face Dancers in *Dune Messiah*, as all the other players in that volume were presented in *Dune*. Two responses: (1) a glossary in *Dune* mentions Tleilax as a planet which produces "twisted Mentats" (xxviii), so the place had already been prepared for them; (2) aside from the fact that they are more and more useful to the ongoing "history" through their production of "the Duncan Idaho gholas" from *Children of Dune* on, and wonderfully important to the thematic development of *Heretics of Dune*, they also fit one of the governing concepts of the whole sequence—that the universe is always full of more surprises than even the most prepared and prescient can plan for: that is its nature, even in an apparently conventional sf series.

§

1965-1985: six books in the *Dune* sequence over twenty years. That is impressive in itself, but even more so is the way they hang together, yet continue to surprise while always evincing a very careful preparation of a "history" for the stories told in these volumes (there could have been many others, both within the period covered by the sequence and going back at least to the "Butlerian Jihad"), a preparation which nonetheless can always be altered as the vision of the whole project matures and broadens. But I take seriously the continuing theme of surprise, and find pleasure in watching the craft by which Herbert shapes his narrative grow from book to book. One example: in *Heretics of Dune* the arc of the narrative actively deploys surprise, especially in the revelation of Teg as hero when everything seems to point to Duncan taking on that role.

We often say that sf is a "literature of ideas," yet we also acknowledge that too much of it only offers tired ideas couched in equally tired conventional narratives of adventure. The *Dune* books can be criticized this way, yet it seems to me that to do so is to miss an important point about them. Which is that even in the first volume Herbert caught a whiff of mythography and, moreover, from the beginning he wrote as a theoretical (as well as practical) ecologist. But I think his sense of ecology expanded immensely as he pursued the larger narrative of which these books necessarily provide only glimpses: he began to see ecology as a putatively historical study—of human evolution in the context of the interaction with environment, the ever-expanding environment of the universe itself.

In *Heretics of Dune*, people are returning/have returned from "the Scattering" which occurred (as Leto II predicted in *God Emperor of Dune*) after the fall of the God Emperor's 3,500-year-long stasis—that is, enforced "peace." Most important to this story of continuing Bene Gesserit long-term cultural manipulation are the evil and highly powerful "Honored Matres." It is intriguing to note that they first appear on Gammu, the new name for Geidi Prime, the old Harkonnen home world. This seems symbolically proper, for the Honored Matres manifest many of the Harkonnen traits of rule, "using brutality and sexual depravity as weapons to control what they refer to as 'the muck'" (443). But there's more to it than that: despite being "bankers" of power, they are like the Harkonnens in that they too make the error of forgetting history: although their tyrannical powers are extreme, and they appear to have everything going their way, their intelligence is static, they cannot change either responses to events or basic ideology/conceptual thinking. And that is the major reason they exist in the final two volumes, much more than their usefulness to a paranoid-thriller plot.

§

Duncan Idaho first appears in *Dune*, with Gurney Halleck, as a weapons-master and an example of the kind of "true" loyalty an Atreides ruler invokes through "honorable" leadership. Such leadership, in stark contrast to that of the Harkonnens, recognizes responsibility to those one leads and displays human and humane care for them. Idaho is perceived, I think, through a point-of-view consistent with the young Paul's knowledge and propensity (as a youth) to hero-worship. He is not much "internalized"—that is, as a character he is pretty flat, and consistent.

Leto II suggests the value of the Duncan ghola to the sequence as a whole throughout *God Emperor*: he is a human standard (of ancient breeding, and of human(e) morality) against which to measure the changes toward or away from greater or deepening humanity which Leto and the Bene Gesserit have introduced (through benevolent tyranny and selective breeding) to the expanding race. And he also reveals some of the ancient prejudices which time and cultural change have erased.

§

"Odrade flagged an open transporter with empty seats and the three of them crowded into a space where they could continue to talk" (*Chapterhouse: Dune*, 133). How neatly that is done. Yes, Herbert has "invented" many new "names" (and therefore things), but this choice of such a neutral term for an ordinary conveyance is but one example of many of how he maintains a sense of continuity from now to that putative "then." Indeed, it is a means of achieving an intriguing "distance" but also it works because there is no need for a special term. I think this, more than some of the quite conventionally sf terms, helps create a tone not unlike that managed by Gene Wolfe in *The Book of the New Sun* with his extraordinarily esoteric terminology. Which is to say, that at this point in the ongoing narrative, some fifty thousand years in the "future," the neutral term, in context, humanizes and makes ordinary parts at least of the extraordinary lives the text cannot help but focus upon.

§

There is a moment in *Chapterhouse: Dune* when Duncan Idaho makes a Mentat projection to recognize that both the Bene Gesserit's possible destruction and the return of the Honored Matres are just "little episodes. Even the worst case assumption has to be screened against that background. The Scatterings has a magnitude that dwarfs anything we do" (196). He perceives that the Honored Matres' return to the Old Empire is actually a retreat due to defeat (which Odrade, previously in the text, has realized they can never admit), and that perception is part of the conceptual narrative of this volume, and perhaps the whole series.

What that moment, and many others like it in the other volumes, informs me is that Herbert's basic (and precisely didactic) vision never stopped expanding. He couldn't tell the story of the Scattering from the inside (or at least chose not to), but he could intuit its possibilities and at least include hints as to what they might be in his text.

"The real [is not] the world as it is...it is not, it becomes! It moves, it changes! It doesn't wait for us to change...It is more mobile than you can imagine...The world, the real, is not an object. It is a process...." This is not Leto II, though it surely could have come from one of his lectures to a Bene Gesserit Reverend Mother, or from one of the later Reverend Mothers' notes. It's John Cage commenting in 1970 (quoted in Marjorie Perloff, *The Dance of the Intellect*, 1985, 196). I like the connection. Perloff is exploring the growth of a new kind of poetry, begun by Pound and the other great early Modernists, in which every kind of discourse can find its place, and in which even a clearly articulated didacticism belongs. Herbert is writing, not out of any necessary knowledge of postmodern poetics but out of a sense (and sensibility) that allowing many different statements into his text (all the various documents "quoted" at the beginning of all the chapters of all the books) is as important to the life of his fiction as are the many different stories told and implied, with all their associated protagonists and their points of view (i.e., various Bene Gesserit "witches," a number of Tleilaxu Masters, at least three Duncans, Basher Teg, etc. are all the central figures in narratives—told or only alluded to—of their own devising).

§

Here's another John Cage aphorism: "We are involved not in ownership but in use" (Perloff, 203). He is speaking, actually, of the production of art events, but he could be suggesting how to create a future, a universe. I think of Mother Superior Odrade telling Murbella, "wherever we stand, we are only stewards" (*Chapterhouse: Dune*, 118), a version of the same point (and moreover, a version of the central belief of the Plains Indians, which Herbert certainly knew). It points to what should be an awareness of continual process but, even in the wide-awake and "human" Bene Gesserit, often is not. So the novels, over and over again, drive the point home, sometimes through the narrative destruction of one of our favorite characters. Another reason to give Herbert credit for going well beyond the demands of the conventions which he nonetheless continued to write, not within, but within sight and site of.

§

From the beginning of the *Dune* sequence, Herbert has striven to intertwine a number of interconnected storylines. And even in *Dune*, the shifts of perspective and narrative point of view were effective. Still, his skill at orchestrating various strains of the massive history he tells consistently improved; and more and more matched the particulars of each novel. So that in *God Emperor of Dune*, the other narratives keep surfacing, but the major current of the narrative flow is Leto's Golden Path, a river of golden opportunity, so to speak, he hammers out in the smithy of his tormented soul (I'm aware of the oxymoronic qualities of my metaphor—they are, I think, structurally present in the text). The singular movement of the plot here is due to his immense power (but note that the power is not due to what he can do but what he can inspire his followers to do). In *Heretics of Dune* and *Chapterhouse: Dune*, however, the various threads of alternative narratives maintain a much greater integrity, because there is no single power in the universe of the fiction strong enough to control the movements of the other stories (some of which—Teg's in *Heretics*, Lucilla's in *Chapterhouse*—come to very sudden ends).

The problem with sequels (as the critics of *Crocodile Dundee II* or *Rambo III*, or any number of recent sf & f "series," never tire of pointing out) is that they are essentially a pale copy, a bad Xerox so to speak, of the original. Nothing changes, and the "hit" is less because whatever spark of originality powered the original (in *Croc*'s case, anyway) is being cannibalized but never ever made new. But, like the later gholas of Duncan Idaho, the *Dune* books undergo changes, due no doubt to Herbert's own maturing and changing thinking during the two decades he worked on the sequence. And due, as well, perhaps to the fact that from the beginning he sought to render a universe of change and process, thus differentiating the *Dune* books from the more conventional examples of what Brian Aldiss calls "Wide Screen Baroque." (The staggering inability of those who made it to recognize this aspect of *Dune* perhaps also explains the failure of *Dune the Film*, which completely bought the Fascist fantasy [see Aldiss, as well, on this aspect of sf&f] which the book rigorously interrogated, as do all the *Dune* books.)

§

Although I love classical music, I am a jazz fan. So what a pleasure to find Odrade, near the end of the whole sequence as we have it (*Chapterhouse: Dune*, 375-6), recognizing the necessity that "the actual confrontation" with the Honored Matres (now recognized to be a bureaucratic perversion of the Fish Speakers with some Bene Gesserit input) "be played as it came—a jazz performance."

After almost six volumes of careful orchestration—with Leto II as the great arranger of it all (within the text of the last three)—this small moment again pays strict attention to the driving vision of the whole: the recognition that it all simply cannot be fixed: life, even the life of civilization, is an improvisatory performance.

§

In June 1988, scientists from all over the world met in Toronto at The World Conference on the Changing Atmosphere to discuss how the rapid transformations of the planet's atmosphere are affecting the whole environment. Throughout the *Dune* sequence, Herbert posits the possibility of very rapid planetary changes, through, it is true, the power of the worm—a fantasy effect. But we now begin to recognize just how accurate his fictional hypothesis was; the changes that can be wrought by the worm of *Dune* or the worm of runaway "development" are vaster and faster than most politicians or businessmen are yet willing to acknowledge.

Would he have made his point any more effectively to them or to "us" had he written only editorials or articles? Can imaginative storytelling be any use in the public realm?

§

The God Emperor creates a vast bureaucratic system throughout the Old Empire—that is how he rules for 3,500 years, enforcing "Leto's peace" upon all his subjects. Of course, we only receive hints of this, yet the basic narrative structure of *God Emperor of Dune*, and the many and various meetings and discussions, provide all the textual evidence necessary. And in the later books it emerges that the corrupt and powerful tyranny of the Honored Matres is a logical development of Fish Speakers, bureaucracy gone mad (remembering, always, that it is a military bureaucracy).

Mikhail Gorbachev strove to wrench the Soviet Union out of the hands of a powerful, stagnant, antidemocratic, and therefore repressively conservative bureaucracy. Once again the implicit didacticism of much sf, the ways in which high fantastic narrative can provide an exotic mirror of our world, reveals itself in the complex interaction of narrative and commentary which has been the structural basis of all six *Dune* books.

§

"[T]he recipient is almost as responsible for the content of a discourse as its author" (Tzvetan Todorov, *The Conquest of America*, 226).

"Form is never more than an extension of content" (Charles Olson, *Human Universe*, 52).

Do I have here one of the major clues as to why the *Dune* sequence appears to be a space opera but is so much more?

For the content is profounder by far, and the "Wide Screen Baroque" sweep of the sequence is complicated by a didactic textuality in which the adventure of exposition or explanation is folded into the narrative of interstellar expansion.

§

There's the interesting question of the temporal lacunae, especially in the final two volumes. It's true that even in the earliest volumes there are occasional long leaps in time (and especially between volumes), but they are part of an essentially linear and singular narrative. In the final two a number of things allow for a far less linear development and for the often sudden jumps in time: (a) the perspective and general point-of-view are those of the Bene Gesserit, and they have learned to distrust singular perspectives; but (b) within that general POV, many of their own protagonists are also antagonists (at least in philosophical attitude); (c) because they are both long-lived (300 years average) and full of historical consciousness, the leaps in time suit their lives and thinking. What we find here, then, is another example of textual mnemonics: another formal method of alerting us to the break with linear (i.e., one-track) thinking (and therefore linear narratives) which the whole sequence argues.

§

A poststructuralist reading of the *Dune* sequence could easily begin in an examination of "the Other memories" of Bene Gesserit Reverend Mothers plus Paul and Leto II. They are presented as oral, i.e., voices in the minds of their holders, but a Derridean reading might point out that they are really texts, always already written, inscribed so to speak on the tabula of the mind. The Reverend Mother as a kind of library, full of ancient and modern texts, from which she can learn much, but upon which, as Odrade points out to Murbella, she must act on her own. They are repositories of knowledge, but they are not living voices, capable of action, however much (like any text, perhaps) they may influence it.

One of the implications of Claude Lévi-Strauss's *The Savage Mind* is that so-called "primitive thought" is more than somewhat akin to bureaucratic thought. An ironic little joke, perhaps: to present the Honored Matres, in their barbarity (which is not necessarily the same as primitivism, as both Herbert and Lévi-Strauss no doubt knew), as decadent bureaucrats; and then to reveal that they are slipping back towards "primitive" humanity (despite their neurological/physical gains) rather than, as the Bene Gesserit hope, joining that part of humanity which is finally "growing up": "We wait for humankind to mature" (*Chapterhouse: Dune*, 446).

Note that the finicky bureaucratic thinking associated with Arc hives is what prevents a Mentat-Archivist like Bellonda from ever becoming Mother Superior.

Note also that the Honored Matres' apparent conquest of the Bene Gesserit, through Murbella, will eventually bring them to an understanding of the "limits" of bureaucratic behavior (and the backstabbing, static, self-protection endemic to it), thus releasing them, as actors on the human scene, into conscious participation in process once again.

§

And why "occasional," after all? Because these notes are simply some of the things that occurred to me as I read through the sequence—on this occasion, the first in which I read all six at once, and which only happened on a whim, my desire to enjoy some thoughtful escapism, anyway. When I realized that part of my response was a kind of "thinking about," I began to make notes; other texts I was reading entered into dialogue with the *Dune* books as I did so. There's much more to comment on, and possibly I will continue to think about the sequence this way for a long time to come; but these are the questions and comments it has elicited from me this summer.

THE AMBIGUITIES OF UTOPIA

THREE UTOPIAS

by Yvonne Rousseau

Austin Tappan Wright, *Islandia*
Catherine Helen Spence, *Handfasted* and *A Week in the Future*.

Islandia appeared in 1942, eleven years after its author, Austin Tappan Wright, died in a motor accident, and thus about twelve years after the novel's completion (Sylvia Wright's introduction, copyrighted in 1958, mentions that the novel "was finished within a year or so of my father's death"). Its author was a United States citizen who was born in 1883, who practiced law for some years, and who then worked as a university professor of law. Islandia itself is an imaginary country in the south of "the Karain semicontinent," which is somewhere in the Southern Hemisphere. The novel's narrator is a United States citizen who spends time in the Islandian utopia between January 1907 and the close of the novel in 1910.

The narrator of *Handfasted* has travelled in the opposite direction; a nineteenth-century Australian citizen, he has set off from the Southern Hemisphere to the United States, where he stumbles upon the utopia of Columba—hidden in a valley somewhere southwest of San Francisco. *Handfasted*'s author, Catherine-Helen Spence, was an Australian citizen born in 1825, who worked as a teacher, writer, philanthropist and political campaigner, and who was eulogized as "grand old woman of Australia" when she died in 1910. *Handfasted* was first published in 1984, seventy-four years after Spence died, and 105 years after the novel's completion.

Spence and Wright both had other publications during their lifetime: Wright's were associated with his profession of law, while Spence published seven other works of fiction, in addition to pamphlets, periodical articles and newspaper contributions.

Because Wright died so unexpectedly, we do not know whether he intended taking steps to have *Islandia* published. Beside the completed novel (which was subsequently cut for publication to about two-thirds of its original length), he left other Islandian papers, including a 135,000-word scholarly history, purportedly by Islandia's first French consul. Wright had been enlarging on Islandia since he first invented it as a child, and his daughter Sylvia mentions that he spoke of it freely with his wife and children, and that the geology underlying its appearance was as clear in his mind as were the unique Islandian forms of "the sailboat, the ski, the saddlebag." He had endowed the Islandians with a distinctive lifestyle and philosophy, successfully isolated from dominant Western tendencies by "laws forbidding trade and limiting the number of foreigners permitted to visit Islandia."

Spence's utopia of Columba has also developed in isolation; but the surrounding world is unaware of its existence. On the other hand, apart from the Amerindian element (who seem to have had no influence—except in some of their dances—on the community's philosophy or customs), Columba's founders were part of the European mainstream until they sailed from Scotland in 1745 (missing the Jacobite rebellion led by Bonnie Prince Charlie later that year). The Puritanism that both Islandia and Columba oppose has thus been observed by Islandians only in outsiders, whereas the founders of Columba had themselves lived under its sway as Presbyterians in Scotland.

Wright's *Islandia* could be viewed as a "lifelong daydream" (as Ursula K. Le Guin suggests in "Science Fiction and Mrs. Brown"). Spence's *Handfasted*, on the other hand, was not the author's first or only novel, and was certainly designed for publication. Spence's autobiography (written in the last two years of her life) tells us that *Handfasted* was written in 1879 "for a prize of £100 offered by *The Sydney Mail* [...] but was not successful, for the judge feared that it was calculated to loosen the marriage tie—it was too socialistic, and consequently dangerous." Helen Thomson's introduction to *Handfasted* tells us that "As far as can be known, Spence never submitted the manuscript to a publisher" after this rejection. Indeed, it seems to have discouraged her from writing fiction: her remaining thirty years brought, by her own account, only two more works of fiction—the utopian novella *A Week in the Future* (set in the year 1988 and serialized in the *Centennial Magazine*, 1888-89) and the lost work *A Last Word*. This apparent discouragement prefigures the case of another Australian woman Marjorie Barnard, the chief author of the science-fiction novel *Tomorrow and Tomorrow and Tomorrow* (by "M. Barnard Eldershaw"), which is acclaimed by present-day readers but was subjected to wartime censorship before it first appeared in 1947, and was then received so badly (for political rather than literary reasons—as is also true of *Handfasted*) that Barnard never returned to fiction.

In Columba and Islandia, Spence and Wright are both depicting utopias where the social mores are different from those in their own societies so that ideas about women have been altered—producing a remarkable effect on heterosexual relationships. But neither author believes that the style of government and the customs found in these communities could or should be installed in the complicated world of the nineteenth or twentieth century. Rather, they are investigating human potentialities that cannot be developed within the social constraints of their own milieu. Imagining how people would behave in an invented society without these constraints, they dramatize an oppression that their readers have suffered without perhaps identifying its source (as Joanna Russ, in inventing the manless planet of Whileaway, illuminates for women the oppression of existing under a lifelong threat of rape). While demonstrating the good and the plausibility of people's adopting new behaviors, Wright and Spence emphasize that Islandia and Columba are not exemplars of the way for the world to achieve such changes. In fact, we might compare them instead to the isolated development imagined (in science fiction) on other planets, with Wright's Islandia somewhat resembling Le Guin's Gethen in *The Left Hand of Darkness* (1969)—in that its inhabitants, though beginning with the common human ancestry (a concept which, in Le Guin's novel, becomes extended to a common Hainish ancestry), have developed extremely deep-rooted differences which make their visitors feel irrevocably alien—while Spence's Columba is more like the Gand planet in Eric Frank Russell's "And Then There Were None..." (1951), in that its inhabitants have been acting on ideas that their visitors can recognize as belonging to a shared cultural history.

Wright's novel begins when Islandia is considering ending its isolation by entering into "full commercial treaties" with some powerful European nations and the United States, and is consequently receiving consular officers—among whom is the young narrator, John Lang, the United States consul. Having befriended an Islandian at Harvard, Lang has learnt the Islandian language and read some Islandian literature (where, as Wright's friend Leonard Bacon wrote in his introduction to the 1942 edition of *Islandia*, fable had remained the dominant form: "The parabolic was carried to a perfection unknown to us" and the Islandian equivalent of Shakespeare was "a sort of super-Aesop"). The lesser alienations experienced in Islandia by a visitor like Lang in the first decade of the twentieth century include the unfamiliar style of dress—not only are Islandian clothes loose-fitting, without whalebone or starch, but also they habitually expose the legs of both men and women from the knee down. (And Lang is shaken to discover later that he is expected to swim naked with naked Islandian men and women.) The general silence also greatly unnerves United States visitors, causing two commercial travelers to complain to Lang (54) that Islandia might be all right for "highbrows." There is not only an absence of bustle, advertising and machinery but also of phatic communion: an Islandian woman, Morana, compliments Lang (244): "You are like one of us in your willingness for moments of no conversation."

Deeper alienation is disclosed when the French consul explains to Lang the difficulty in obtaining advice from an Islandian, since advice entails "presuming to doubt that you knew what you were doing" (63)—whereas honor is supposedly "a matter of pure instinct," in the Islandian definition of "a gentleman." People who have read Le Guin's *The Left Hand of Darkness* before reading *Islandia* will find this disclosure the more striking because they are already familiar with the related (but far more developed) concept of *shifgrethor*, which is "the all-important principle of social authority" on the planet of Gethen. I do not know whether Le Guin read *Islandia* before or after writing *The Left Hand of Darkness*; if she read it beforehand, then the Islandians' taboo against advice-giving, their dependence (501) on custom instead of rules, and their belief (404) that everything is "a question of balance" might well have been (in Henry James's image) dropped by Le Guin into the "deep well of unconscious cerebration"—or, in Gary Snyder's image, "composted"—to emerge again, transmuted, in the envoy Genly Ai's narrative of the very much stranger world of Gethen.

An alien conception of how people should make their livings has shaped Islandian ideas about women. Although Islandian women may work as prostitutes, Islandians believe that "no man should keep a woman—supporting her in return for her body," because then (380) "She has no safety. She cannot be herself. She must act so as to please him, [...] or else her bread is gone." Similarly, (395) "No Islandian young man is handicapped by 'having his way to make'." Instead, an Islandian's wants are supplied by the family and place where he or she belongs. For as long as a woman chooses to be a prostitute (for which she incurs no disgrace), the people at the brothel where she is living take on the role of her family; when a woman marries, the place and the family of her husband become hers. To Islandians, "family" means (464-5) "the continuation of generations on the same land." Understood in this sense, the family is "the natural unit" for Islandians, and "the state is a servant created by the family for its ends." Thus, their lifestyle is centered (471) on "place and family as one."

Because Islandian women are not seen as financially dependent on men, they are not seen as property, and the American notion in Lang's era of a "good" woman (which partly implies a blinkered— or, as Usanians may say, "blindered"—woman) is untranslatable: she might be (458) "a good promise-keeper, a good housekeeper, or good as a lover." Islandians regard marriage (for which no legal ceremony is required) very seriously, as the opportunity to express the two strongest aspects of "love" that their language defines— feelings linked with place and with generation. But their language defines another strong aspect of "love," and they do not believe (530) that "confining yourself to one person is the one vital thing in a marriage." Heterosexual relationships between unmarried people are not censured unless one partner is careless of the other's feelings (homosexuality is never mentioned). Islandians have used contraception "for hundreds of years" (432)—the woman usually taking responsibility—and this not only prevents obvious social difficulties, but also ensures that the link between place and family does not become broken by overpopulation. (Islandians also limit to one hundred the number of foreigners—who must first be free of venereal disease—allowed to live in their country.)

Clearly, the absence of the Christian Church is vital to Islandian ideas about women. Foreigners think of Islandians (18) as "pagan," while "hedonism with a kind heart" (403) is the nearest approach an outsider has made to defining the Islandian philosophy. Islandians repudiate the Puritans' hope (398) of finding "salvation by the control of their feelings": "We don't believe at all in being critics of our feelings" (403).

Because the best part of their lives is spent on farms, Islandians do not distinguish between (177) "men's jobs and women's jobs," but "work together" (521). And because women are not men's financial dependents, Lang observes (272) that "here the slight shame a woman feels at being a man's host, or perhaps thinks he feels as a mere guest, did not exist." Nevertheless, Islandians are always identified to each other (71) "by reference to their relationship to the heads of their families" (for example, "Brother—George of Hem; grandnephew—Dorn of Lower Doring") and the family heads are always men. Moreover, the novel's events suggest that Islandian women have no vote. The National Council consists of five military lords, five judicial lords, three naval lords, and twenty elected provincial lords, plus the king and (at the time of the novel) his sister and wife. All the male Councilors have the right both to speak and to vote, but the women are entitled only to speak (473-4). Thus, when an informal referendum is held, for all the stress placed on the importance of the "individual" and "the people," it is likely that "the average man" (462 and 468) does not include women. Wright's other Islandian papers, apart from the novel, may make this point clearer; it is obscure in the novel because the narrator attaches no importance to it. (In the United States, women's fight for the vote was not won until 1920, ten years after the close of *Islandia* and only eleven years before Wright's death. It was 1896, by contrast, when South Australians became the first women in their country to cast a vote in a state election—while Australian women cast their first federal vote in 1903. Spence was a South Australian, and although she believed in 1879 when *Handfasted* was written that a change to proportional representation was needed more urgently than female suffrage, she gave the women in Columba the vote.)

Like many other fictional utopias, Wright's *Islandia* is being reported by a visitor whose perceptions are both heightened and given direction by his having fallen in love with a local inhabitant. In fact, Lang falls in different kinds of love with at least two female inhabitants, and very solemnly has what Americans would regard as "an affair" with his second-best choice. When she refuses to marry him, he acts on another Islandian woman's advice (686)—that an Islandian wife "would be too much at home, too much your teacher"—and persuades an American woman to come to Islandia as his bride. Readers thus first observe the complications that the social assumptions of Boston and Nantucket introduce into Lang's courtship of Gladys, and afterwards witness his struggle, back in Islandia, to persuade his wife to see the advantages in an Islandian marriage, with a husband who will not act as if he "owns" her. Replying to a complaint from Gladys of his failure to guide her—"You don't make me do what you want"—Lang protests that then:

> Everything you did would be done of my will and not of yours. You would obey, and inwardly reserve your freedom. You would hold fast to the right

to criticize and rebel. All the burden and blame of what we did you would escape and shift to me. (904-5)

In the civilization that Gladys is familiar with, women are so accustomed to exerting their will only reactively that an Englishwoman married to an Islandian assures Gladys (915) that "Islandia is a man's place rather than a woman's," because "One had to learn to live very much upon one's own resources." The feeling of not being one's own (but instead always coerced, socially and financially) has been so pervasive in these women's former lives that Gladys finds it hard to see any point in investigating her true feelings: thus, she tells Lang (933) that, after she had failed to prevent an Islandian from kissing her, she worried that she had "been untrue to our marriage. That was the main thing, not my feeling for you."

As it reflects on the United States of the early twentieth century, Wright's novel illuminates two main barriers to freedom between men and women: women's financial disadvantage, which is linked with their being treated as men's property; and society's "standardized moral rules" (792), which prevent candor and distort both marriage and friendship. In *Islandia*, Wright enables society to function without these barriers by inventing special conditions: reliable contraception, no Christian Church, and a small and likeminded population with an agricultural lifestyle. But he is conducting a thought experiment on "human nature," not suggesting that this set of conditions could be duplicated elsewhere.

Readers may notice another special condition of *Islandia*: nobody of any nationality in this novel displays a sense of humor, although at least twice Lang tells us that some individual has one. A voice may sound "amused"—someone may "tease"—"humor" itself may be attributed to some unreported remarks—but the scattered instances of laughter seem always associated with a sense of superiority, while the few Islandian girlish giggles we encounter are of the highly strung variety. Henry James once spoke of remembering a novelist's works as if they were all set in a single season—"the endless autumn" of Charlotte Brontë; Jane Austen's "arrested spring." Partly because of its people's lack of effervescence and extravagance, Wright's Islandia (smiling gravely) makes me think of a dry winter, whereas Spence's Columba exists in full summer—and not only because it rejoices in coffee and tobacco crops (tropical products which Islandia eschews).

The impression of greater warmth and brighter light in Columba derives from a more radical change in ideas about women than is imagined by Wright, who reveals that "some but not all" Islandians (431) "judge" women who become pregnant outside marriage. In Columba—as Helen Thomson writes (378) in her afterword to *Handfasted*—Spence has

> simply removed the burden of sexual guilt from women and thus freed them from the curse they had borne since Eve's acceptance of the apple from the serpent had branded the female as the cause of the Fall. (378)

The narrator of *Handfasted* is Hugh Victor Keith, a young doctor from Melbourne. Like Spence herself, whose family emigrated to South Australia when she was thirteen, Hugh Victor is of Scots descent. His eighty-eight-year-old grandmother has recounted to him the story she heard from her own grandmother who (in 1745, when she was fifteen) witnessed several Scots families setting sail together for North America and "the most wonderful fine country better than Virginia in every way" which had been stumbled upon and afterwards tirelessly recommended by a survivor of the ill-fated Darien scheme of 1698-1700 (an attempt to establish a Scottish settlement on the isthmus of Panama). When Hugh Victor himself subsequently strays into Columba and meets the flourishing descendants of this supposedly lost expedition, the story of the expedition's background is told again as it has been passed down to Liliard Abercrombie, the "handfasted" bride of Hugh Keith—a Columban kinsman of Hugh Victor Keith's. It is then told for a third time in an extremely engrossing autobiographical narrative left by Marguerite Keith, the founding member responsible for Columba's social innovations.

By repeating the story of Columba's beginnings, Spence greatly encourages the reader's belief in it, not only by the operation of the Bellman's rule in Lewis Carroll's *The Hunting of the Snark*—"What I tell you three times is true"—but also by the timely embellishment of each new telling with details that answer new questions likely to have occurred to Hugh Victor and the readers only as they became better acquainted with Columban ways. This progressive expansion of the view seduces the reader into an illusion of being an investigator whose questing mind is uncovering what lies behind the mere appearances with which other (less interesting) visitors to Columba would probably have been contented. The result is a kind of flattery—and people are tempted to believe in the truthfulness of their flatterers.

In Spence's day, one difference between Scottish and British law was the validity in Scotland of irregular private marriages: as Hugh Victor writes (340), in Scotland "a simple declaration of marriage, the mere going by my name and living as my wife before witnesses was as binding as the most elaborate ceremony." Irregular marriages like this were important in the plots of *Mr. Hogarth's Will* (1865) and *Gathered In* (1876-77), two novels that Spence wrote before *Handfasted*. In Columba, however, a more obscure and contentious Scottish custom has been adopted: trial marriage (or "handfasting"), as described in Sir Walter Scott's novel *The Monastery*. In Columba, this practice has been formalized so that every couple who wishes to marry must first have been "*Handfasted*" in a trial marriage that lasts for a year and a day. At the end of this time they may marry, they may part, or (if undecided) they may be handfasted again for another term. There are no Columban penalties for fickle people who pass through many handfastings with different partners: as Liliard Abercrombie says (44) "It is not given to everyone to be naturally constant."

The most liberating aspect of the handfasting system is the Columban attitude to children. As Hugh Victor says (56):

> In Europe, and indeed in the civilized world generally, a child born out of lawful wedlock is a burden to the mother, which she has much difficulty in partially shifting off sometimes to the father. As for the disgrace, she generally bears it all.

In Columba, on the other hand, a child (55) is purely "a blessing and a treasure." If handfasted parents decide to part, their child is held to need its mother's care during the first year of its life, but after that, if only one partner desired the break-up, the other partner has first claim to custody of the child. Various other agreements may be made—parents often take the child "year about"—but Columba's most revolutionary innovation is the treatment of the few children who are given up by their parents. Regarded as "God's bairns," they are brought up differently from the rest (after the age of ten), but the difference is a better education for the cleverest of them; they alone are taught to read and write (there being very few books in Columba), and they alone can enter the professions (as ministers, teachers, doctors and arbitrators) or become civil servants.

This is a breathtaking reversal: that children abandoned to the care of the State should become the society's professional elite. Nevertheless, the system produces its own disadvantages. Columban government is by elective Councils at both town and Commonwealth level, and although both women and men from the general population may vote, "God's bairns" may neither vote nor serve as Councilors; instead, they form an advisory bureaucracy. As a consequence, devotees of the British television series *Yes, Minister* will be charmed to discover that in 1879 Spence attributed the following reflection to Hugh Victor:

> We know that the permanent and irresponsible heads of departments have great power in the shifting ministries in Australia, and that any exercise of power against routine is resented not only by the class itself, but by the whole community; and how could a body, not a ministry but only a single feeble Chamber, oppose a guild like the Columban civil service. (232)

Despite its imperfections, however, Columba's reversal of the usual fate of outcast children illuminates a point that Ursula Le Guin also makes in *Tehanu* (Gollancz, 1990: 159): that most people believe "that you are what happens to you." In Australia today, this belief inspires the social stigma associated with the poverty endured by more than 200,000 single-parent families, mostly headed by women—with many of these women acquiescing in society's dim view of them, to the point of believing that it is only their children, not themselves, who "deserve" release from poverty traps. The Columbans, on the other hand, with no instances before them of women as victims and children as burdens, have no belief at all that women are morally inferior—or that the work they do is of no real consequence. (It may also be noted that they have no knowledge of Charles Dickens and his creations—such as Em'ly, in *David Copperfield*.)

Columba was originally intended to be rigidly Presbyterian. However, both the Presbyterian minister and the schoolmaster were killed (one by overstrain and the other by pirates) before they reached Columba, and almost all the books the settlers had brought (including the Calvinistic Church Standards) were burnt by malicious pirates. In her role as the minister's widow, Marguerite Keith therefore used the Gospels as her manual in teaching the community's children, and found that the texts could be interpreted quite differently without "the benumbing influence of tradition" (198). Thus, she established in Columba the tradition of dancing on Sunday, as in her childhood she had observed French Catholic peasants to do, because (206) she learnt from the Gospels that for the Jewish people the Sabbath was originally "a day of rest, but not a day of penance or restriction—God had *given* them the Sabbath not *taken* it from them." (The opposite opinion, however, lingered on officially in Hugh Victor's home city of Melbourne well into the 1950s, when overseas visitors regularly reported their stupefaction at the blank austerity of the Melbourne Sunday.) Marguerite Keith's reflections on Calvinism (influenced by her own experiences in both France and Scotland) make vivid the terrors of the pitiless doctrine of innate human depravity that caused Spence herself, as a Presbyterian, to refuse marriage proposals—shrinking (as her autobiography reports) "from the possibility of bringing children into the world with so little chance of eternal salvation." (She was thirty years old, and resigned to spinsterhood, before "the dark veil of religious despondency" lifted, and she became a Unitarian.)

As Liliard Abercrombie realizes (334), Columba has been "a curious political and social experiment on a small scale under the most favorable circumstances"—and its customs will not survive the inevitable future intrusion of the outside world. She sees (300) that, in order to become part of the United States, Columba would have to "give up the handfasting, as you say the Utah people will have to give up the polygamy, which they thought a religious duty, whereas our folk never thought ours more than a wise arrangement." (A chapter entitled "Salt Lake City," presumably dealing with the necessity for the Mormons to conform to Federal laws if Utah is to become a State, has been omitted from the published version of *Handfasted*—together with some of Hugh Victor's grandmother's conversation.) As for the outside world, Hugh Victor assures Liliard (334) that "Vested interests in any large complex society fight to the death against every social reform."

Apart from the relatively small population, one circumstance favoring the Columban experiment has been the abundance of food, leaving parents more free to regard children simply as a joy—just as they are in the equally fertile utopia of Charlotte Perkins Gilman's *Herland* (published in her magazine *Forerunner* in 1915, and reprinted as a book in 1979). To ensure that this joyousness continues, the parthenogenetic women of *Herland* practice a rare spiritual form of contraception—but Columbans apparently practice none.

Another favorable circumstance for Columba was that, as Marguerite Keith observed (187), it was inspired neither by religious fanaticism nor by greed, but was intended simply as "a plantation for the bettering of the condition of the people that went, and it was composed for the most part of whole families." (In this, there is a parallel with South Australia's beginnings as a planned settlement based on Edward Gibbon Wakefield's ideas. Having arrived in the colony only three years after its founding, Spence both observed and participated in its development; and thirty-nine years later (in 1878) she wrote: "Perhaps never in any human society did circumstances realize the ideas of the community of labor and the equality of the sexes so fully as in South Australia in its early days.") Thoughtful Columbans (151) take a "comprehensive view of the tendency of different institutions to produce different kinds of character," but readers may also think that the temperaments of Columba's founders have played some part in the continuing success of handfasting among their descendants: no Columban ever disrupts the orderly "year and a day" of trial by engaging in outside "affairs"—no one ever calls for divorce when once married—and there is no prostitution. (There is no suicide, either.)

Whether environment or heredity is most to blame, Columban society has evolved with certain deficiencies: Hugh Victor notices at once the absence of ornamentation in homes, and Liliard concludes from what he has told her of the outside world that Columba has (217) "no architecture and no music worthy of the name, no art, no literature—no sense of beauty as you have." (This sense of beauty is demonstrated by Hugh Victor's bothering to photograph mere scenery. Readers of Jane Austen will remember that Catherine Morland in *Northanger Abbey* (written 1798-99) had to be instructed in "foregrounds, distances, and second distances—side-screens and perspectives—lights and shades" before she could securely distinguish that certain landscapes were beautiful; and Columbans began their isolation in 1745, before the development of enthusiasm for the "picturesque" in scenery.) Still more striking to Hugh Victor (241) is that Columbans "have absolutely no sense of humor" but the need for such a thing is protested against very gravely indeed by his confidant, Master Hepburn, who has just been lamenting the equal absence of religious fear and awe among Columbans. Hugh Victor's theory (243) that a "sense of the ludicrous is a sort of compensation for hard luck which you seem to stand in no need of" is later borne out by the rapidity with which Liliard develops a sense of humor when she meets the vicissitudes of the outside world.

Handfasted is remarkable for the brilliance with which Marguerite Keith's life story (including experience of France, England and Scotland) is interwoven with the special conditions in Columba to originate the ideas that have shaped Columban life—for many ingenuities, such as Columba's ways of aiding the memory (in the absence of writing and reading) by notched sticks or by knitted stitches—for awareness of how strongly the novel's confrontation between cultures resembles the effects of time-travel (the Columbans speak eighteenth-century Scottish, with some local additions)—and for the development of Liliard's character in the outside world as she faces risks such as smallpox and man-of-the-world misconstruction of her principles. It is a startlingly original and accomplished novel, and it is sad not only that it received such a discouraging reception and was consequently unavailable to readers for so many years, but also that Spence's other novels have spent decades out of print because the faith she expresses below was badly misplaced:

> I have always held that, though the Pilgrim Fathers ignored the right of the Pilgrim Mothers to the credit of founding the American States—although these women had to take their full share of the toils and hardships and perils of pioneer and frontier life, and had in addition to put up with the Pilgrim Fathers themselves—Australian colonization was carried out by men who were conscious of the service of their helpmates, and grateful for it. (*Autobiography*, quoted on p. 442 of *Catherine Helen Spence*, ed. Helen Thomson (in the Portable Australian Authors Series), UQP, St. Lucia, 1987)

In fact, even as Spence wrote this in the early twentieth century, the Australian literary establishment was consolidating a narrowly nationalistic masculine myth-making tradition which has not been forcefully challenged until quite recently, and which has systematically "forgotten" Australian women's writing, including Spence's, because it fails to fit the legend. (When I received my university degree in Melbourne in the 1960s, Australia's English departments clearly assumed that male experience was in fact universal experience; therefore any female experience that men could not share was essentially genre experience—peripheral, not serious—whereas the existence of male experience that females could not share simply meant that women inevitably failed in universality.)

It is particularly sad that such triumphant achievements as first *Handfasted* and then *Tomorrow and Tomorrow and Tomorrow* were disparaged when their authors produced them. Spence and Barnard were both disheartened: whether it was themselves or their audience in whom their confidence was most shaken, they were not likely to rally their forces so superbly again after such inappropriate responses.

The only surviving fiction written by Spence after *Handfasted*'s discouraging reception is *A Week in the Future* (1888-89)—in which the novelistic brilliance of *Handfasted* has been extinguished. In order for Miss Emily Bethel to travel in both space and time—from Adelaide in 1888 to London in 1988—Doctor Brown, who has a "strong leaning towards the occult and the transcendental," makes mesmeric "passes" over her and gives her "a colorless fluid" which she drinks, while they both wish intensely that the two years more of life which her diseased heart might allow her should be exchanged for a "WEEK IN THE FUTURE!" Her body lies (27) in "a trance or suspended animation" in Adelaide, while (in the same dress) it eats and drinks and talks and travels for a week in twentieth-century Britain. When a week has passed, the body dies in Adelaide—and, since Emily Bethel's written account of her twentieth-century experiences began to be published in 1888, we might suppose that her papers mysteriously materialized beside her Adelaide deathbed. However, it is clear to the reader (32) that the granddaughter of her niece has never heard of them, although she has often heard personal reminiscences from her grandmother about "Aunt Emily."

As Lesley Durrell Ljungdahl's "Prologue" to *A Week in the Future* explains, the "story is contrived to popularize the ideas about social progress inspired by Jane Hume Clapperton [...], the author of *Scientific Meliorism and the Evolution of Happiness* (1885)." Compared with *Handfasted*, Emily Bethel's tour of the voluntarily cooperative socialist future reads like a tract rather than a novel—and the usual utopian opportunities for narrative suspense are precluded by the heroine's being so elderly, and by our prior knowledge of exactly how long she will spend in her "utopia" and how she will leave it.

I end by returning briefly to Austin Tappan Wright's novel. The influence of Janet Frame's *To the Is-land* may be leading present-day readers to mispronounce "*Islandia.*" Sylvia Wright's introduction reveals (ix) that the "s" is silent—information which is more interesting (because less helpful) when placed at the end rather than the beginning of this review.

REACTIONARY UTOPIAS

by Gregory Benford

This article first appeared in *Storm Warnings: Science Fiction Confronts the Future,* edited by George Slusser, Colin Greenland & Eric Rabkin, Southern Illinois University Press (Carbondale), 1987. It is included here because its reprinting in *ASFR* #14 led to the heated and extraordinary debate that follows it below.

[Benford writes: A warning to the reader: This essay is written polemically, outside the usual manners and genteel discourse of literary criticism. In part, I intend this to provoke emotional reactions (yes, especially negative ones) because of a general complacency I sense in the treatment of utopian fiction and its true implications. It treats Ursula Le Guin because she is probably the best of all living utopian writers. I caution the reader against assuming my own political views can be read in detail from this essay.]

One of the striking facets of fictional utopias is that nobody really wants to live there. Perhaps the author, or a few friends, will profess some eagerness. But seldom do utopian fictions awaken a real longing to take part.

I suspect this is because most visions of supposedly better societies have features which violate our innate sense of human progress—they don't look like the future; they resemble a warped, malignant form of the past.

Time and again, utopists envision worlds where one aspect of human character is enhanced, and much else is suppressed. Plato's Republic was the first and most easily understandable of these; he thought that artists and similar unreliable sorts should be expelled. Too disruptive, you know.

Should we be uncomfortable with this fact? If we value Western European ideals, yes.

FIVE REGRESSIVE IDEAS

How can we codify this notion? Utopian fictions stress ideas, so we need a way to advance the background assumptions, while suppressing the foreground of plot and character.

Nearly all utopias have one or more characteristics which I shall term *reactionary*, in the sense that they recall the past, often in its worst aspects. Here, "reactionary" means an aesthetic analogy, no more. It may apply to works which are to the left in the usual political spectrum, though I feel this one-dimensional spectrum is so misleading that the customary use of reactionary means little. *Regressive* might be an alternate term, meaning that a utopia seeks to turn back the tide of Western thought. Looking at the range of utopian literature, I sense five dominant reactionary characteristics:

1. *Lack of diversity*. Culture is everywhere the same, with few ethnic or other diversities.

2. *Static in time*. Like diversity, change in time would imply that either the past or present of the utopia was less than perfect (i.e., not utopian).

3. *Nostalgic and technophobic*. Usually this takes the form of isolation in a rural environment, organization harkening back to the village or even the farm, and only the simplest technology. Many writers here reveal their fondness for medieval society. The few pieces of technology superior to today's usually exist only to speed the plot or to provide metaphorical substance; they seldom spring from the society itself. (Only those utopias which include some notion of scientific advancement qualify as sf. Otherwise they are usually simple rural fantasies. Also, this point calls in question classifying any utopia as sf if it is drastically technophobic. Simply setting it in the future isn't enough.)

4. *Presence of an authority figure*. In real utopian communities, frequently patriarchal, this is a present person. Historically, nearly all utopian experiments in the West have quickly molded themselves around patriarchal figures. In literary utopias, the authority is the prophet who set up the utopia. Often the prophet is invoked in conversations as a guide to proper, right-thinking behavior.

5. *Social regulation through guilt*. Social responsibility is exalted as *the* standard of behavior. Frequently the authority figure is

the focus of guilt-inducing rules. Once the authority figure dies, he or she becomes a virtual saint-like figure. Guilt is used to the extreme of controlling people's actions *in detail*, serving as the constant standard and overseer of the citizen's actions.

These five points outline a constellation of values which utopists often unconsciously assume.

Before backing up these points with specific arguments, consider some utopias which *don't* share all or most of them. Samuel Delany's *Triton* (1976) seems to have none of these features; indeed, it proclaims itself a "heterotopia," stressing its disagreement with the first point. Often Delany depicts societies which express his delight in the freakish. Franz Werfel's *Star of the Unborn* (1946) depicts a heavily technological future with many undesirable aspects, while accepting the inevitability of war, rebellion, and unsavory aspects. Advanced technology is carefully weighed for its moral implications in Norman Spinrad's *Songs from the Stars* (1980).

Nonreactionary or genuinely progressive utopias often reject regulation through guilt. This divides utopias roughly along the axis of European versus American, with Europeans typically favoring social conscience, that is, guilt. Consider Edward Bellamy's *Looking Backward* (the most prominent American utopia of the nineteenth century) and William Morris's reply to it, *News from Nowhere*. Both stabilize society more through gratification of individual needs than through guilt. Indeed, one of the keys to American politics is just this idea. Huxley's *Island* (written after his move to California) sides more with gratification, though his *Brave New World* (written in England) depicts the horrific side of a state devoted to gratification without our "sentimental" humanistic principles.

LE GUIN AS REACTIONARY

I want to argue that utopists often thought to be forward-looking and left-wing may be in fact reactionary. Consider, for example, Ursula Le Guin. Arguably, *The Dispossessed* (1974) is the finest American utopian novel of our time, and much of her work touches on these issues.

A first clue comes from the strangely nineteenth-century middle-European "feel" of her background society in *The Dispossessed*. This gives a curious static flavor, and, of course, recalls her reverence for the European tradition of utopian thought.

Her utopian experiment on the world Annares is strikingly technophobic. Except for minor intrusions of a faster-than-light communicator and interplanetary travel (old sf staples), there is little which suggests the future at all. The vague middle-European feel to the architecture, organization of work, and so on, is clearly nostalgic; rural Europe itself isn't even like that anymore. Plainly, the author disapproves of the techno-flash and dazzle of the opposite world, Urras.

There, Shevek can't connect with the womanly embodiment of Urras's temptation, and he symbolically spills his seed on the ground before her. Indeed, in later works, Le Guin sees space travel as "a bunch of crap flying around the world, just garbage in the sky." [1] NASA's planetary missions, or Shevek's science, can be clean, serene. Technology, though, is practical, dirty and liable to fall into the wrong hands.

We learn that the Hainish, who began the colony worlds, are burdened and driven by some strange guilt. Considering their superiority in so many fields, it is difficult not to conclude that Le Guin feels we should regard their guilt as admirable, too. This book is the culmination of her utopian thinking, a path which leads through the short story, "Those Who Walk Away from Omelas." (This parable might be titled "Those Who Walk Away from Omelets," because we know what it takes to make one—you must break some eggs.)

The Dispossessed reeks with Old Testament themes and images, using guilt as the principal social control. The founder, Odo, is the central saint of a communal society. Her pain and suffering during nine years' imprisonment *make possible* the virtue of the later Anarres society. Citizens remind each other of the events and connect her suffering with their dedication. The implied lesson is that utopia will not arrive until man comes to grips with his own inner nature, which means in turn that a citizen is *born guilty*, must repay Odo's pain with his submission to the general will and society's precepts. Living on Anarres has an uncanny resemblance to being nagged by your mother.

The marriage vows in Castro's Cuba explicitly require a couple to raise all children according to socialist morality. On Anarres a child is not a true citizen, psychically, until he has undergone a guilt-inducing experience—an unconscious, implicit rite. Both processes seek to induce early control. The crucial scene in the protagonist Shevek's childhood is the boy's imprisonment game, described in careful detail. (This incident is clearly central, and an act of juvenile delinquency taking up more space than Shevek's entire courtship of his wife!)

Odo is clearly the guilt-inducing authority figure which appears so often in reactionary utopias, though she is not the customary type: that is, male, dynamic, assertive. Odo dies just before her utopia begins (see the short story, "The Day before the Revolution" [1974]) and has some resemblance to Le Guin herself. It is interesting, then, that Odo avoids the problems of building a real utopia, for Le Guin does this too.

READING THE SILENCES

I propose a further method of investigating utopian writings, after first applying the litmus test of the above characteristics: reading the author's silences.

Plausibly, the yearning which motivates a writer to construct a utopia, devoting narrative energy to it, will in turn lead the author to neglect certain disturbing problems. The novel reflects the author's avoidance of crucial questions that arise naturally from the imagined world. Conscious avoidance (or, more importantly, unconscious neglect) of these tells us what the writer fears and feels uncomfortable with. Also then we might expect the inhabitants of a utopia never to think of the blind areas in their own society.

The principal ignored problem of Anarres is the problem of evil and thus violence; to Le Guin they are often synonymous. Guilt (social conscience) simply overcomes such discordant elements. In the middle of a drought in which people starve, no matter how evenly food is shared, somehow no one thinks of taking up arms with some friends and seizing, say, the grain reserves. Similarly, there is no onstage evidence in *The Dispossessed* of hardened criminals, insane people, or naturally violent types (indeed, violence is "unnatural," and an impulse towards it is the principal offense which calls up guilt). There *is* a prison camp for undesirables, evidence for the ambiguity of this utopia. But people seem to go there for offenses such as writing unpopular plays or, perhaps, voting Republican.

Le Guin's silence is conspicuous. This arouses the suspicion that shying away from violence of any sort is part and parcel of an emotional posture of which *The Dispossessed* is only one reflection.

Tolstoy is the obvious father of many of Le Guin's ideas, techniques, and even literary mannerisms. As Samuel R. Delany has remarked in "To Read *The Dispossessed*," [2] whenever Le Guin begins to discuss politics (a common occasion) or show it (quite rare), she uses a language which "sentence by sentence is pompous, ponderous and leaden." He surmises that her style owes much to the

Victorian translations of the great European novels, and that when she attempts depth she unconsciously lapses into this voice. These are "signs of a 'European' or 'Russian' profundity that the [translated] texts do not have." (This brilliant essay stresses the microtext and ignores the book's principal strength, its beautiful structuring. As Delany deftly shows, hidden assumptions or avoided problems often show up best at the sentence or even phrase level. He also misses some of the lovely passages which her style achieves.)

Why Tolstoy? He, as well as the Russian anarchist Prince Kropotkin, took an absolutist position—no cooperation with any state control which used force. It is worth noting that the home of much idealist anarchist thinking, Russia, is now the largest prison state in history. One suspects that this comes in part from the inability of the nineteenth century socialist thinkers to confront the problem of violence in any moderate way.

One would then expect Le Guin's Anarres to evolve, if it ever slipped free of the authorial hand, in the direction of nineteenth-century Russia—without, of course, the apparatus of the Czar, and so on. Failing to confront the problem of evil and violence gives these forces more power, not less. A quite plausible outcome, then, would see the reduction of Anarres to warring camps, each promising to restore order and ideological purity, perhaps even concluding with a Bolshevik-style victory. Le Guin attempts to finesse this entire problem. Her ignoring of a remarkable historical parallel (the demise of Russian socialist idealism at the hands of Lenin) marks *The Dispossessed* as a deeply reactionary work, concerned more with repealing history than with understanding it in order to make a better future.

This came up recently when I was discussing Soviet sf with one of the principal sf critics there, M. Gakov. Appropriately enough, it was a cold day in 1984 and we were crossing Red Square. He remarked that *The Dispossessed* was not translated into Russian, in part because it referred to ideas the regime didn't like. Then he said rather wistfully, "For us, you know, it is terribly nostalgic. And irrelevant."

Le Guin seems to have tentatively approached the problem of real-world violence in the cartoon version of real politics depicted in *The Eye of the Heron* (1978).There, descendants of the mafia confront non-violent anarchists in highly implausible fashion, leading to a retreat of the anarchists into the wilderness—a note oddly reminiscent of many American escape-adventures. One must conclude that Le Guin can hardly bear to confront this crucial issue, and, when she does, sees no solution.

But there seems to be a deeper reason for Le Guin's silence about the realities of the world: fundamentally, the real world does not matter.

As the British critic Roz Kaveney has remarked in a review of *Malafrena* (1979),

> "Throughout there is the sense that fills all of Le Guin's work: that politics is important less for what it can do for other people than as a way of achieving moral self-realization. Altruism is seen as good for its own sake and not because it may be useful to the under-privileged, although the altruist is supposed to be too busy to ever think in precisely those terms."

A utopia of hard-scrabbling scarcity solves so many problems quite cheaply. No worries about distribution of wealth, no leverage for power relationships. And it casts all in a superior light: poor people can have few sins. Throughout, no one questions a system which produces poverty, because, after all, it provides lovely opportunities for sacrifice.

A genuine revolutionary in such a place would be he who puts productivity over political theory. No such figure appears—another author's silence. But reality, after all, is not the principal concern of such narratives.

So the crucial scene in *The Eye of the Heron*, in which anarchist confronts mafia thug and the protagonist dies, is *skipped*. We learn of it obliquely, via dialogue, in flashback. Partly, this comes no doubt from her aversion for violence, but I suspect we are meant to see the moral grandeur of the survivors as the central fact. Even death is another way to strike a moral posture—or rather, to be *seen* doing so.

The street confrontations on Urras in *The Dispossessed* rang false to many reviewers, and for good reason: they are the only examples of real-world political confrontation in the book, and Le Guin knows very little of such things.

So her anarchists, confronting theory rather than facts, come over as nice, reasonable, and fairly boring. They behave like middle-class middle-brows, except that they are scrupulously horrified at the idea of property. (One of the book's assets lies in reassuring the middle-brow reader that revolutions will let him feel moral and yet comfortable. Everyone, after all, believes himself capable of overcoming his own greed and being a nice guy.) The conspicuous villains of the book are a physicist who steals Shevek's work, and, of course, lots of pseudo-American capitalists on Urras.

But not quite. As Delany points out in his essay, she treats the homosexual Bedap with an unconscious condescension. It is clear that Bedap should reform himself—stop being gay—because it does not fit in with the utopia she is constructing in her head. Which in turn intersects with the reactionary utopist's dislike of cultural diversity. Homosexuals cannot be eliminated from human society (without genetic engineering at least); they are in fact impossible to ignore, but clearly their presence troubles Le Guin's blueprints.

In her world, a quiet talk over herbal tea will surely fix matters up. A romantic, she ignores the problem of evil wherever possible. In Le Guin's land, crowds watching a potential suicide on a window ledge never shout "Jump!" Averting her gaze from the twentieth century, she sees evil people as those unfortunates who have not been given sufficient chance to be good.

The real question here is not the use of violence—which is, in Le Guin's work, an invariable sign of wrongness—but rather, is moral order compatible with human diversity? Her answer is clear: her societies should opt for the age-old solution, known to the pharaohs—moral authoritarianism. Even in the dystopian future America of her novella *The New Atlantis* (1975), dissidents retreat to classical music and romantic humanism as a counter to the oppressive state. Old world values can, perhaps, redeem us.

Active thwarting of violence is not allowed, though. Le Guin labels her utopia as ambiguous, clearly knowing something is wrong, but does not confront the deep problems. Rather than think through the hidden assumptions of Anarres, Shevek returns to pursue his own moral self-realization. Perhaps he, too, will become a martyr, like Odo—and thus engender more guilt, more attendant control.

Looking Backward

As perhaps the best modern utopian novelist, Le Guin is worth studying to illuminate *why* utopists are so pervasively reactionary. I suggest that some underlying aspects of her thought come from the failures of European utopian theory. But there's more to it than that.

While there is much in reactionary utopias we should scorn, I think we should properly look at *The Dispossessed* and some more obviously feminist utopias as responses to earlier, more mechanistic and masculine utopias. (As examples of novels which clearly are such reactions, see Suzy McKee Charnas's *Motherlines*, Marge Piercy's *Woman on the Edge of Time*, and Joanna Russ's *The Female Man*.) They depict communal societies with pleasant characteristics: relative lack of government, ecological virtue, diffusion of parenting, freedom of movement, sexual freedom, and no crime.

Feminist utopias often use the family as a model for social structure, but "the unowned, non-patriarchal family, headed by nobody." [3] This, with their classlessness, makes them seem like fantasies about how families ought to be (and seldom are). If masculine utopias fret over the means of production, feminist ones are bothered by the means of reproduction. They uncouple sex from power. But this is not enough to provide social ordering.

Perhaps it is natural for women to extend the family as a model, since they have not, up to now, experienced society as a whole from a more masculine viewpoint—as a focus of conflicting forces. It isn't surprising that the problem of control doesn't rear its vexing head in such utopias, and the principal problem seems to be work assignments (who's going to do the dishes?). No trace remains of general competitiveness and the desire to be better than others; somehow, they have been laundered from the human psyche. (Interestingly, feminist utopias support this by asserting that women are inherently better, that is, non-competitive. The idea seems to be that men have merely taken a wrong turn lately.)

There is no doubt which authority figure is to set the house rules, as Joanna Russ's choice of words signifies: "Careful inspection of the manless societies usually reveals the intention (or wish) to allow men in...if only they can be trusted to behave." [3] If you don't, presumably you are sent to your room, i.e., exiled—unless it's James Tiptree, Jr.'s utopia in "Houston, Houston, Do You Read?" (1977) where you'll be killed with minimal regrets. In no case should divisive ideas of surging hormones be allowed to thwart the communal good. Unsurprisingly, the authority figure is the only fallback enforcer in such worlds. The problem of control is simply neglected.

These feminist utopias are primarily reactive, responding to perceived masculine evils. The qualities they long for—stronger communal feeling, harmony with the natural world, violence only if it expresses anger in limited ways or in self-defense, country versus city (where the streets are unsafe)—reflects current needs. But by concentrating on these concerns they run the risk of forsaking the gains of the present, and becoming reactionary because they cannot imagine new ways to organize community.

Freedom to do as we please, so long as we all agree with each other and remain in a state of harmony with the cosmos, is no freedom at all. It is little better than a religion in which faith in a deity has been replaced by faith in some supposed truths of the human spirit. It is a single-party system that is as superficially benign, yet as subtly authoritarian, as Disneyland.

Why does much utopian thought tend in this direction? The central difficulty confronting social planners is just that contained in the name—they must *plan*, and so must fear the wild card, the diverse, the self-regulating. History provides methods for governing errant wild spirits, so a planner looks longingly back for models. Few peer ahead to landscapes where men and women have more freedom, can interact swiftly and chaotically, yet with good results.

Some sf authors have seen this. Norman Spinrad's descriptions of electronic democracy, from *Bug Jack Barron* onward, are deliberately saturated with lust for power and sharp contradictions. Frederik Pohl has meditated through a long career on these problems, notably in *The Years of the City*, which abounds in utopian visions threaded with practical lore. It would be interesting to apply the criteria for a reactionary utopia and for reading silences to such works, as well as older (more apparently right-wing) utopian novels such as Heinlein's *Beyond This Horizon* and Niven and Pournelle's *Oath of Fealty*.

I conclude that reactionary facets spring in part from lack of imagination. And feminists, searching for ways to revise our society, fall upon analogies with the family, even if these do not provide solutions to the genuine problems of a diverse, urban, cantankerous world. Fundamentally, what we sense as most reactionary about these fanciful worlds is their fixation on a final, glorious endpoint: utopia as stasis.

We intuitively understand now, in a world ever in flux, that no society will stay put. The modern spirit is less concerned with ends than with means. We wrinkle our noses at frozen goals, sensing that our longing for a better world must fasten on making the process of change better, rather than nailing down eternal, theory-bound specifics. We need utopias which satisfy many human needs while all about them is changing, being made new by the insights of science and art.

It is no longer enough to depict flawed utopias, ambiguous ones, or the like. What literature needs, and plainly isn't getting, are utopias of *process*, which tell us something about how to reach goals and be happy during the journey. Such visions people could respond to creatively.

Instead, present utopists long for sweeping simplicities. The supremacy of communal values, the need to suppress the individual, the fear of diversity or of science, the longing for a respite from change—these find many echoes in socialist thinking, in third world societies, in all those who look forward to a restful era when we could, thank god, sleep off the binge known as modern times. [4]

I thank Charles Platt, George Slusser, Sheila Finch, and Kathleen Spencer for discussions of the manuscript.

REFERENCES

1. "In a World of Her Own," *Mother Jones*, January 1984.
2. Sheila Finch-Reyner, "Paradise Lost: The Prison at the Heart of Le Guin's Utopia," *Extrapolation* 26, Fall 1985, 240-248.
3. Samuel R. Delany, "To Read *The Dispossessed*," *The Jewel-Hinged Jaw*, Berkley, New York, 1977.
4. Joanna Russ, "Recent Feminist Fictions," in *Future Females*, Madison, Wisconsin: Bowling Green Popular Press, 1981.

REPLIES TO "REACTIONARY UTOPIAS" BY GREGORY BENFORD

I await with trepidation the response to my essay "Reactionary Utopias," confident that most will not allow for its tongue-in-cheek ferocity. I had wondered about letting it see wider print, because I don't want to offend Ursula; but on the other hand, I've always regarded the even-handed manner of criticism as often a sham. So be it. I fully expect the piece to be taken as right-wing, simply because it stresses liberty (though I'm not rightist at all, simply anti-statist).

[ASFR editor: It was a real worry, getting such a nice letter, as we beavered away on an issue containing (unsolicited) umpteen attacks on your article—some even from Collective members! I burn with shame. If it's any consolation, I thought the article was interesting and fun, and chuckled away to myself dementedly as I typed it in. (Jenny Blackford)]

INTRODUCTION TO RESPONSES

JOHN FOYSTER

Gregory Benford's "Reactionary Utopias" presents a number of challenges to the reader. Not all of these challenges encourage the reader to go on, but in my case I was encouraged more by the *context* of "Reactionary Utopias" than by the content of the article itself, by a problem which seems to me to arise in science fiction generally rather than particularly in Ursula K. Le Guin's *The Dispossessed* and discussions of its political meaning.

But *The Dispossessed* and Gregory Benford's remarks about it constitute a convenient starting place from which to work towards my own conundrum.

The comments about *The Dispossessed* in "Reactionary Utopias" seemed to me to be of great generality until Benford breaks away from reflections upon the social nature of Le Guin's imagined world and turns to perceived origins of Le Guin's work. Appealing to the authority of Samuel R. Delany, he reports to us Delany's opinion that "whenever Le Guin begins to discuss politics (a common occasion) or show it (quite rare), she uses a language which 'sentence by sentence is pompous, ponderous and leaden.'"

The citation refers the reader only to Delany's "To Read *The Dispossessed*," published in *The Jewel-Hinged Jaw* in 1977. This is an ungenerous citation: Delany's sixty-six-page article deals with many matters, and tracking down the exact source is unnecessarily time-consuming (the words cited appear on pages 276-77 of the Berkley Windhover edition). Finding that quote is made more difficult by the fact that the reader—at least this reader—scans for a section commenting on politics, and that's the wrong approach, for Delany's full sentence, in context, is:

> It does no good to tell an author, much of whose language sentence by sentence is pompous, ponderous, and leaden, that her writing is lucid, measured, and mature.

This isn't exactly what one would expect to find, on the basis of Benford's citation. It seems that Delany is not writing *at all* about how Le Guin manages when she writes about politics; her general literary style and what she needs to do to improve it is Delany's subject.

After this experience one moves with some trepidation to Benford's next sentence, in which he reports Delany surmising:

> ...that her style owes much to the Victorian translations of the great European novels, and that when she attempts depth she unconsciously lapses into this voice. These are "signs of a 'European' or 'Russian' profundity that the [translated] texts do not have."

Delany, of course, surmises no such thing. Writing on p. 225 of the edition cited—some thousands of words prior to the first "quotation" discussed above—Delany is discussing the use of language. He has just completed an uncharacteristically wrongheaded analysis of the first seven sentences of *The Dispossessed;* it introduces his major point about a distinction between image and language and his view that the kind of analysis he has just completed would be inappropriate for the work of other writers, say, Constance Garnett. He wants writers to work in their *own* language, not language which derives from another culture, another time. Some writers of contemporary American—perhaps, but not unambiguously certainly including such science fiction writers as Le Guin, Silverberg, Ellison and Malzberg—use "locutions and signifiers" which recall (to Delany) "Garnett or other translatorese." There, Delany contends, they are:

> ...signs of a "European" or "Russian" profundity that the texts simply do not have.

Or, failing that (Delany goes on) they are in any case derived from the style of the Victorian writers.

Now I would be amongst the last to deny that Delany writes in a way which ensures his own deniability so effectively that had he been so minded he could have had an honored place in the Reagan White House (though I would not go so far as did Robert Stone in a response to William Gass in *Harper's* [June 1988]: "There are few statements in the essay which Gass does not obviate or contradict"). But it is extremely difficult to read Delany as Benford appears to do.

1. Delany refers not to "Victorian translations of the great European novels" (Benford) but to a translator of Russian works of fiction (i.e. *not* "Victorian," *not* "European," and *not* "novels"—novels are not mentioned in the paragraph in question at all).

2. Delany believes that some writers of contemporary American—maybe, but not necessarily, including a handful of science fiction writers, amongst whom Le Guin is listed as one example amongst several—use locutions which are read by Delany as counterfeits, as signing a profundity the *contemporary* American texts do not have.

Delany is not making a point about Le Guin as an individual writer, but about his own analytic method and its appropriateness for works which borrow extensively from other cultures. (Delany's charge against the science fiction writers is that they carry along with their images verbal baggage which contradicts those images.

The discussion about Garnett and translation is in fact "another point.")

3. There is *nothing* in these words of Delany's to justify the Benford contention that "when she attempts depth she unconsciously lapses into this voice."

The paragraph of Gregory Benford's under analysis in not without merit: in a parenthesis he notes that Delany's analysis ignores the macrostructure of *The Dispossessed*. Indeed, a reasonable analysis of those first seven sentences demonstrates this superbly, at least to the extent that Delany's analysis can be seen to *depend* upon his failure to perceive or at least respond to point and counterpoint in Le Guin's writing on this micro-scale. But my alternative analysis of those seven sentences would probably occupy as much space as Delany's, and the object of analysis is Benford's "Reactionary Utopias," not the quite different remarks about *The Dispossessed* made by Delany.

Why, then, so much space on a peripheral matter? Because the questions about fictional utopias raised by Gregory Benford are so important that we cannot allow them to be obscured by the carelessness of Benford's writing. It's too easy, identifying misreadings of this magnitude, to dismiss the trivializing argument embedded in "Reactionary Utopias" as being a definitive statement of a weak case. What ought to be addressed—and it has been addressed in many places in this century—is the question of the political nature of utopian writing and thinking. For me, located within the science fiction environment, this is personalized as questions about why science fiction appears to be inherently politically conservative, about why "libertarianism" in science fiction circles is so unquestioningly taken to be a first cousin of gunslinger capitalism.

In a brief reply such as this I don't hope to reproduce all of the extensive arguments which have been developed in approaching this broader question. At best I can outline why the argument is worth pursuing.

Fredric Jameson sets up the problem within a broad frame in *The Political Unconscious*:

> ...how is it possible for a cultural text which fulfills a demonstrably ideological function, as a hegemonic work whose formal categories as well as its content secure the legitimation of this or that form of class domination—how is it possible for such a text to embody a properly Utopian impulse, or to resonate a

universal value inconsistent with the narrower limits of class privilege which inform its more immediate ideological vocation? (288)

Although I regard this as a desirable description of the problem, Jameson's discussion is more general than I believe is useful in the present context—a simple consideration of the "politics" of utopias, and why these are (to use Benford's term) "regressive."

An alternative description achieves my end more quickly (appropriate in a supposedly brief comment...). In this description:

> The utopian man sees that there exists a mode of being more full and satisfactory than that which he now knows, but believes that his vision of the ideal is wholly discontinuous with the present state of things and that he "has no choice but to worship established power as a mystery [he] cannot grasp and as a fact [he] cannot change." (Stanley Fish, 1987)

Because of this, Fish suggests, utopianism, like resignation and idolatry, inhibits change and reaffirms the status quo.

Fish is discussing Roberto Mangabeira Unger's *Knowledge & Politics*. Unger begins his sixth chapter in a way which allows us to explore the meaning of utopian fiction free of the context of any individual utopian work:

> But what if some future society brought about a complete and final actualization of the ideal in history? If the good is defined as the union of immanence and transcendence, the idea of its being perfectly accomplished in the historical world is self-contradictory, hence false. (236)

It is because a utopian world defined in this way cannot be achieved, says Unger, that utopianism manifests itself in a way which is ultimately conservative:

> Utopianism fails to give men either insight into their circumstance or guidance to move beyond it. Awakened from its dream by the call of politics, utopian reason has no choice but to worship established

power as a mystery it cannot grasp and as a fact it cannot change. (237)

Unger would therefore argue that to the extent that Anarres exists as an isolated utopian community it is a self-contradiction. And if Anarres is thought of as existing within a broader political framework then it fails because it cannot deal with bureaucracy. I ignore here extensive arguments about the development of utopias being dependent upon shared values, which demolishes Benford's utopias of process—at least as he formulates them in this essay:

> Thus, the Leftist conception of community typically appears in either of two forms. One is the utopian commune, a would-be island of harmony in the bureaucratic order, coexisting perilously with it rather than changing it from within. The other form is the revolutionary commune, which appears as a transitory body during the ardor of revolution, only to be sacrificed, after the revolution, to the needs of bureaucratic organization and centralized power, or to itself be made into a new bureaucracy. (251)

In science fiction we see both forms—and possibly the revolutionary commune, used by many writers (obviously including Robert A. Heinlein), and incorporating on occasion aspects of the anarchist proposal for permanent revolution, is more successful as a mode of speculation about humanity and its growth towards a civilized society, precisely because it is grounded in a notion of inherent imperfection, capable indefinitely of improvement.

Unger's theological resolution of his quest for good probably will please few. This is not the point. What we should recognize are the inbuilt limitations of utopian fiction and its byblow, the scientific romance. We cannot ask of the writer of a utopian romance that which it is incapable of yielding. Gregory Benford's questions, sensibly reformulated, could help us to understand why science fiction occupies a domination-conserving political niche rather than one more liberating for humanity. But how could science fiction, enslaved in its own bureaucracy, manage that?

GUILT AND THE UNIMAGINATIVE UNAMERICAN FEMINIST

by Yvonne Rousseau

Gregory Benford's "Reactionary Utopias" was published in *ASFR 14,* May 1988, but has also appeared as a chapter in *Storm Warnings,* a book published in 1987. Finding the essay in a magazine, readers have an opportunity a book cannot give them: to let their response be seen by practically every fellow reader of the essay, not just by the author or the book's editors (to whom they might write private letters) or by the odd reader who happens to encounter both the book and the particular newspaper or journal that reviews it. Benford knew this when he offered "Reactionary Utopias" to *ASFR*—thus opening the way for public discussion of his arguments. Unfortunately, however, my own response will unavoidably degenerate, at times, into gruffness—because some parts of Benford's essay seem inexplicable unless I assign to their author one or more of the faults identified by plain speakers as Laziness, Stupidity, and Malice.

Benford begins by suggesting that, throughout "the range of utopias," he "senses" five characteristics that "outline a constellation of values which utopists often unconsciously assume." That is, he postulates a fundamental Psychology of the Utopist, persisting through the ages. However, some of the characteristics in his list clearly depend on the experience available to particular utopists. Thus, "nostalgic and technophobic" utopias were infrequent in the nineteenth century, when there was simple faith that technology would increase human happiness, and that society could be favorably transformed by the State. Views about "progress" became more skeptical after the First World War, and have remained so through subsequent wars. On the other hand, utopias "static in time" were imagined in past centuries, rather than now, and are notably absent from the works which (it emerges) Benford is actually attacking. Although he claims that these works are by "present utopists," they reduce themselves in fact to utopian novels written by feminists in the 1970s; in particular, *The Dispossessed*—which was published in 1974, more than a decade ago.

Benford's references to *The Dispossessed* are particularly disconcerting, because the "evidence" he cites is actually untrue. Elsewhere, one may dispute Benford's interpretation or selection of facts; but on this subject—having referred both to the novel itself and to Samuel R. Delany's essay about it—one is forced to realize that the examples Benford derives from these works are not to be found there; sometimes, indeed, their opposites are there.

Thus, Benford writes that *The Dispossessed* is "using guilt as the principal means of social control"; that on Anarres (the novel's ambiguous utopia) "a citizen is *born guilty*" because Odo (the founder of the anarchist revolution, who has been dead several generations by the time of the novel) functions as "the guilt-inducing authority figure" whose "pain and suffering during nine years' imprisonment" each Odonian "must repay." In fact—and on the contrary—the novel actually records Odonian repugnance for such an idea; analyzing another person's motives, Bedap says (301, Panther Books edition, 1975): "Guilt? Has the Odonian Society gone so rotten we're motivated by *guilt?*..."

Later I shall discuss the extraordinary assumptions in Benford's equations: "social conscience, that is, guilt" and "guilt (social conscience)." At present, I am merely listing his contradictions of fact—the next being the assertion: "On Anarres a child is not a true citizen, psychically, until he has undergone a guilt-inducing experience—an unconscious, implicit rite." There is simply no evidence whatsoever for this in *The Dispossessed*. Benford describes—as if it were explicitly an example of such rites—an incident from Shevek's boyhood, where he and four friends, having learned about Lawful Imprisonment (an alien concept on Anarres), decide to play "prisons" to see what imprisonment is like. The significance of this episode for Shevek is related to the significance for all Odonians of the wall described at the novel's beginning: "For seven generations there had been nothing in the world more important than that wall." There is no indication of the game's being a "rite" with guilty parallels in other children's experience; one of the participants (41) "boasted about it once to some older boys and girls, but they did not understand, and he dropped the subject."

Similarly, Benford accuses Le Guin (15) of "shying away from violence of any sort"; he asserts that, to her, "evil" and violence are "often synonymous," and that *The Dispossessed* contains no "naturally violent types (indeed, violence is 'unnatural,' and an impulse towards it is the principal offence which calls up guilt)." Again, the novel contradicts him. The naturally violent Shevet does not seem evil and unnatural to other Odonians, and is not expected to experience guilt. When Shevet is beating up Shevek (49): "Several people paused to watch, saw that it was a fair fight but not an interesting one, and went on. They were neither offended nor attracted by simple violence." The inverted commas Benford places around "unnatural" must be meant to emphasize the absurdity, from his point of view, of applying such an adjective to violence; they certainly do not represent a quotation from anywhere in *The Dispossessed*.

It is conceivable that Benford assigns to "violence" a private meaning which excludes the "violence only if it expresses anger in limited ways or in self-defense" that he finds (19) in the other 1970s feminist utopias he mentions—and which is part of Odonian society. Far from "shying away from violence" (as "violence" is normally defined), Le Guin begins *The Dispossessed* with a scene in which one person is killed and at least one other —Shevek—is injured by Odonian violence (expressed, in these people's limited way, by rock-throwing).

Benford also asserts about Anarres (15): "In the middle of a drought in which people starve, no matter how evenly food is shared, somehow no one thinks of taking up arms with some friends and seizing, say, the grain reserves." The novel contradicts this. People do band together more than once (257-8) to seize grain trucks during the drought, and deaths result from at least one of these conflicts. Within Shevek's own experience, his fellow passengers contemplate banding together to raid "the truck-gardens" (215), but their train moves on again before they reach agreement.

Laziness on Benford's part is a possible explanation both of these discrepancies, and of those I shall mention next—between Delany's "To Read *The Dispossessed*" and Benford's account of it. Laziness would entail having read the novel and essay years ago, jotting down some quotations and ideas as one did so, and then relying entirely on those notes and on one's memory. The unwisdom of such reliance has been well expressed by John Livingston Lowes *(The Road to Xanadu*, 57), explaining the discrepancy sometimes between the book one remembers and what one finds upon rereading:

> Into [the deep well of unconscious cerebration] has dropped, without an inkling of its disappearance, the thing which we once read, and it has undergone strange transformations there. It has merged insensibly [...] with others of the myriad denizens of that mysterious deep, and what we think we have remembered we have actually, in large degree, unconsciously created.

Relying on memory, Benford might suppose (incorrectly) that Delany's analysis "boils down to" his own representation of its arguments, and can thus be used to bolster his own opinions about *The Dispossessed*. He begins by utterly misapplying some words from Delany—who writes that much of Le Guin's language "sentence by sentence is pompous, ponderous and leaden." Benford completely invents the idea (15) that Delany detects these faults "whenever Le Guin begins to discuss politics (a common occasion) or to show it (quite rare)." What Delany actually writes is that "the tones of voice" evoked by many of La Guin's sentences belong in the characters' thoughts or speech, instead of "in the auctorial voice." And it is purely Benford's judgment—not Delany's that Le Guin often discusses but rarely shows politics.

The quotation about Le Guin's language comes from pages 276-7 of *The Jewel-Hinged Jaw*; but Benford's paragraph suggests that it precedes—or at least belongs to the same discussion as the next quotation he chooses, which is actually lifted from p. 225, more than fifty pages earlier. Benford links the quotations by a sentence which is simply untrue: Delany never "surmises" that Le Guin "unconsciously lapses" into Victorian translatorese when she "attempts depth"—yet Benford states that he does. Moreover, Benford misinterprets the statement Delany does make on p. 225 (about "current written American"), as is demonstrated by his interpolation in square brackets in the words he quotes: "signs of a 'European' or 'Russian' profundity that the [translated] texts do not have." In Delany's argument, the profundity is missing not from the translated texts but from imitative "contemporary American texts"—which should be written, instead, in the language of their own time and place. If laziness is excluded, the most charitable interpretation of Benford's procedure here will depend on which accusation the reader thinks worse: malice or stupidity. Stupidity entails that Benford is incapable of understanding an argument of any complexity and also that he cannot detect his own incapacity. Malice entails deliberate misrepresentation — gambling that most readers, having encountered *The Dispossessed* and Delany's essay years ago, will trust Benford's representation of them in preference to their own recollection.

My own diagnosis is that Benford has been afflicted—in this particular essay—by a mixture of laziness and stupidity; and that the root of this affliction is emotional. In his character as an affronted practicing physicist (of the male American persuasion), Benford is both hostile and reactionary, and thus declines to see any gradations between technophilia and technophobia or any directions other than forward and back; moreover (their American nationality notwithstanding), the utopists whose ideas affront him find themselves reduced to Unimaginative UnAmerican Feminists.

The background to Benford's feelings obviously includes Roz Kaveney's "Science Fiction in the 1970s," which appeared in *Foundation* 22, June 1981. Having read it, Benford observed in a letter of comment *(Foundation* 24, February 1982, 78):

> I found her use of "reactionary" in an (?) artistic sense rather confusing. Similarly she seems unable to get a grip on sf which isn't technophobic[.]

Kaveney had noted a combination of the "politically and artistically reactionary" in the works of some 1970s writers who used "thoroughly shoddy and unconvincing methods" to persuade readers of "the joys of technophilia." Benford's *Timescape* was specifically exempted from the charge of being artistically reactionary: its subject was technophilia, but it was (28) "a real novel," because of Benford's

> ...humility which means he has to descend to persuade us of the possible validity of his views and prejudices, of the reality of his characters, of the emotional truth of his fantasies of success [...]; he is free of the arrogant assumption that assertion equals persuasion.

Benford appears to have been not only confused but also fascinated by Kaveney's "artistically reactionary" concept—which he has therefore confusingly commandeered. "Reactionary," he tells us in "Reactionary Utopias," is meant here as "an aesthetic analogy, no more." But he fails to explain or demonstrate how we can apply the analogy. My own best guess, at the end of my reading, is that we are meant to paint in our minds an allegorical Scene—where groveling utopists attempt to oppose (with hurled and heaped-up clods of earth) the three mighty Benford Abstractions which serenely sail on over them: "our innate sense of human progress"—"the tide of Western thought"—"the modern spirit."

The "nonreactionary" spirit that Benford champions is "American" in a mystical sense. Thus, he writes (13) that utopias can be roughly divided into "nonreactionary, or genuinely progressive" ones, which are American, and utopias regulated through guilt, which are European in style. American utopias espouse the idea of stabilizing society "through gratification of individual needs," which is "one of the keys to American politics." In schoolboy howler mode, Benford reports how, compared with "his *Brave New World* (written in England)," Huxley's "*Island* (written after his move to California) sides more with gratification"—and argues as follows for his distinction between the American and the European styles:

> Consider Edward Bellamy's *Looking Backward* (the most prominent American utopia of the nineteenth century) and William Morris's reply to it, *News from Nowhere*. Both stabilize society more through gratification of individual needs than through guilt.

Hence, by Benford's definitions, William Morris was American, despite being British, while Aldous Huxley acquired an American temperament once he moved to California. Examining Benford's mystical definition further, one perceives that Americanism is associated with the possession of cojones; no male utopist that he mentions lacks it completely, whatever his nationality, but American female feminists do.

Apart from his initial suggestion that we ought to value "Western European ideals," Benford's references to Europe associate it with the past (the nineteenth century, in particular), with a nostalgia for rural life, and with "the European tradition of utopian thought"—seemingly equivalent to "the failures of European utopian theory." In *The Dispossessed*—the only utopia he purports to treat in detail—he senses a "strangely nineteenth-century middle-European "feel" , to the "background society," and concludes: "The vague middle-European feel to the architecture, organization of work, and so on, is clearly nostalgic; rural Europe itself isn't even like that anymore." Rare sensitivity (or else predisposition) is surely required to detect a rural middle-European feel to the "organization of work, and so on" upon Anarres, where there are no birds, no large animals, and no forests—all essential to the structure of people's everyday life in the rural Middle Europe of the past.

The Dispossessed is not a RAND corporation publication. It is set in another solar system, where specific conditions (a planet that is a "howling desert" richly stocked with minerals) have permitted a colony of anarchists to settle and to test their principles without provoking interference from their nearby parent world. What Benford looks for, however, is a generalizable utopia that contemporary USA could turn into: "What literature needs, and plainly isn't getting, are utopias of *process,* which tell us something about how to reach goals and be happy during the journey." For Benford, any other (more radical) kind of utopia can only be backward-looking and European. (Thus, the less the 1970s feminist utopias really resemble the past, the more incompetent their authors must be.) To criticize utopists for their ill success in showing what they never meant to show, however, seems as idle as to criticize Praxiteles because his statue of Hermes fails to give the well-dressed man of Athens in the fourth century BC a clue as to what the best people will be wearing in the way of chiton, himation and shoe next season.

It is interesting that the Odonian society in *The Dispossessed* makes Benford think of the European past rather than of past socialist utopias in America—such as the Shakers, the Rappites and the Oneida Community. The most successful of these were the Shakers, founded in the late eighteenth century and lasting (with principles intact) for 170 years until the early 1950s, when they were finally overcome by pressures from the very different American society surrounding them. John Fowles paid tribute to the Shakers in 1985 with A *Maggot*—a fantastical account of the parents and conception and birth of their founder, Mother Anne. Being pacifists, the Shakers were attacked in early days as unAmerican (thus, pro-British or pro-Native American); by the late nineteenth century, however, Leo Tolstoy was enquiring of them, by letter, how they contrived, as non-resistants, to hold communal property. (Tolstoy's enquiry is reported by Edward Deaming Andrews in *The People Called Shakers,* rev. ed., Dover, New York, 1963: 221.)

The Shakers were celibate, whereas the Oneida Community, from its foundation in 1847, successfully practiced Complex Marriage (a regulated form of promiscuity) for almost thirty years. This practice was abandoned because of opposition from the larger American society surrounding its 250 members, but Oneida itself continued to thrive. Its founder, John Humphrey Noyes, published in 1869 a *History of American Socialisms,* using data that A. J. Macdonald had painstakingly gathered. Noyes viewed the communitarian movement as "the enlargement of home—the extension of family union beyond the little man-and-wife circle to large corporations." To the question, "Has any attempt at close Association ever succeeded, which took marriage into it substantially as it exists in ordinary society?" he answered "No": indeed, having observed which communities were successful, he postulated "some rational connection between their control of the sexual relation and their prosperity." Benford, in contrast with Noyes, thinks feminist utopias unrealistic because they often "seem like fantasies about how families ought to be (and seldom are)"—and then he produces another of his schoolboy howlers: "Perhaps it is natural for women to extend the family as a model, since they have not, up to now, experienced society as a whole from a more masculine viewpoint—as a focus of conflicting forces." Temporarily ignoring Benford's extraordinary views on the nature of women's experience, I mention that Noyes was a man (and American), that he nevertheless shared the 1970s feminist notion of the extended (and altered) family as a utopian model, and that his notions were derived from experience and observation of actual utopian societies. It is true that Noyes is from the past—but the past is not always irrelevant to Benford. A writer who ignores an obvious historical parallel, he tells us, is "concerned more with repealing history, than with understanding it in order to make a better future." (The occasion for this dictum is Le Guin's failure to see "a remarkable historical parallel" between the Odonian experiment and nineteenth-century Russia, where there occurred—in remarkably different circumstances—"the demise of Russian socialist idealism at the hands of Lenin.")

Benford is not thinking of past American utopian experiments when he dismisses "analogies with the family" as showing feminist "lack of imagination": feminists "cannot imagine new ways to organize community." Rather, when Benford writes that many utopias "resemble a warped, malignant form of the past," he is apparently thinking, in part, of the past in which the Benford boys were "nagged" by their mother. Thus he writes: "Living on Anarres has an uncanny resemblance to being nagged by your mother"—and he uses this analogy to illuminate his conception of "guilt as the principal social control" in *The Dispossessed.* Earlier, I mentioned—for future discussion—Benford's astonishing equation of "social conscience" with guilt, likewise, more recently, his idea that women lack experience of "society as a whole [...]—as a focus of conflicting forces." These ideas are related both to one another and to the peculiarities of Benford's own lifestyle—part of which he helpfully laid bare in *Foundation #21*, February 1981, in a contribution to the magazine's "The Profession of Science Fiction" series.

Benford's contribution—"A String of Days"—gave diary entries describing his daily life in 1980, from the 6th of May to the 3rd of June. They show him getting reports from his teaching assistants, acting as colloquium chairman, seeking advice on his investments, feeling pleased in a faculty meeting that a new plasma experimentalist whose help he "can use" is being appointed, completing the job of setting up a student-operated bookstore on campus, and congratulating himself (11) on having moved to theoretical physics:

> The quantity of sheer fiddling in experimental physics is numbing. [...] Now I'm back supervising exactly that sort of thing, but the pleasure is that I get to look at the results, and can sidestep most of the grunt labor. Of course, there's dog work in theory, too. A lot.

These are incidents from just the first sixteen days. Among the later entries is this (16):

> Coincidentally, I receive today a call from my twin brother, Jim, who is working on assessment of Soviet progress in charged particle devices. He listens to my story about the Soviet paper [...] We both wonder if the surfacing of this Russian paper is a tip of an iceberg.
>
> This is about as close to defense-related work as I get.

The diary shows that Benford might very reasonably see himself as a person in control—and quite close to the "focus of conflicting forces" which defines, for him, "society as a whole." (On the other hand, I am not at all certain that males would predominate in similarly active positions if the lives of all utopian writers were compared with one another.) Benford dislikes "grunt labor"—and the diary records nothing about how the grunt work gets done in the

Benford home. But it is fair to assume that in a 1970s feminist utopia Benford's life would include more—not less—tedium, because these are utopias where no one sex or class does the domestic work. In the USA, by contrast, Maxine L. Margolis in *Mothers and Such: Views of American Women and Why They Changed* (1984) reported (177) that

> ...the upper limit in the number of hours men spend on household tasks is about 20 percent of that spent by their wives, regardless of whether their wives are employed or the age and number of children at home.

However, despite Benford's assumptions (which childcare experts shared, regardless of reality, until the 1970s), American women have not meanwhile remained at home, protected from "society as a whole" and its "conflicting forces"; Margolis points out that women—including (225) "mothers, wives, the middle class and the middle aged"—began increasing their numbers in the labor force after World War II; by the end of the 1950s (216) "the number of working mothers had increased by 400 percent" since 1940. (Not for decades, however, could women's magazines and other advice givers bring themselves to face the facts—so it is not surprising that Benford has been taken in by the popular mythology prevailing in America throughout most of his life.)

Benford's position *vis-à-vis* society's conflicting forces (as recorded in 1980) is relatively privileged, and he has no doubt won it by a combination of intelligence, aptitude, judgment, hard work and (conspiring with these) a modicum of good luck. In such circumstances, some people are able to admit, without hostility, that others in society have had worse fortune than themselves—but some people regard the very suggestion as an accusation, a devaluing of their own efforts and dedication, an imputation that they ought to feel they owe something to unsuccessful people. (Michael Apted's documentary *28 Up* aptly illustrates these alternative attitudes in, respectively, a solicitor and a barrister—both born into the British upper class.) Writing in the era of Reagan's presidency (when commentators observed among American people a marked upsurge of hostility towards the poor), Benford adopts the second alternative, and asserts (from his own favorable position) that social conscience is only guilt. People in circumstances less remote from poverty—being less likely to react against anticipated accusations of adopting "*I'm* all right, Jack" attitudes—are much less likely to consider guilt a motive; the spring of their social conscience, if not simple goodness, is more likely to be aesthetic—a distaste for the existence of misery, disease, subjection and waste.

Given his propensity for feeling guilt (that is to say, for believing that others think he ought to feel guilt that he refuses to admit), Benford naturally reacts with hostility towards utopias where present-day grunt-workers would benefit, at the cost of more grunt work for him. The price of this hostility is an access of laziness and stupidity when he affects to assess such utopias; his mistakes about *The Dispossessed* indicate that he cannot bear to pay proper attention to it. (For example, when he objects to the oppressiveness of the "subtly authoritarian" rule of custom, Benford implies that Le Guin and other feminists are quite unworried by this—whereas *The Dispossessed* highlights it as the chief danger threatening Odonian society.)

If Benford truly thought feminist utopias the pitiful timorous things that he pretends, he would not find it necessary to misrepresent them—or (if we suppose instead both that he is actually attempting a fair representation, and that he normally reads more intelligently than this) his comprehension would not be so blurred by hostility and preconceptions. My own conclusion is that it is Benford (not his utopists) who "long[s] for sweeping simplicities": to see people as technophobic if they aren't technophiliac; either pulling backwards or pushing forward; tradition-bound Europeans versus go-ahead Americans; home-body head-in-the-sand women versus active fighting real-world men.

THE AMBIGUITIES OF UTOPIA: A REACTION TO "REACTIONARY UTOPIAS"

by Norman Talbot

I.

ASFR volume 3, number 3 (May 1988) gave its valuable pages 11-20 to a grotesquely inept and malicious attack on Ursula K. Le Guin's *The Dispossessed*. Since the author is a failed sf novelist called Gregory Benford, we can assume that the motive for the attack is jealousy. What *ASFR's* motive for publishing it may have been is impossible to guess.

Benford begins with the mildly interesting commonplace that few readers really want to live in fictional utopias. From then on it's all downhill.

He assumes that we all have "our innate sense of human progress," a sentimentality that sits oddly in a periodical issue that devotes a great deal of space to discussion of George Turner's fiction! Then he goes on to defend "Western European ideals," which, since they are also "the tide of Western thought," can probably manage without his help. Why should a man writing (I am told) in California and publishing in Melbourne fancy himself a defender of philosophies from the west of Europe? Worse, why should he be so petulant with Plato for not fitting into his preferred geography? If it's any help, the most western of European philosophers was probably Wittgenstein, when he lived at Galway Bay....

But Benford's posture has a serious purpose. He sets out to define "reactionary" to mean "they recall the past." Let us hope that when he employs a word to do a job for which it is so obviously untrained he follows Humpty Dumpty's example and pays it extra. What does he hope to gain by twisting such a well-known term of rejection? The answer is quickly clear: over the page he starts using it as a term of rejection again!

He claims that "the customary use of the term means little." It could hardly mean less than the verbal dandruff about "one-dimensional spectrums" by which he pretends to justify his misuse of it. Helpfully, he adds that "*Regressive* might be an alternate term," but since he does not employ it every second time he probably means "alternative." Well, it might be, but it's just as inapposite for the pseudo-objective tone Benford stalks behind.

II.

Benford's next step is to claim to have studied "the range of utopian literature" and found (objectively of course) "five dominant reactionary characteristics." The first is "Lack of diversity," although it is manifest nonsense to claim that this recalls the past in any way.

Even sillier is the second, "Static in time." "Static" ought to be a noun like "Lack," but that is merely proof that Benford cannot write competently any more than he can think consistently. If we assume it to be an adjective, the characteristic cannot possibly recall the past either, by definition. But this ludicrous definition is worth quoting in full:

> 2. *Static in time. Like diversity, change in time would imply that either the past or the present of the utopia was less than perfect (i.e., not utopian).*

How can any utopia have a perfect past as well as a perfect present? The idyll of the garden of Eden before the Fall might be like this, according to one famous tradition, but there can be no plot and no possibility of utopian (or any other) fiction in that state. More crucial is Benford's bracket: he wants to re-define "utopian" as meaning "perfect."

"Utopia," Sir Thomas More's coinage, means "no-place," as most people know. It describes a culture, whether civilized or bucolic, which is better both in general and in specific details than that in and for which the author writes. More deliberately invites a Greek pun, it is true, on "Eu-topos," the good place, but he was certainly not writing about Heaven. His *Utopia* (1516) is satiric of the Renaissance civilization around him, especially of its assumptions about property ownership, religious tolerance, education and relationships between the sexes. A system based on slavery can hardly be thought of as ideal, but it can remind the author's contemporaries of many valuable things that are offered to citizens "nowhere on earth." Hythloday's expectations and judgments are based on contemporary Europe, and many of the best inventions about his Utopia are purely satiric. For example, the utopians have found that gold is not entirely useless, being a first-rate material for making chamber-pots.

Benford's third "reactionary" element is "Nostalgic and technophobic," and it is perfectly true that most people, and therefore many writers, prefer a technology they can grasp intellectually and control manually, rather than one which seems to alienate humans from both purpose and power. However, it would be healthful for Benford to look up the meaning of the word "techne."

Since a utopia offers a more admirable lifestyle and community than the society from which it springs and for which it is utopian, it follows that hi-tech is not above scrutiny for its effects on the utopians. The more overcrowded a society is, the more meaningless individuality and quality may become, the more financial and bureaucratic management will control the experience and imagination of groups as well as individuals. Similar problems develop when a society's members feel alienated from its technology (or its armed forces or legal system or any other aspect of power). In such cases that society's utopias will be low in population, with lots of open space and open time, and communal power will be expressed in simplified and slow-paced ways like folk-wisdom, debate, magic and useful presbyters.

Benford is so chafed by this refusal to take the benefits of hi-tech as axiomatic that he decides to re-define a few other things, including the whole subject-matter of *ASFR:* "Only those utopias which include some notion of scientific advancement qualify as sf." Fortunately, Benford's intellectual and rhetorical powers are not quite up to the task of enforcing this rule; otherwise we should lose many fascinating Arcadian fictions, all narratives based on irony and ambiguity about technology, like Delany's *Nevèrÿon* series, and all the post-holocaust fiction that has been so welcome and nourishing since Hiroshima *(Riddley Walker* is a major example, but any reader can think of fine sf which emphasizes the horror potential to hi-tech weaponry).

Worst of all, we should lose the vitally important branch of utopian fiction known as dystopias. Zamyatin, Huxley, Orwell, offer their Nowheres precisely because major developments in their societies need the medication of the imagination. All three warn us that "scientific advancement" and the management of human societies by its means can be loathsome in their effects. Joanna Russ, Suzy McKee Charnas, Suzette Haden Elgin and many other feminists point out that the masculine ego too easily identifies itself as the only power suited to control of science, with equally chilling results. Tim Powers' *Dinner at Deviant's Palace* combines awful warnings about nuclear poisoning with the good old Wellsian fear of alien invasion to show that low-tech societies can also be brainwashed, charmed, spooked or drugged into horror. Nobody said the virtues and vices of alternative societies had to be a simple matter (nobody but Benford, anyway).

Benford's fourth point is "Presence of an authority figure." Though it is pleasant to be back with nouns for captions, this characteristic is otherwise fudged. There are few examples of such a being in eutopian writing and many in the dystopian branch. Benford's real intention is to point to "real utopian communities," not to fiction at all. In fiction the mention of a founder counts for him as a "Presence"!

The fifth characteristic is said to be "social regulation through guilt," and again there are very few examples in eutopian fiction. "The standard of social responsibility" is undoubtedly important in all such stories, but it is of course based on positive reinforcement rather than negative conditioning. Few modern utopias are likely to be based on the worldview of the early Christian church, so a negative reinforcement is likely to be based on shame, not guilt, if one exists.

Benford's last three points may very well "recall the past": there *have* been nostalgic and even "technophobic" elements in all societies, and authority figures and guilt have been used as repressive instruments. What they have to do with utopian fiction is, however, not clear.

Only once does Benford try to find out what he is saying and if there is any observable truth in it. The attempt lasts for most of a paragraph, and is comic enough to be quoted in full:

> Nonreactionary, or genuinely progressive utopias, often reject regulation through guilt. This divides utopias roughly along the axis of European versus American, with the Europeans typically favoring social conscience, that is, guilt. Consider Edward Bellamy's *Looking Backward* (the most prominent American utopia of the nineteenth century) and Wil-

liam Morris's reply to it, *News from Nowhere*. Both stabilize society more through gratification of individual needs than through guilt. Indeed, one of the keys to American politics is just this idea. Huxley's *Island* (written after his move to California) sides more with gratification, though his *Brave New World* (written in England) depicts the horrific side of a state devoted to gratification without our "sentimental" humanist principles.

If the only version of social conscience Benford can imagine is guilt, that is worrying for those around him; however, I assume his glib definition comes from his epidemic verbal ineptitude rather than psychopathy. But for a man to announce himself the defender of "Western European ideals," then define Europeans as guilt-mongers, is very peculiar.

Benford's examples are delightful too. We are told to "consider" Bellamy's and Morris's books as utopias exemplifying American and European practice. But when he considers them, Benford finds his division along a mid-Atlantic guilt axis is totally disproved: "Both stabilize [...] through gratification." Presumably he could find no examples that would bear out his argument.

Benford's strong suit is geography, not literature, so he naturally assumes Huxley in California to be a totally different being from the one who wrote in England, but examples can be very revealing. *Island* is, after all, one of the very few eutopias with an authority figure such as Benford had posited for "reactionary" utopias: a "sane" Raja has ordained the moksha-powered paradise that gives a happy ending to *King Oedipus*. By Benford's logic, this ought to mean that American Huxley and those on his side of the guilt-axis prefer authority-figures to guilt when they feel like a bit of the old social coercion. What a pity *Brave New World* doesn't say a lot in praise of guilt; European Huxley must have slipped up there.

III.

After this sturdily constructed theoretical basis, we come to the shameful shambles Benford makes of his attack on *The Dispossessed*. He claims to detect a "nineteenth-century middle-European 'feel'" to Anarresti society, but does not attempt to prove that this is an objective phenomenon, while mixed metaphors like "a curious static flavor" are deeply unconvincing. Then begins the series of brutal lies by which he traduces what he calls "the finest utopian American novel of our time."

He says Anarres is "strikingly technophobic." In fact it is technologically impoverished but totally committed to high technology, even in having a computer-designed language and social structure. Anarres is desperate for more technology, and Urras keeps it desperate. Everything from earthmoving to piscine genetics is done by people only because the technology they love so confidently is kept from them. The gratitude and pride with which an efficient machine is greeted is a genuinely moving aspect of Anarresti society, shared by anyone who has ever had to use a shovel to do an earthmover's job.

Benford also describes the "faster-than-light communicator" which is the major physical and scientific result of the life, work and journeys of the book's protagonist as (along with interplanetary travel) "minor intrusions." In narrative energy and design as well as intellectual and metaphoric development, Le Guin makes it almost impossible to ignore the ansible, but Benford's resistance to competent reading is very dogged. As for interplanetary travel, the book's narrative and structure correspond to its argumentative and metaphoric focus upon two planets that circle each other, Urras and Anarres, the one settled from and defined by the history of the other. How can interplanetary travel, the major event of the first and last chapters, be a minor intrusion?

It is perfectly true that scientific and technological gimmicks abound in sf, masquerading as intrinsic and crucial aspects of the books' imagined worlds. The difference between gimmickry and high-technology or hard sf is experienced by all *ASFR* readers and readily recognized (though Benford cannot be assumed to belong to this honorable company). The difference is that, in the words of Kathryn Hume in her excellent *Fantasy and Mimesis* (1984),

> Many fantastic additions really belong to escape literature. They contribute nothing to our greater understanding of reality. Interstellar travel simply takes us to new scenes. (90)

I know of no story in which the protagonist's interplanetary journey is more integral to the narrative. We are never "taken to new scenes," as even the European-obsessed Benford unwittingly testifies.

And why should Benford tell us such lies? Since he describes these key elements of ansible and interplanetary travel as "old sf staples," it seems he is looking for hi-tech inventions he has never heard of before. How many books will he find them in, I wonder, and how many of those will be good ones? The ansible is based on a very fresh approach to the Cetian "Noble Science," a heightened and cosmological mathematics, but Benford has no time for a book which he thinks "disapproves of" Urrasti high technology and its "techno-flash and dazzle." In the book, the "dazzle" is disapproved of because of what it conceals and exploits, not because of anything intrinsic to the applied sciences. Here is the triumphant object of interplanetary technology:

> They showed Shevek all over the ship, the interstellar *Davenant*. It was as different as it could well be from the freighter *Mindful*. From the outside it was as bizarre and fragile-looking as a sculpture in glass and wire; it had no look of a ship, a vehicle, about it at all, not even a front and back end, for it never travelled through any atmosphere thicker than that of interplanetary space. [...] Its style had neither the opulence of Urras, nor the austerity of Anarres, but struck a balance, with the effortless grace of long practice. (306-7 of the Avon edition, 1974)

In between these two passages, the ship is compared to a house and a sailing ship, and its garden, "where the lighting had the quality of sunlight," is its "recreation." The comparisons are not sentimental, because they are Shevek's perceptions, and he has never been on any interplanetary ship except the *Mindful* before. The sculpture referred to is of the kind Takver makes, and Shevek is going home to her. The description is also, of course, a perfect test for the Hainish, since Urras and Anarres are both lacking in balance, and if balanced high technology cannot compare with the beauty and humanity of house and ship, it simply isn't high enough.

Benford is frantic to prove that Le Guin dislikes technology as "practical, dirty, and likely to fall into the wrong hands," using almost anything from anywhere in her *oeuvre*. The most revealing device is about the lovely fable "The Ones Who Walk Away From Omelas," about the necessary questions an ethical being has to ask of utopias. The inept mis-titling should not be allowed to conceal the pun's significance:

(This parable might be titled "Those Who Walk
Away from Omelets," because we know what it takes
to make one—you must break some eggs.) (14)

There is plain menace in this Reagan-like folksy humor. The hardboiled joke (to change the culinary metaphor) is precisely what Randall Jarrell saw in his summary of war propaganda:

You can't break eggs without making an omelet—that's what they tell the eggs.

On *The Dispossessed* itself, Benford cannot tell the truth. For him it "reeks of Old Testament themes and images." I cannot find a single Old Testament theme or image, though admittedly I have been reading the book rather than sniffing its "reek." He asserts that Odo's life of integrity and suffering is used to make the Anarresti feel that they are "*born guilty*" and italicizes this chilling concept as if he has a cluster of brilliant examples in mind. Yet in the society of Anarres only Rulag might be impelled by such a self-image in her ceaseless opposition to Shevek and the Syndicate of Initiative. Her leaving her young son and his father might be seen as causative—by one complex thinker, Bedap, to whom I shall return. Benford never mentions her.

Benford asserts, but cannot prove, a guilt-based social bond on Anarres, and with sublime obtuseness traces it to an imprisonment game which one little group of boys once plays—in total defiance of the overt and tacit values of their society. He ignores the earlier and equally striking use of wall imagery, even Shevek's crucial dream of the number as cornerstone which immediately precedes the imprisonment game.

How can a society's basic bond be established by a game it neither understands nor even refers to? The game does indicate an obsessive reverence for freedom, it is true, but Benford wants it to be something far deeper and darker. He "proves" its importance by asserting that the episode takes up "more space than Shevek's entire courtship of his wife." Since Odonians have no courtship ritual at all, and there is no "entire courtship" of Takver, only a psychic challenge by her, this case is easy (but useless) to argue.

Having convinced himself that the consciously virtuous, even morally austere, Odonians are fatally guilt riddled, Benford claims that Odo is herself the "guilt-inducing authority," on the evidence that her followers mention her. This logic allies her with the system of coercion and imprisonment which victimized her, and which she devotedly opposed, all her life. Of course, she opposed guilt just as effectively:

> [...] we each of us deserve everything, every luxury that was ever piled in the tombs of the dead Kings, and we each of us deserve nothing, not a mouthful of bread in hunger. Have we not eaten while another starved? Will you punish us for that? Will you reward us for the virtue of starving while others ate? No man earns punishment, no man earns reward. Free your mind of the idea of deserving, the idea of earning, and you will begin to be able to think. (288: quoted from Odo's *Prison Letters*)

Still, why should Benford read what the prophet is supposed to have said, when such evidence ruins his attack on her teachings?

Bedap is by far the most perceptive in social terms of the Syndicate of Initiative members, and he suggests that the conservative opposition of Rulag is guilt-based, and therefore the most hideous perversion of Odonianism possible:

> Why? Guilt? Has the Odonian Society gone so rotten we're motivated by guilt? [...] in her, it's all gone hard, rock-hard dead. (292)

Benford is besotted with the idea that Odo teaches guilt. This may be explained by his malicious assertion that the anarchist teacher "has some resemblance to Le Guin herself." He cannot derive such an assertion from the text, of course, and apart from their sex and their strength of mind any supposed resemblances are likely to be of no significance for an experience of the text.

His most ludicrous accusation against Odo is that she "dies just before her utopia begins"—by which he means before the revolution on Urras began—and thus "avoids the problems of building a real utopia"! If this is her guilt we should forgive her: we shall all be guilty of a similar evasion soon enough.

IV.

Benford goes on to an elaborate misdescription of Anarres as if, first, every inhabitant were exactly like a late-twentieth-century Californian, and, second, Le Guin had tried, and failed, to make them all alien to every aspect of late-twentieth-century culture. All his rhetoric is based on the pretence that Anarres is designed to be an unambiguous utopia. No, he quotes the sub-title, so at one level anyway he knows this is not true.

Or does he? His citation is not, of course, competent, since complacent label-mongers cannot afford to read with competence: a competent reading of a perceptive book rubs off labels rather than sticking them on. Still, his expression of incompetence at this point as at many others is a jeer at the author:

> Le Guin labels her utopia as ambiguous, clearly knows something is wrong, but does not confront the deep problems. (18)

Of course the sub-title does not signal that something is wrong, but establishes a contract with competent readers and warns off Benford and other incompetents.

The even-numbered chapters (the Anarresti plot) are not only a *Bildungsroman* of Shevek but also a confrontation with deep problems epidemic in the society. Put simply, the society develops Shevek as a medication for those problems. The three most obvious are social conformism as an insidious variety of violence, the use of moral and social labeling by those who fear and resent any non-conformist behavior, and the claustrophobic isolation of Anarres that stimulates both. If, like Benford, we need overt comparisons with recent history, the isolation of "socialism in one country" in the USSR, reparations and encirclement of Germany after World War I, and USA-funded encirclement of the People's Republic of China (including wars in Korea and Viet Nam) after World War II seem to have stimulated varying amounts of pathological response by whole societies.

Anarchism that comes to believe in walls soon comes to rely on walls. This develops into blatant archism, and open or covert funding of what are really "defense policies." Social approval becomes a universal medium of exchange and a goal for profiteering, and social disapproval becomes a form of poverty and even punishment, the "active thwarting of violence" that Benford longs to find.

Is Benford really fool rather than knave? Can even the most innocent of ignorances, expressed with sufficient smugness, come to sound, quite inadvertently, like malice? I cannot decide, even with the worst example, where he cites a reviewer of a quite different book, *Malafrena*, as asserting that "Altruism is seen as good for its own sake." The austere Anarresti would reply coldly that "Altruism is not an Odonian virtue," the less austere would be very rude about egoistic excrementalism between the ears.

Not that all Anarresti are that predictable, or usually remarkably good or non-violent: such sentimentalism has to be projected onto the text by Benford. A typical tactic is the cheap sexist sneer: "a quiet talk over herbal tea will surely fix matters up." This is his way of coping with a society in which physical violence against individuals is seen as both bad and uninteresting, and just as unlikely to produce truth as blackmail or voting.

Benford uses "romantic" as a blanket sneer too: "A romantic, she ignores the problem of evil." Some romantics undoubtedly invented worlds in which evil is secondary to God's love and comes into being later, but none of them thought it would therefore go away quietly on the fumes of herbal tea.

The Eye of the Heron is Benford's "proof" that Le Guin is soft on evil. Presumably he would prefer the futile pretence that the hippie culture could defeat the mobster culture at its own game of violence, whereas Le Guin gives us the grim and undignified story of a furtive retreat. It would be wicked to murder all the mobsters, perhaps; it would certainly be bloody difficult. It would also be wicked to submit and become slaves to gangsters.

Benford is shamelessly sexist in his tactics when he tries to describe this small book—which he does only to "prove" (that word again) that *The Dispossessed* is not about real politics:

> So the crucial scene in *The Eye of the Heron*, in which anarchist confronts mafia thug and the protagonist dies, is skipped. We learn of it obliquely, via dialogue, in flashback. (17)

Benford doesn't even ask himself whether a protagonist might not be female, and so carefully trained by her loving family that she never realizes women are allowed to be protagonists. ("Women aren't kings...") Much of the novella's power comes from Luz's evolving awareness of the physical and psychological demands and possibilities of her female life.

As to the scene being crucial, of course it is not. Luz could not be present: what godfather would allow his pure and innocent daughter to witness such a potentially violent scene? Her painful sense of the distance between herself and this supposedly definitive scene is eloquent, in itself, of both her upbringing and the challenge when she accepts a life of action. The shock and destitution of Lev's death is mainly because Luz has assumed he, as a man, would dutifully survive to look after her. There are books in which a "crucial" confrontation has been shirked (*Portrait of a Lady* is the best-known example), but Le Guin hasn't written one.

Though Benford's attack on *The Eye of the Heron* is logically irrelevant, I like it because it reveals a representative silliness in the adverse critics of Le Guin. The best fiction is not likely to be about achieved, wholly liberated women who do not have to face any more major challenges; that kind of sentimentality can be left to the love story genre, as in *Daughters of a Coral Dawn*. The girl who never expected to be a protagonist and would have thought it unwomanly, who yet, like Huck, finds herself lighting out for the territory ahead of the rest, offers us a far more witty, alert and intriguing point of view.

To defy the expectations of the sexist readership is quite usual in sf, but Le Guin also unsettles the many regretful disapprovers among both liberal and even radical-feminist readers who have wished so ardently that Shevek had been feminine! That gives a special *frisson* to the otherwise fairly traditional plunge into unknown country in the novella. The sense that the hippie commune, however anarchist in its rhetoric, is just as fatally old-earth in its assumptions as the mobsters, must also have hurt certain well-intentioned readers. I have often tried to imagine a female Shevek on Urras, at Vea's party for example, but cannot believe she would have been invited to either party or planet.

V.

The details of Benford's misrepresentation are not tedious but they are legion. In general he gets the book wrong because he assumes a utopia must be intended by its author to be a picture of an ideal society, rather than a construct markedly superior to the real target society, the one from which and to which the book is written. True voyage, especially in ideas, is return. If the utopia approaches ideality, its point-of-view character must proportionately fail to share, anticipate or even understand those ideals. The new element Ellen will contribute to Nowhere, inspired by the poignant visit of Guest, indicates how dynamic Morris's utopia is, once its "epoch of rest" is challenged by revivified history.

His second mistake is to assume that Anarres is meant to be entirely unambiguous even in the relativistic definition of utopia I recommend. In fact, any society, and especially an anarchist society where the citizens are called upon to assent, or refuse cooperation, requires constant revolution. Inertia, like excrement, is poison if retained in the body politic.

His third mistake is to wish to wrench *The Dispossessed* towards a thesis about the USSR as "the largest prison state in history." This harmless Reagan-style generalization becomes harmful because he blames his "fact" on nineteenth-century anarchists, and deliberately pretends that Le Guin resembles Tolstoy. Therefore he can blame her for not writing about "nineteenth century Russia—without, of course, the apparatus of the Czar, and so on." This extraordinary complaint has some delightful challenges—for example, does anyone but Benford claim to know what Russia without "the apparatus of the Czar, and so on" would be like?—but what has happened to *The Dispossessed* in all the silliness?

It has been degraded by political guilt-by-association, and this is surely intentional, I think:

> Her ignoring of a remarkable historical parallel (the demise of Russian socialist idealism at the hands of Lenin) marks *The Dispossessed* as a deeply reactionary work, concerned more with repealing history, than with understanding it in order to make a better future. (16)

It is obvious that *The Dispossessed,* however enlightening it may be for a speculative mind to set beside global history of the last two centuries, is not a propaganda work that relies upon a single exact set of historical parallels. After *Animal Farm,* none seems to be necessary anyway, but how would Benford arrange for invading armies to attack the moon, and why should they bother?

Even more obvious is Benford's use of "reactionary." It means exactly what it has usually meant, and has dropped its mask of "they recall the past [...], no more." Now the fool (or knave) complains because the book doesn't recall the past he says it "deeply" recalls.

Benford proves his case that the book ought to be about the USSR by announcing that it hasn't been translated into Russian. So there. To cap even this logic, Benford has a Russian friend, and that friend said wistfully it was "irrelevant" there. Benford's touching faith in his friend's infallibility is matched by his faith that the only reason a book is not translated into Russian is its irrelevance there. Not all Soviet-watchers would be impressed. Benford's own contempt for utopias where "the problem of control is simply neglected" is shared by the Kremlin's bureaucratic old guard, even in *perestroika* days, and was the core of many a Zhdanovist denunciation of "irrelevant" radical fiction.

Benford also has a liberal posture, though, which makes him sound as if he has occasionally understood some moral precept or other, though failed to recognize it in its dynamic form in *The Dispossessed*. The dangerous anarchism of the Syndicate of Initiative would understand this:

> Freedom to do as we please, so long as we all agree with each other and remain in a state of harmony with the cosmos, is no freedom at all. [...] It is a single party system that is as superficially benign, yet as subtly authoritarian, as Disneyland. (19)

However coarsely expressed (and the omitted sentence misunderstands the religious mode's contribution to Shevek's radical thought, and Takver's, and Bedap's) this is in line with the devastating indictment of Anarres that leads Shevek and the Syndicate into conflict with the rigidifying forces of both PDC and the public opinion of Abbenay.

It is also the expression in the intellectual mode of the need for Shevek to go to Urras, and therefore the narratological analogue to the book itself. It is because of this radical definition of freedom that a utopia must always be something evermore about to be.

This freedom relates to no possessions except the mind, the body, and the spirit. An Odonian always returns with empty hands, but Shevek's mind brings with it the General Temporal Theory, his body brings with it his identity as a bonded Anarresti coming home, and his spirit brings a kinship with the external universe, and a Hainish friend. Perhaps these three gifts that Shevek brings his society will be sovereign against walls, for a few generations anyway.

Benford is the wall personified, and explains away the whole of Urras as a parody of the contemporary USA (which he predictably calls "America"). How this relates to his parallel sentimentality about Anarres as the USSR, or a more virtuous Tolstoyan Eastern Europe, he doesn't explain. Anarres is settled from Urras, right? It never occurs to Benford that this book is a quintessentially American utopia irradiated by quintessentially American ambiguities. Perhaps he is the only US citizen never to have heard of the Pilgrim Fathers, the contrasting Quaker settlers in Pennsylvania, and millions of voluntary or fugitive arrivals who sought a more just state; some even sought a new frontier where they could set up their own. Maybe a few of these new North Americans also experienced the "hard-scrabbling scarcity" he writes of so condescendingly.

At one point Benford finds himself in distinguished company. Like a cowbird on an eagle's back, he rides on Delany's fascinating hypertense essay in *The Jewel-Hinged Jaw,* though he never catches any of the neurotic ingenuity of that reading experience. Delany can be forgiven his text-warping, even up to the 491st example, because the freakish desperation of his experience of *The Dispossessed* is inseparable from that which produces his major sf. Defensiveness against other kinds of greatness is an occupational hazard.

What Delany misunderstands, and perhaps has to misunderstand, is one barren, chill night, the nadir of the lives of the Syndicate members before the great decision to send Shevek to Urras. Bedap's isolation at this point is different in kind from that of the family that Takver and Shevek have bonded. Bedap is the major antenna of human relationships in the Syndicate, partly because he has no bond himself. That night he realizes the worst (in Rulag's rigid guilt) and the best (in the "intimacy of pain" Shevek shares with his daughter Sadik) of family bonding, and feels intensely, as no one else could, how much his life lacks such bonds.

Delany feels without an instant's doubt that this is a heterosexual woman's unwanted compassion for a homosexual male, that what Bedap longs to change is his sexuality, to become a father. What the text says is that Bedap longs for one crucial and purposeful bond like Shevek's—or Odo's. There is no assertion that this has to involve heterosexuality or begetting. Anarres has sold short the bonded relationship for years, but when malevolent public opinion makes minority life hard, the most intimate sharing becomes the most crucial resource. Delany's reading is not mine, but it is based on a passionate response to a version of the text; Benford's grotesqueries come from denial of the text.

Far from re-expressing Delany's vigilant (though, for me, inapposite) unease, Benford merely preens himself on agreeing that Le

Guin is against homosexuality, and adding that Anarres is so too. Like the rest of the descriptive bursts he produces, this is mere name-calling.

To return to the general issue, Benford wishes to believe Le Guin has ignored the problem of evil because he wishes to sound tough: "Maybe I can't write, but I'm a sure-as-hell implacable reasoner!" In fact, with his longing for "control" he is a mere sentimental gunslinger who assumes that when it comes to the OK Corral the good guys will always outgun the bad guys. He proves that Le Guin has a keen interest in, and a special power of evoking, revolutionary leaders whose success is tantalizingly limited. This cannot prove that she is a reactionary writer, either in the accepted sense of the term or in Benford's polystyrene sense.

The Dispossessed indicates that force is unusable by genuine anarchists at much more than an individual level, and that the use of force puts the users into the archist category. Anarres could not develop an efficient militia or even an efficient mob, whereas Urras has a superbly equipped pair of military super-powers: if either of these had attempted to take over their moon by force, that invasion would have been militarily irresistible. The rigidity of Rulag thrives by exploiting freedom, as does the bullying by the young man from Northrising. Therefore the freedom they "defend" is painfully partial, the revolution betrayed. Shevek's journey, not their tough attempt at "control," is true valiance for freedom. His journey and his ansible, and the consequent future vigilance of Hain and Terran observers, are the only unsentimental defense Anarres has or (for the moment) needs.

The reason why Anarres is an ambiguous rather than either a static or a developing utopia is a complex of sharp ironies. First, public opinion has become a tyranny and fame the reward of tyrants; it makes victims out of innocent and sensitive people like the comedian Tirin and the twelve-year-old Sadik. It threatens to make martyrs or aliens out of radical public figures like Bedap, Shevek and Takver.

Second, Odonianism is being degraded into a gospel, creating passive compliance rather than active, mindful, individual contributions to both the theory and the practice of anarchism. Initiative has to be specially evoked and advocated rather than recognized as the dynamic of the society.

Third, such crass commonsense assumptions as utilitarianism and majority rectitude have white-anted (as Australians put it) the Anarresti social structures. This steals from every individual as well as the body politic—since I could prove anything using the Analogy!—the Cetian birthright of The Noble Science, which is the very essence of Shevek's ministry to both planets and to the rest of the galaxy.

Fourth, and I know I've said this before, the whole society has pressure cooked these viruses by hotly maintaining its isolation from the corrupt outside world. Remember the horror of the king of Karhide on Gethen, when he/she was told about single-sex humanity being the norm elsewhere?

> "So all of them, out on these other planets, are in permanent kemmer? A society of perverts?" (*The Left Hand of Darkness*, 36)

Similarly, Anarres has consecrated doctrinal purities and economic scarcities into permanent aridities. All Urrasti are vicious profiteers and propertarians; all others are irrelevant.

Shevek comes to embody permanent revolution, constantly reaffirmed anarchistic experience, self-acceptance and self-utilization. In him Odonianism goes home to Urras where it began, and comes back to Anarres renewed, revised and interplanetary. This does not mean he has set out to be a hero, but that his society has created the perfect antibody for its sicknesses.

VI.

Back to Benford. He ends his travesty of critical description by broadening his sneer to direct it at "feminist utopias" in general:

> ...they run the risk of forsaking the gains of the present, and becoming reactionary because they cannot imagine new ways to organize community.[...] I conclude that reactionary facets spring in part from lack of imagination. And feminists, searching for ways to revise our society, fall upon analogies with the family, even if these do not provide solutions to the genuine problems of a diverse, urban, cantankerous world. Fundamentally, what we sense as most reactionary about these fanciful worlds is their fixation on a final, glorious endpoint: utopia as stasis.

This glibness contrasts with the wretched incoherence of his theoretical and critical description, and is presumably a deeply held conviction. It is also vicious nonsense.

Le Guin has undoubtedly imagined a community distinct both from the present US norms and from what Benford is determined to read. The Analogy Odonians use to articulate their social values is not with the family but with the living organism. Like all stereotypes it can easily be misapplied; its usefulness depends on individual and experiential alertness. What it specifically disallows is property thinking, where a child's mother becomes "my mother" or its patch of sunlight "mine sun."

The analogy of the family was brilliantly used by Jesus to describe the ultimate relationship between the individual and God and the interrelationships between individuals, though only Benford would think this made him a feminist utopian. It is the overt opposite to Odonian teaching, where bringing up children, and even naming them, is not related to biological parenthood. There are difficult ambiguities about this aspect of Anarresti society, and it may well be that Le Guin has more sympathy with familial bonding than a healthy Odonian would recommend. Shevek, wholly Odonian in perspective, is certainly prepared to test out this as well as most other matters, but most Anarresti will probably pay no attention to that aspect of his contribution.

Benford's assumptions about women writers do remind us that Shevek, the Syndicate of Initiative and Odonian tradition in general not only oppose the family-model for the State but also abhor "the fixation on a final, glorious endpoint: utopia as stasis." Such a fixation would destroy not only Odonian social dynamics but all storytelling. Therefore, puzzling over why rational beings should print Benford's abysmal pseudo-thought—and even reprint it, since it has already appeared in an anthology which also contains criticism—I have experimented.

If we invert a given assertion by Benford, we frequently end up with lucid, truthful and even enheartening ideas. He claims to have read three "feminist novel" utopias: *Motherlines, Woman on the Edge of Time,* and *The Female Man*. Sure enough, each disproves his accusation about women revering the family analogy and longing for stasis. Charnas's book is a sequel to *Walk to the End of the World,* and there are elaborate and passionate satires on late-twentieth-century male-centered social behavior (in the USA) in the other two; these show that they are indeed responses to "perceived masculine evils," rather than attempts at unrelativistic ideal societies.

Far from this limiting their value, though, these utopias can be properly understood as responses to and influences upon their culture of origin, which is also their target culture. All other literary qualities they possess partake of the energy and the comic vision which this relationship to their culture of origin affords them. The case is even clearer in Tiptree's "Houston, Houston, do you Read?" which Benford also daringly mentions. There, emphatically, the true voyage of the narrative ironies is return to the readers' and the writer's culture.

Benford calls all feminist utopias reactionary failures, because, he says, women are fixated on family. What would Joanna Russ have to say about that? Benford has blinded himself to the major energy-source of any feminist utopia. Fortunately, he prefers to be blind to such things. In fact, it is virtually impossible for even the crudest feminist utopia not to challenge a competent reader from our culture (whether US or Australian or European) in a few ways, and the family model is the immediate vulnerability for them. Even Jane Palmer's *The Planet Dwellers* can manage that.

"What real literature needs, and plainly isn't getting, are utopias of *process* [...]." Apart from the grammar, this is another perfect reversal of a truth. To competent readers, if not to poison pen jealousy-ridden hacks, this is crucially what the best feminist utopian writers offer. The Tiptree story is too brief for an articulated utopia, but the novels Benford lists evoke process, not contentment or reassurance. Most of all, *The Dispossessed* ends with both a beginning and a vigorous answer to the book's own beginning. We read first of Shevek stepping across the planet's only official wall; he ends by stepping back onto the same spaceport, not alone, unbuilding walls all over the cultures of a diverse universe, and certainly damaging all the inward walls of Anarres. What will a non-Urrasti alien do to Anarresti visions of reality, to the static revolution?

Shevek may well fade from the attention of his fellow-citizens now, but Anarres will be forced to become what Benford says no woman's utopia can become, a place "where men and women have more freedom, can interact swiftly and chaotically, yet with good results." Here, Benford manages to sound like an inarticulate and possibly feeble-minded member of the Syndicate of Initiative, his heart in the right place: what he cannot see happening on Anarres is the most lucid aspect of Shevek's vision.

Shevek's deadliest enemy is neither of the human menaces Benford picks out, the physicist Sabul or the Urrasti profiteers. Rather, his life and selfhood are endangered by two things: Urras-charm and Anarres-charm. Urras-charm is in the sentimental vitality not only of the physical world but in Pae's family and Vea's quite traditional beguilements. Anarres-charm is in the deceptive togetherness and reductive certitude of the people themselves, the unearned radical rhetoric that Benford thinks *The Dispossessed* enshrines and worships:

> The supremacy of communal values, the need to suppress the individual, the fear of diversity or of science, the longing for a respite from change[...].

Many readers, simply because of their innocent expectation of a less challenging book, will brush past the poison spines of Benford's false hokum and be infected. After all, it is not obvious how such an incompetent and ephemeral description can do any harm to major literature. The trouble is, sf readers are still likely to be uncertain and defensive about the quality of the genre, and to such readers it is prima facie unlikely that a book unmistakably in the sf category should make major demands of both imagination and thought. Perhaps what seems like subtlety, the naive reader reflects, was only a cloudy indecision. Perhaps, just as the devotees of the "classics" and the "mainstream" had always asserted, an sf novel can't really be that good.

Benford is dangerous because he invites us to read the expected cliché, the stereotypical character, the same old story with a re-bored gimmick. He will cheat you out of a rich and unique delight and a sharper, more passionate response, if you believe him. I for one will not allow him to cheat me: the book I have read exists, and works, and he can't gabble it away.

Debunkery's grayest and most shapeless all-purpose weapon is bunkum, and its most dangerous is malice. It is all very well to say that *The Dispossessed* will outlast the mixture of both that has been daubed over it, and it is true that even vitriol only remains fatal for a short time. But though rain and time and soil will eventually render it less noxious, the environment remains damaged: readers will still be reading sf with lowered and stereotyped expectations.

Good sf writing is not an endangered species any more, but good reading is. The natural and spiritual enemies of both must not be allowed to get away with reviling the one or betraying the other, or we will end up voting for the young man from Northrising as the first Führer and Minister for Culture of our Anarres Reich-Soviet.

AFTERWORD, FEBRUARY 2010

by Gregory Benford

On rereading this work from a quarter century ago, I feel that I should not have carried forward this discussion with such a chip on my shoulder. I wrote it after a particularly stressful time in my secret life, as a Soviet specialist for the Central Intelligence Agency. In the early 1980s I carried out field espionage both inside and outside the USSR, using my contacts with the scientific agencies there, my now-vanished facility with Russian and German, and an invitation as a guest of the USSR Academy of Sciences.

There I saw the true depth of Soviet Orwellian logic, and its effects on people I knew as fellow physicists. I worked to plant ideas about US capabilities, delivered and collected some useful documents, and carried out direct inspection of Soviet Army and national defense laboratories, all useful in judging their capabilities.

This drew the attention of the KGB and led to my being tailed, my camera film stolen, and then an attempted arrest by a colonel in the KGB. I avoided this and escaped, was debriefed in England, and never returned to the USSR on the advice of the CIA. This colored my remarks and though I shall not try to edit the past, I regret the tone in this piece. I apologize to all who were offended by it, and especially to Ursula K. Le Guin, whom I have known as a friend for over forty years.

SKIFFY AND MIMESIS

THE ROLE OF THE SCIENCE FICTION READER: CYBERPUNK AND THE KIDS IN COSTUME

by John Foyster

[This piece has its origins in a talk given to the science fiction discussion group Critical Mass on 7 June 1989]

Speakers at Critical Mass follow various courses in presenting their ideas. Collectively, from time to time, a pattern emerges, and it was one such imminent pattern which led me to volunteer to discuss "Adult Science Fiction" following two earlier papers on children's sf and adolescent sf. (Despite strongly-expressed revulsion from attendees at Critical Mass I intend to conclude the series with "Grandfatherly Science Fiction" late in 1989.)

Some things are much more easily said than done. In this case it is necessary to have both a notion of some examples of "adult" science fiction and a critical framework within which to provide analytical comments—the first being rather more difficult to achieve than the second.

In tackling this problem I resolved to reduce it to something simpler: dealing with works that someone else regarded as adult, or might have regarded as adult. In this cowardly way I could halve the problem by dealing with someone else's definition.

Science fiction has the peculiar advantage that the existence of serial publications of one kind or another allows a reputation of a general (or genre) kind. "Genre" fiction, when labeled as a particular class, is already defined. In the case of science fiction, it was relatively easy to find a subgenre which might be examined.

In his introduction to Michael Swanwick's *In the Drift* for the Ace Science Fiction Special series, published early in 1985, Terry

Carr included some remarks about the reason for the return of the Specials. After describing the growth in the science fiction field generally as a result of visual media growth (he cited *Star Trek* and *Star Wars* in particular) Terry Carr goes on to say why the Specials were needed.

> So in recent years sf publishers have catered to this vast new market. The result has been that most of the science fiction published today is no more advanced and imaginative than the sf stories of the fifties, or even the forties: basic ideas and plots are reworked time and again, and when a novel proves to be popular, a sequel or series will come along soon.
> There's nothing wrong with such books; when they're well-written they can be very good. But when authors are constrained to writing nothing but variations on the plots and styles of the past, much of the excitement of science fiction disappears. Science fiction is a literature of change; more than any other kind of writing, sf needs to keep moving forward if it's to be exciting. (viii)

Such a call to arms has specific elements; we can seek straightforwardly for books which have the characteristics Terry Carr was writing about. They will be books which

- do not consist of reworkings of basic ideas and plots, and
- are in some sense "moving forward."

Whatever coincidence there might be with respect to talks at Critical Mass, there were good reasons for me to have particular interest in "adult" science fiction as distinguished from science fiction for children. Stanislaw Lem and Franz Rottensteiner (to identify one tendency) have been especially (and appropriately) vexed about immature fiction. Although one might disagree with them about particular examples, the direction of their argument seems to hold up well.

Secondly, in the editorial of the January 1987 *ASFR*, I made some remarks about trends which Robert Silverberg and Norman Spinrad had described recently (in articles in *Amazing* and *Asimov's*). Both of them expressed some concern about the image of science fiction as being *exclusively* fiction for young people. (Silverberg later recanted.) My editorial failed to excite any interest in readers, but I will bravely run three paragraphs past you once again

> Bluntly put, the question is "is there, or should there be, science fiction after nineteen?" or "is science fiction only for teenagers?" The public image of science fiction—whether as represented in the advertisements upon the backs of which *Locus* and *Science Fiction Chronicle* are published or as modeled by the "kids in costume" about whom Robert Silverberg has expressed concern—is that it is fiction for young people or, if you prefer it, unsophisticated people. Since we all read science fiction, and the likelihood is that we started reading it in our teens, we can understand the perception that this is the ideal audience at which to aim. But what happens to science fiction readers as they grow older? [...]
> The risk lies, I believe, in the possibility that writers who try to write adult science fiction may find themselves without a market, for if science fiction increasingly identifies itself as a teenage market then it will no longer be possible for writers for the adult market to sell sf. And it is not yet the case that "adult" science fiction will be recognized for its quality and published outside the ghetto with ease. [...]
> The question to be faced by the world of science fiction is whether, *in addition to* the identified market for teenage fiction, there should be a market for writers who want to write about adult ways of thinking and, conversely, science fiction books for adult readers.

The difficulties which Silverberg and Spinrad wrote about are by no means confined to science fiction. A different slant on this matter (and indeed a different slant upon science fiction) is given in some recently-published essays of the English poet Philip Larkin. The collection includes a letter to a publisher about this matter, part of which I quote here.

> I feel it is a very great shame if ordinary sane novels about ordinary sane people doing ordinary sane things can't find a publisher these days. This is the tradition of Jane Austen and Trollope, and I refuse to believe that no one wants its successors today. Why should I have to choose between spy rubbish, science fiction rubbish...or dope-taking nervous breakdown rubbish? I like to read about people who have done nothing spectacular, who aren't beautiful and lucky, who try to behave well in the limited field of activity they command, but who can see, in the autumnal moments of vision, that the so-called "big" experiences of life are going to miss them, and I like to read about such things presented not with self-pity or despair or romanticism, but with realistic firmness and even humor. That is in fact what the critics call the moral tone of the book. It seems to me the kind of writing a responsible publisher ought to support. *(Partial Payments: Essays on Writers and Their Lives,* quoted in *The New York Times Book Review,* 16 April 1989.)

This quotation was taken from a letter written by Larkin to one of the many publishers who, in the late 1960s, were rejecting the later novels of Barbara Pym (by the middle 1980s, soon after her death, Pym was very much in vogue, with over a dozen hardcover books in print). Pym's problem, some might say, was that her fiction was neither glitzy nor fashionable, just very good.

In the remarks quoted here Larkin is, of course, only expressing concern that a particular type of fiction is being crowded out of the market; this type of fiction, in Larkin's view, has its place and should be available as well as various kinds of rubbish. Witold Rybczynski, in his recent (1986) *Home* expands upon what Larkin means:

> An Austen novel is a *tour de force,* at least by modern standards. Nothing extraordinary happens—no murders, escapades, or disasters. Instead of adventure or melodrama we read about the prosaic daily comedy of family life. (112)

The particular characteristics of "rubbish" which Larkin selects are interesting to us because while they are to be found most intensely in what is sometimes charmingly called "airport fiction" they are also to be found, perhaps slightly distorted, in some forms of science fiction. But now let's angle more directly towards our target.

Michael Swanwick, like several of the authors published in the later incarnation of the Ace Science Fiction Specials, has been part of the cyberpunk group (one way of identifying them appears to be the editors—like Ellen Datlow and Gardner Dozois—with whom they associate, at least according to Bruce Sterling in the introduction to *Mirrorshades*). If adult science fiction exists, perhaps this is where we shall find it.

Rather than work this idea over with a single example, I propose to consider two, of which the first might well be regarded by many as the archetypal cyberpunk novel, William Gibson's *Neuromancer*. What characteristics does *Neuromancer* have that are of interest in our present investigation?

Case, the protagonist of *Neuromancer*, is a loner who has some skills but also a great amount of luck. Case, more or less a member of the underclass, takes on the most powerful entity in the world, the Tessier-Ashpool artificial intelligence(s). He enjoys reasonable success with women, but also has reliable male buddies.

Such a plot was common, if not endemic, in the 1940s and 1950s. Though the plot may be familiar, we should not give up, for we may yet find other signs that this novel has progressed beyond the science fiction of thirty or forty years before.

There are several differences which I want to call attention to. Earlier novels were built around rocket ships, blasters, inter-stellar (or inter-galactic) empires, psi powers, and so on. Relations with females, in those earlier novels, were rather circumspect, and tended towards the eternal. *Neuromancer* is built around a latter-day equivalent of psi and the rocket-ship combined: the mind powers released by humans linked into computer networks. Psi and the rocket-ship were the glamor icons of lonely teenagers in the 1940s and 1950s whereas in the 1980s the computer, and especially, the computer in a network, has a similar iconic function. Indeed, of the major icons of male teenagers of the 1980s only the rock guitarist is missing.

The second difference between *Neuromancer* and its counterparts of thirty years before lies in the unambiguous and open attitude towards sexual relationships with females. Here again, however, *Neuromancer* is merely reflecting societal change, rather than leading it. Philip José Farmer created a stir in the 1950s because his work explored aspects of sexuality which were out of step with the social mores of most of his (teenage) readers. *Neuromancer* fits all too comfortably into its times, both in this regard and in its attitude towards drugs (something rarely treated in the science fiction of the fifties).

But if we seek to identify *Neuromancer* as either fitting Terry Carr's goals, or as being adult in other than the sense inelegantly expropriated by "adult" bookstores, then we are certain to be disappointed, for *Neuromancer* is all too easily identifiable as "airport fiction."

Our second example is a more recent example of cyberpunk.

Lewis Shiner's *Deserted Cities of the Heart* (1989) has appropriate cyberpunk credentials. The acknowledgements refer, for example, to both Ellen Datlow and Gardner Dozois. Does it fit within the schema indicated above? Is it an "adult" novel? Is it a "teen" novel?

The underlying *stfnal* element of *Deserted Cities of the Heart* is drug-assisted, all-in-the-mind time travel in which, in the far past, the man from the future uses his knowledge/experience to influence the past (and hence his own present). The separate elements of this are not new, although their combination may be (even though this does not interest me particularly). Jack Finney does all-in-the-mind time travel rather better, for example, and Sam Merwin's hasty time-travel novellas for *Startling Stories* in the early 1950s were probably just as appropriate for their time.

But what about the other characteristics of the novel, and in particular the iconic content? We have, as foreshadowed above, the rock guitarist (who played with *Hendrix!*). And we have, picking up on a second popular envisaged future for the young male, the hip journalist (who writes for *Rolling Stone!*). And finally, for the Truly Mature, the anthropologist working for a Sound Ecological Future (with colleagues who used to be at the *New Alchemy Institute*—and indeed one of the books by the Todds is acknowledged in the "Author's Note"), someone whose publishers said of him (let's cover a few more bases) "You could be the next Castaneda."

It is, of course, quite reasonable for an author to make use of individual elements such as these. But with our deliberately biased view, we may see things somewhat differently; for if an author consistently and, to appropriate the most-favored word of the Australian sporting commentators, comprehensively chooses male teenage icons then it is reasonable to note this fact and incorporate it in more general discussion.

In *Deserted Cities of the Heart* we also find other elements which may be less appealing to the teenaged reader. Lewis Shiner conjures up some of the atmosphere generated by Robert Stone and, in a different way in the science fiction context, by Lucius Shepard. I write "may" with less than utter conviction because, of course, writers like Stone (in particular) *may* be read in ways which support relatively violent male fantasies; and there is a respectable amount of *Guns and Ammo* stuff in *Deserted Cities of the Heart*.

Deserted Cities of the Heart does have more going for it than this, and for that matter probably has more going for it than *Neuromancer*. Whereas the characters in *Neuromancer* are so hard-edged as to dissuade you from ever wanting to meet one of them, the characters in *Deserted Cities of the Heart* are sufficiently varied (if somewhat stereotyped) to allow one an edge into the book and thus into their lives. Some of their characteristics have been hinted at above, but they are also reflective, at times uncertain, and certainly engaged with one another, which gives us a chance to engage with them as well. And whereas in *Neuromancer* the characters are unashamed world-changers, in *Deserted Cities of the Heart* we are reading of people who would like to change the world, but whose capacity is limited, and who recognize their own limitations.

But that having been said, we have to recognize the general superficiality of those engagements with one another. We are reading teen pulp fiction—and perhaps it is inappropriate to be looking for anything else.

At the Critical Mass meeting at which this discussion was first presented, several objections were raised to the general line of argument advanced here.

One argument, advanced at various stages during the evening, related to the "writing" of the novel and its quality. This argument emerges both in terms of arguing that a particular novel—say, *Deserted Cities of the Heart*—is "well-written" and in claims about the superior qualities of particular genres. What this means is a little unclear. It seems related to a similar argument, often advocated by the same people, that fiction which is overtly written for children or teenagers is "better-written" than a lot of fiction written for "adults."

But in terms of the case addressed here, such an argument is irrelevant. It may be comforting, for example, to adults to believe that the works aimed at children which they enjoy reading are "well-written" (which is what was said at Critical Mass), but this has no bearing upon the primary case being advocated here, which is that there is decreasing room for science fiction which is not derived from the fantasies of teenagers, especially and generally male teenagers. At least some of the novels labeled as "cyberpunk" rely upon, if they do not pander to, just these fantasies.

SCI-FI AND PSI-FI: HOW POINT OF VIEW INFLUENCES REVIEWING

by George Turner

It was, I think, Yvonne Rousseau who commended Lucius Shepard's *Life During Wartime* to me. I was not able to obtain a copy until May, some months after the appearance of John Foyster's laudatory review (*ASFR* 17/18), and after reading the novel I went back to the review with some puzzlement, the greater for his reference to myself as one who "could write sensitively in the science fiction mode about this facet of humanity." I could not see that Shepard was writing about war at all, sensitively or otherwise; he was writing, it seemed to me, about the human ego naked, stripped down to its basic murderous selfishness. What knowledge he showed of war and soldiers would leave a wide margin, if written on the back of a postage stamp.

The very title is hard to understand because the "war" in the book is a mere backdrop, a stage property backgrounding a structure wherein the world's problems are a by-product of the enmity between two psi-gifted families.

It serves, in the simple sleight-of-word-processor that every writer knows, to prepare the mind for outrage and brutality which would otherwise stretch credulity too far. (The book could be written without a war background but reader preparation would need to be subtle and extensive.) Even the psi element works (though not for me) because the sense of outrage is readied in advance. It works also because sf readers have been relentlessly bombarded with it for the last half century, to the point where they accept it without thinking. "Without thinking" is what springs the trap.

Life during wartime? There is mostly a series of brutal distortions of life caused not by war but by a set of imaginative circumstances beside which war seems as natural as breathing. Nor does author Shepard take any trouble to present war to the reader. His few combat references are firmly distanced, with no evocative detail to solidify the picture (even his tunneled hill reads like a disaster of tactical planning) and his soldiers are in the Hollywooden mould of *Platoon* and *Full Metal Jacket*, themselves reflections of the macho trash soldier novels in their presentations of living men. All the characters speak a neo-gutter jargon as though they all come from the same tenement in the same run-down area—something between Bronx and hillbilly and true to neither.

The fact is that in any group of soldiers you will find as many varieties of speech as you would expect in an army where rich, poor, educated and ignorant exist together in a ten-man section. And their four-letter usage is no greater than that of the average man in the street. (There is always the macho twit, of course, usually disliked.) Having worked and fraternized with American infantry, I find the model hard to take. The peculiar viciousness of the Vietnam war probably exposed layers of primal screaming better left covered but in general the GI speaks as well as, or no worse than, his Australian counterpart. (For the true rich variety of speech, see Mailer's *The Naked and the Dead*.) The movie-imposed view of men in action in Vietnam can be considerably watered down by a reading of Joe Haldeman's autobiographical novel, *War Year*.

I have dwelt on military behavior to demonstrate my belief that *Life During Wartime* is a construct whose every nut and bolt is suspect. Nevertheless, at the core of the novel is a monstrous truth, one surely worth propagating, and I will come to it later, but the exposition is jerrybuilt, rendered viable only by commendably expert writing. Have no reservation about Shepard's literary talent; it is great. My quarrel is with what he has expended it upon.

§

It is a truism of criticism that no two persons will read the same text in quite the same fashion. Each will find either what he/she wants to find (the usual reason for grabbing a favorite author's new novel, but not the best reason) or some facet of the narration that engages his/her attention and colors the whole interpretation of what happens thereafter. Each will also find what personal knowledge, experience, psychological makeup and bias demand. (It might be said with some justice that nobody reads into a work quite what the writer designed should be read.) Consider, then, the probable differences between what John Foyster and I brought to the reading of this novel.

1. I have firsthand experience of soldiers and warfare. This is important only in that after a dozen or so pages I suspected that Shepard's conceptions were derivative and his models chosen from literary secondhand shops. Credibility suffered where it badly needed support.
2. John apparently accepts psi as legitimate science fiction. I do not, and this is crucial.
3. I think we have rather different beliefs about the essential nature of humanity. His seem more generous than mine. I have said and written that human beings are barbarians puffing themselves as civilized but in fact passing through a technological stage of racial history without the self-knowledge or self-control to make the passage save at constant risk of disaster. The "civilized" record of genocide and selfishness beats savagery hands down.

§

There is no question here of right or wrong points of view, only of differences of approach. The first of these differences requires no further discussion from me, but I have labeled the second "crucial."

In the dear old days of the Campbell autocracy we sucked monthly on the flowing tit of the Dean Drive, Dianetics, Psi, the Suppressed Carburettor and other fantasies long forgotten. Only Dianetics has changed its name and progressed to a moneymaking level that would be hilarious if it were not sinister. Even science fiction has just about given up on psi save for the occasional special effects sequence in a junk novel (I think the dreary Telzey Amberdon drove it whimpering into hermitage) and it came as a shock to find it served up with a straight face in a novel purporting to have some serious intent. (Perhaps Shepard has never read James Blish's deadpan sendup of the whole silly business in *Jack of Eagles*. Most readers at the time seemed unaware of mockery, which says something or other about the readership of the time.)

My opinion of telepathy and other psi manifestations has been indicated in *Beloved Son*, *Vaneglory* and, most strongly, in a novella, "A Pursuit of Miracles." It is that there are solid physical and psychologial reasons militating against the propagation of psi forces, particularly telepathy, and that the development of such talents would be an unmitigated disaster for the human race. Evolution usually knocks such anti-survival factors on the head before they become endemic.

However, I thought that maybe somebody was at last about to take on the job of giving psi some logically derived credibility, though I have never seen it attempted in sixty-and-odd years of reading sf.

Its existence is always assumed. Its practitioners "discover" their power, which grows with use, and they never destroy or badly damage themselves by inept handling. They "direct thoughts" into other minds, "force their way" past "mental barriers," establish "mindblocks," shatter minds with a "telepathic shout" and do anything the author finds useful to his purpose—but he maintains a wise silence about what they do, how they do it, what they do it with and why the talent should exist. Put bluntly, they fantasize because the true sf going is hard for a poor scribbler chasing a dollar. Psi in all its forms is the refuge of the unoriginal mind, like sword 'n' sorcery. It is a retreat into magic. (Please don't tell me that today's magic is tomorrow's science. That's a half-truth designed to legitimize nonsense, like the one about truth being stranger than fiction. Fiction springboards from truth.) It may be argued that a writer can introduce a fantasy element to describe or suggest a truth (as, perhaps, in *The Satanic Verses*) but he may not, in my view, plaster it on to a background of savagely realistic narrative and expect it to be accepted as a truth in itself. Disbelief is not suspended until he declares his hand.

Shepard declares his hand fairly soon and there is not a credible card in it. Psi powers, which he never really defines, are stimulated, we are told, by a drug. How does it work? What cerebral system does it work on? Your guess is as good as mine. Too much drug, or careless application, or application to the wrong type of mind may be destructive. Why? How? We never find out. No clue is ever given to what the reader is sucking up, bug-eyed, from the deceitful page. There is no logic to cling to. Why a drug? Why not, "open sesame'? It might work as well but the memory of Ali Baba would alert the reader to the snow job, whereas "drug" sounds vaguely scientific. (In the novel they've used it for three centuries but it has never hit the pharmacopoeia, even by accident.)

OK; allow the drug.

But is it possible to allow super-esper Mingolla's use of his powers—without understanding, without psychological expertise, without a clue as to how a mind actually works? I don't know these answers, nor do you, nor does Shepard—but in science fiction you are supposed to work from some core, however small, of fact.

So I give a fed-up yawn whenever Mingolla "throws," "gives," "imposes" (find your own carefully non-committal word) an emotion, usually fear or confusion or some such, to or on his subject.

How might it be done? Not at all, I think. First, I would suggest, he must create and hold the missile emotion in his own mind, building it to the requisite strength, and then launch it. But—in the case of a thoroughly destructive emotion, such as anger, despair or hatred (Mingolla's best stock-in-trade) would he at the end of the build-up be in mental condition even to cope with his own overriding emotion? Again, building a synthetic emotion is not easy; actually creating a feeling is extremely difficult. Ask a method actor about it some time; it can take hours. By then the proposed victim is in the next town.

Mingolla also "blocks" minds.

He just does it. Shepard never once uses so much as an adjective to clue in the process though his word processor runs over with prose on easier matters. Nor does he give the reader much idea what is involved in "stripping" a mind to leave a minimally aware hulk, barely living.

These never-rationalized commonplaces of psi-fi are so thoroughly embedded in genre writing that it is unlikely that anyone will make the attempt to rationalize them. They are accepted as givens and the reader's psi-fi-conditioned thinking asks never a question, though every questioning of the esper game will probably come up with the answer that it just won't work.

Which is as well. ESP would be the dead end of the race. Insanity Inc.

I do not quarrel for a moment with John Foyster's account of the plot of the novel but I suggest that in and under his account is another plot and thrust.

§

Mingolla is a rather ordinary young man but has a strong core of rather generalized resentment, demonstrated early in the story by his treatment of his parents on a TV hookup. (I feel that Shepard tried to justify Mingolla here by making the parents tight-minded caricatures.) As his psi powers grow Mingolla is filled with anger at the ambivalence, grounded in selfishness, of everyone and everything he sees. Even Debora, whom at first he merely wants but comes to love, seems two-faced, though his desire for her lets him see her as puzzling rather than equivocal—a very human rationalization. All others, even his friends, are basically contemptible. So, as he eventually realizes, is he.

Mingolla's trouble is that his powers allow him to see humanity stripped psychologically naked, to see that every motivation is either self-deception or deliberate sham, that the core of every mind is an ego ruthlessly directing the thought processes to provide a cover of virtue or at least of explanatory lies.

He is possessed throughout the book by anger and it is his undoing. Power corrupts and Mingolla's power is irresistible. Absolute power corrupts absolutely, so Mingolla finds himself unable to restrain his urge to wreck and maim. His treatment of some of his victims makes this novel one of the most repellent fictions I have read in many years. (That is quite a tribute to Shepard's literary power.) Mingolla has after-flashes of concern for what he does but these do not prevent him going on to do worse. He is as mean-spirited a creature as any of his victims, when the chips are down, driven by a raging ego to actions which even he cannot rationalize as justice.

I have no quarrel with this portrait of a basically barbaric humanity; the daily news suggests that it is a correct one and that Shepard's portrayal of us in the person of Mingolla should give rise to some lateral thinking about the true nature of our plight—neither wholly savage nor wholly civilized and desperately short of self-knowledge.

Final problems for the novel begin when Shepard needs to find a way out for his ruined hero. There is, of course, no way out, but it doesn't do to end on a note of utter damnation. (Editors don't like it.) So, enter Salvation via Love for a Good Woman. Cover the cliché as he may with a display of urgent writing, Shepard doesn't get away with it. I can't think of anybody who could. They would have, for a start, to account for Debora being the one person in the long cast of espers who is not debased by her talent.

John Foyster quotes part of the redemption scene but only part of the desperate writing of those concluding pages. But what he quotes is all that matters (the rest is emotional camouflage) and you may look at it and wonder just what it means. How, for instance, would you translate "leaving behind the thought of peace, and entering the precincts of a violent dutiful morality with its own continuum of behaviors and possibilities"?

I suggest that "violent dutiful morality" means "violence as a virtue"—and I don't much care for the implications. Then there is:

"its own continuum of behaviors and possibilities." Loosely, that may mean "a place where nothing is as we know it" or it may mean any transcendental imagining the reader cares to load on to it. It saves Shepard making a rational statement while giving some sort of affirmation of the ultimate righteousness of the depraved and brutalized Mingolla.

These final pages are, to put it mildly, rhetoric designed to lull the reader into agreeing that love can purify the vision of the lover, though some millennia of experience suggest the opposite. I would have applauded Shepard for the fine writer he can be if he had taken the final step to dramatic truth and left Mingolla psychically ruined, a monster aware of his ruin and no longer capable of restraint. His eventual act of love would have been to twist Debora's mind into resonance with his own and so own her completely. Add to Lord Acton's dictum: Absolute power corrupts irretrievably.

Life During Wartime is, behind all its flamboyance, a hollow novel, a savage fantasy rather than science fiction, in the end vitiated by the failure to follow its thesis to the desolate act of truth.

A LETTER FROM LUCIUS SHEPARD

I am writing in response to George Turner's examination of my novel *Life During Wartime*. Ordinarily I would refrain from responding to such an article. I feel no particular need to defend my book, for in a sense it is no longer mine; my passionate involvement with it ended on the day that I handed it over to my editor, and it no longer is of real moment to me. The truth is, I probably admire it even less than does George Turner, since—like most books—it is an unsatisfactory approximation of the intent and vision that informed it, and thus I perceive of it mainly its failures. Like all books, it is open to subjective interpretation by readers and critics; therefore if Mr. Turner wishes to characterize it "a hollow novel," if that is his honest reaction to having read it, my belief is that—being subjective—his viewpoint is unarguable. I have read with pleasure several of Mr. Turner's novels and my initial impulse was to chalk the misstatements in his article up to a passing intemperate mood and to let the matter slide; however, I am so confounded by the absurdity of certain of his arguments, so disturbed by their implicit smugness, I feel that some sort of defense is called for, and, at the risk of being labeled paranoid or contentious, I intend to address what I consider to be his logical inequities.

Mr. Turner's most annoying and poorly supported argument is his insistence that my novel is in no way an accurate depiction of war. He has himself, he states, experienced war, and he goes on to testify from this authoritative height that it is apparent I have culled my information on the subject from literary and cinematic models. I have asked my bookseller to acquire Mr. Turner's war novels (I am assuming from the righteous tone of his rebuke that such do exist) so that I can read about the real thing and learn how to write about it without betraying the least literary influence. Once these books are in hand, doubtless all my caveats concerning the matter will be swept aside; but in the meantime, I am left with the impression that Mr. Turner has an unwarranted degree of self-esteem and that his own expertise in war is somewhat limited. I have no knowledge of Mr. Turner's personal history—though from his bewilderment with my choice of title and the unfamiliarity with popular music that this implies, I judge that he is not of my generation—and so I cannot be certain during which war he gained his experience, be it Crimean or Boer or the War of Jenkins' Ear; yet surely it was not so different from mine, surely it involves a number of men all of whom held varying opinions as to what happened and why and how it felt to be there. Even a cursory study of the literature produced by each separate conflict gives evidence of the fact that although the authors fought upon the same battlefields, although they obviously influenced one another, their wars were nonetheless vastly different, their memories funded by a wide spectrum of individual experiences and idiosyncratic perceptions. That Mr. Turner attempts to invalidate my perceptions by doing nothing more than banging the gavel of his Experience smacks of a curmudgeonly refusal to admit that there may be other truths, yea, even other realities apart from those with which he is familiar. Those portions of *Life During Wartime* that aspire to verisimilitude have been well received by a good many authors who participated in the Vietnam conflict, and by other veterans as well, and I have complete faith that I have managed to communicate to a relatively large number of people what war is like *from my viewpoint*.

There is another point that appears to have eluded Mr. Turner—in writing *Life During Wartime* I was not attempting to write a naturalistic novel, nor was it my central purpose to convey the nature of war; rather I was utilizing a fictive war as a backdrop against which to present themes that in my opinion required a more surreal palette. At one juncture Mr. Turner acknowledges this, and yet at the same time he damns me for not having laid on the specific details that he deems necessary to depict the Honest-to-Jesus real thing. (In certain sections of the novel, particularly in parts of the opening, I admit to having attempted some degree of realism, wanting to launch the narrative from a recognizable platform; beyond that, the war I am describing does not pretend to reality, no more so—at any rate—than does Pynchon's war in *Gravity's Rainbow*.) If critical accuracy were Mr. Turner's aim, he would have done well to spend some time in clarifying and expanding upon this minor ambivalence; but as he states early in the article by saying that his purpose for dwelling on the subject of "military behavior [is] to demonstrate [...] that *Life During Wartime* is a construct whose every nut and bolt is suspect," his true aim is deconstruction, and his tool for tearing down my house is not logic or truth, but—again—his portentous assertion that he knows war and I do not, his demand that we accept his authority for no other reason than that he has put on a soldier hat. Yet from the paucity of martial information contained in his article, he seems every bit as uninformed as he claims me to be. For instance, in referring to "R & R," the opening section of the novel, he dismisses my creation of a tunneled fortified hill, the Ant Farm, as being "a disaster of tactical planning," implying that this is a telltale of my ignorance, that during his war there were no such tactical disasters. I find this more than a little difficult to accept. In my experience such disasters were the rule rather than the exception, at least where the US Armed Forces were concerned, and I could cite a hundred incidents and tactical blunders in whose insane light the Ant Farm would appear the result of a perfectly reasonable military stratagem. And as for Mr. Turner's characterization of "any group of soldiers" being a mingling of "rich, poor, educated and ignorant exist[ing] together in a ten-man section"—going by this little titbit, and by his statement that machismo among the troops was limited to the odd "macho twit," were I as irresponsible as he, did I not take into account that his experience might be distinct from mine, I might make some ill-considered statement concerning *his* ignorance.

Mr. Turner goes on to comment that all of my military characters speak "a neo-gutter jargon as though they all come from the same tenement in the same run-down area—something between Bronx and hillbilly and true to neither." Since he refuses to accord me credence in the realm of warfare, I'm afraid I must be equally reluctant to grant him credence in the field of American street language—be it Bronx or hillbilly or whatever—simply because he once "fraternized with American infantry," something that strikes me as a meager credential at best. I have in my time "fraternized" with Australians, yet I would never be so foolish as to claim that this fraternization has made me conversant with regional Australian slang and terms. Most combat soldiers in Vietnam, the conflict I have used as a crude model, were not—as Mr. Turner says they must have been—"well-spoken"; their average age was nineteen, some eight years younger than the average combat soldier during World War II, and large numbers of them were poor whites and inner-city blacks and Hispanics who were barely literate and given to certain unanimity of profanity and slang and swaggering machismo. Even their better-educated brothers-in-arms came during the course of bonding to adopt or affect elements of this vulgar style. Nevertheless, I insist that both regional and individual distinctions are evident in my characters' modes of speaking to anyone with an ear for hearing them. To cite, as Mr. Turner does, Mailer's *The Naked and the Dead*—a book that substitutes the word "fugging" for the more common Anglo-Saxon verb—as being exemplary of how soldiers *really* talk is the height of the ludicrous...unless, perhaps, when referring to Mr. Mailer's war, a war a half-century removed from the one with which I was dealing.

I am tempted to ignore Mr. Turner's contention that psi is not legitimate science fiction, a type of argument that should have gone out of vogue along with the Hula Hoop. But as I have come this far in rebuttal, I will make a brief comment: who the fuck (or should I say, *fug?*) cares what is legitimate science fiction and what is not? It's the stories and the craft that matters to me, the challenge of achieving some form of precision and principled statement. To huff and puff about the legitimacy of genre conventions is worthless prattle. I'm certain there are a number of hard science fiction practitioners who will quarrel with this, but it's taken for granted by most writers I know that it's all bloody fantasy, that ninety-nine percent of all science-fiction doodah, ringworlds and FTL and the like, is implausible. So why the hell should I, as Mr. Turner suggests with catty paternity, haul a glob of rubber science out of the vat in order to justify and explain my psychics? What good would it do to support my characters with a feeble rationale that everyone would know is bullshit? To satisfy a few nit-pickers, or because to do so is a moldering conceit approved of by the doyens of the status quo? My eyes tend to glaze over when I read such expository passages, and I have no intention of writing them anymore. One reason I am straying further and further from the science fiction field these days is my weariness with the proliferation of this sort of ridiculous argument, and also with the henhouse clatter that arises whenever a new rooster pokes his head in. By trying to disallow the use of a science-fictional convention in a science fiction book, it seems to me that Mr. Turner is looking for an excuse to find fault, to cluck louder than the rest, for my book is only one of countless others that for the sake of fluency have ignored exposition and utilized instead the average reader's familiarity with genre convention.

Mr. Turner's most startling argument is that I have not lived up to his sour conception of human nature, that I have stuck on an ending to my book that is untrue to my unkind portrait of our species and lacks the unflinching bleakness of his own. This is hard to credit. I have, I believe, firmly established that Mingolla has become something of a monster and—through a sequence of flash-forwards—that his immediate future is to involve the empty, joyless pursuit and execution of his enemies in order to ensure his survival. I felt it would be laying it on rather a bit thick to stamp MONSTER on his forehead and have him run howling off into the jungle; I considered it more appropriate and subtle (too subtle for some tastes, apparently) to let the reader draw his own conclusions, conclusions to which I had led him, but which I had not rubbed his nose in. I believe I have also firmly established that Mingolla has achieved dominance over and a distance from Debora, and by making plain that love for the two of them has become not a form of solace but a means of fuelling their psychic strength, I am certain that I have scotched—to all except the most inattentive reader—any notion of romantic salvation or Love Conquers All. Mr. Turner is the first critic to accuse me of having done a happy ending and to have neglected desolate over-kill. I will console myself with the fact that in this regard I appear to have more than satisfied everyone else.

I have taken, I realize, an acerbic tone in the foregoing paragraphs, but I feel it is warranted. I have not read the favorable review that so piqued Mr. Turner as to inspire his reaction; it may be that I would quarrel with it as well, though likely for different reasons. But what perplexes and rankles me about this particular article is why Mr. Turner has taken the trouble to address a review of a book printed two years after its publication and why he has done so in such a thoughtless and self-aggrandizing fashion. Despite its misleading subtitle—"How Point of View Influences Reviewing"—this article is not criticism, it has nothing to do with the art of reviewing; it is simply a platform from which he has chosen to toot his own horn and to launch a clumsy attack against a book that he does not appear to care much for. But why the persiflage of the title, why bother with the brief justifying paragraphs that read like an insert and pretend to lend some scholarly bias to what is plainly an attempted evisceration? Why all this effort expended over such an inconsequential matter? Now I know why I have bothered to write my response—I am ill with the flu, and the illness has sapped me to such an extent that this is the best I can manage as far as exercising my intellect. Perhaps Mr. Turner, too, was ill when he wrote his article. If so, I can sympathize, I understand his dilemma, and I certainly understand how easy it is to get carried away when one is confronted with what one perceives to be an act of folly. But if he was hale when he wrote his piece, then I am forced to question the quality of the motivations that underlie what is essentially the flogging of a dead horse and a waste of time far better spent, I would hope, at his own creative work.

DESPERATELY SEEKING LUCIUS

by John Foyster

George Turner's comments on my review of Lucius Shepard's *Life During Wartime* [reprinted in *Chained to the Alien*] do him a considerable disservice. But as this is partly my fault, I ought to take part in George's rehabilitation.

I did, after all, use psi powers to influence George in his reading and his reactions to *Life During Wartime*, as is conclusively demonstrated in his opening remarks "It was, I think, Yvonne Rousseau who recommended Lucius Shepard's..." Having recommended *Life During Wartime* to him (consistently with having previously recommended to him *Green Eyes*), I sneakily blocked from George's mind any recollection of that fact and substituted a false memory that the recommendation had come from Yvonne Rousseau (who, not having read *Life During Wartime* at the time of reading George's article, was inclined to claim some precognitive skills but settled for reading Shepard's novel and is all the better for it). But I believe the demonstrated impact on George's critical reactions is greater testimony to the strength of my psi powers, for my next step was to turn his critical faculties to mush, and this he demonstrates in the remaining pages of his article.

In order to write as he has, George Turner has had to willfully misunderstand and misinterpret almost all the evidence available to him. For example, neither the title of Shepard's novel, nor the pairing of it with Aldiss's *Forgotten Life* in my review, has been a strong enough hint to George Turner that these novels both deal with life in the context of war rather than (as I baldly put it in the first sentence of my article) *The Naked and the Dead Go To Mars*. (My psi powers reveal themselves unmistakably here, for on his first page George Turner cites as a preferred model exactly this work—*The Naked and the Dead*—I asserted Shepard was to be praised for not following.) *Forgotten Life*, asserted by me to be appropriate to be treated alongside *Life During Wartime*, also has war as "a mere backdrop"; perhaps, curious as it may seem, I am actually making a point here which George has missed.

Let's turn aside from the negative aspect—the demonstrations of George's fatal misreadings—to look at the points George asserts.

George Turner basically has two points to make; one is about the point of view of the reader, and the other is about the use of psi in science fiction. With respect to the first, George asserts that he and I differ in (at least) three ways which he (presumably) thinks lead to different ways of writing about a book such as *Life During Wartime*.

In the real world, the problems of the biases of the reviewer/writer/critic have actually been thought about by many people. As a result, several solutions have been developed.

One solution, which has been quite successful in several arenas, is to have available a large array of reviews and criticism by one person, and thus to come to know and understand the relationship of that person's views to one's own (*any*one's own). One might use the film criticism of Pauline Kael in this way, or perhaps the science fiction reviews by P. Schuyler Miller in *Astounding/Analog* over that long period. Such an approach is, however, of limited utility, just because so large a mass of review material is necessary.

A second solution, more commonly used in literary criticism, is to operate with a theory of literature constructed by oneself or someone else. This approach is also extremely useful, but is scarcely available to the reviewer of science fiction, whose audience is so diverse in background as to be unlikely to be suited by one particular theory of literature.

I currently prefer a third solution, borrowed from the social sciences, in which one uses multiple perspectives (or triangulation) to minimize the "reviewer effect." In its most appropriate application this requires several reviews of the one work (as in the symposium on George Turner's *The Sea and Summer/Drowning Towers* which *ASFR* published in mid-1988 [reprinted in *Chained to the Alien*]). The variation I deliberately use now (see most of my pieces in *ASFR* over the past couple of years) requires that the single reviewer deal with several works, preferably works which the reviewer is able to tie together, making more explicit the differences between reader and reviewer perspectives.

Thus I had to wait some time to find a book I could review alongside *Life During Wartime*. Had *Forgotten Life* not become available during 1988 I suppose I would eventually have reviewed *Life During Wartime* as an isolated work, but I am glad that I did not have to do that.

George's twittering about the differences between our viewpoints is therefore of little interest to me other than the extent to which it reveals the superficiality of his thinking about the question. Indeed, his claim that he is concerned about differences in "point of view" seems to me almost certain to be spurious. George has one obsession about which he is just plain neurotic—and that is what he devotes all his energy to arguing about. He doesn't really care that he and I have different experiences of war or that we have different beliefs about humanity; what really matters to George ("this is crucial") is that I "accept [...] psi as legitimate science fiction."

That this is codswallop on at least two levels (the statement at its face value and the underlying notion that individuals canonize genres) is not likely to disturb George for he is driven to run the hare of psi to earth.

Over a long period of time George has argued publicly and privately about the place of psi in science fiction. "All others," he has effectively said, "have gotten it wrong, and I alone (in several works) have dealt with psi in an honest, a *scientific* way." This fatal/fateful obsession with science continues to be George's downfall.

In George Turner's view, then, there are at least two major flaws in *Life During Wartime*—Shepard's treatment of war and Shepard's treatment of psi—and hence two failures in my review.

If you happen to think that George has misunderstood the function of war in Shepard's novel, as I do, then the first flaw evaporates. And if George's obsession about psi distorts his vision...?

In "Sci-Fi and Psi-Fi" George Turner goes a little into the history of psi in science fiction. The *social* function of psi in science fiction (and elsewhere)—its offering of salvation in a godless world threatened by nuclear destruction—and its growth and dominance as a consequence of that social function seem to be of little interest to George Turner, whereas to me the context is just about all that is of interest about it. (I contrasted, you may remember, Shepard's handling of a psi denouement with that of Eric Frank Russell in 1946 [in the story "Metamorphosite"], at the start of the rise of the psi era; the psi powers were similar, their context very different.)

I therefore take it as a reasonable assumption that, except in the crudest pulp fiction, a serious writer uses psi as a social device, rather than a scientific (as George Turner seems to prefer it, a Gernsbackian) device. I don't assert that George Turner has to have my view, of course, but I note that if that scientific purism is maintained then one locks oneself out of a large amount of reading and interpretation. After all, there really aren't orcs, are there? Or dragons? Or spaceships? Or near-immortals?

What a dreadful time George Turner would have were he to read Lucius Shepard's Griaule stories! Not only is psi influence often significant, but there is a dragon...Does Shepard really believe in dragons? How foolish he is! No *scientist* believes in dragons!

Such a view means missing out on the views of the most substantial writer of science fiction active today. "The Father of Stones" (*Asimov's*, September 1989) is a significant work of fiction about dragons and magic and psi, yet it bears more directly on mankind's present condition than George's *The Sea and Summer*. If George Turner wants to come to grips with real science fiction then he has to shake off his Gernsbackian science-fiction-as-prediction nonsense and read beyond the nuts and bolts; because of writers like Lucius Shepard it becomes decidedly worthwhile to do this. Shepard himself (in the August 1989 *Asimov's*) writes about the relationship of science fiction to the real world, and I recommend that story to George Turner; perhaps it will help change his mind. Meanwhile, I'll keep up the mental blocking; George will never notice it, dear reader, but you and I can wink and nudge one another.

SKIFFY AND MIMESIS; OR, CRITICS IN COSTUME

by Russell Blackford

Science fiction is bad for you. It saturates your hardening blood vessels with triglycerides and the evilest cholesterol. It's junk food. Junk.

That's why I need lifestyle talks from my family doctor. That's why we're all soaked through with the noxious chemistry of a walking heart attack. They've assured us: folks like George Turner, John Foyster. We *know* their yarn. Plenty of people will tell it, but, as we said in *Urban Fantasies*—me and David King—the story is sacred within the tribes of fandom itself: "even within the community of science fiction and fantasy writers"—yes—"one sometimes hears the sounds of pitiful self-flagellation from those who are hypnotized by the supposed relevance of the elite culture."

Us 'n' them. S 'n' M.

I.

This outburst is provoked by three recent articles in *ASFR*: "The Role of the Science Fiction Reader: Cyberpunk and the Kids in Costume" (John Foyster, *ASFR* 20); "Sci-Fi and Psi-Fi: How Point of View Influences Reviewing" (George Turner, *ASFR* 21); and "Desperately Seeking Lucius" (Foyster, again, *ASFR* 21). The first article is an attack on sf generally as immature, homing in on the cyberpunks, and especially on William Gibson's *Neuromancer* and Lewis Shiner's *Deserted Cities of the Heart*. The Turner piece attempts to gut a particular book, Lucius Shepard's *Life During Wartime*. But Turner's implicit critique of science fiction is much wider. In "Desperately Seeking Lucius', Foyster, in turn, springs to Shepard's defense. Yet the logic of *this* article subverts "Cyberpunk and the Kids in Costume."

I'm not going to write the slim monograph needed to defend Gibson and Shiner (and Shepard if necessary) with any rigor. I'll stick to the internal logic of the Foyster/Turner threesome of articles, especially what they say or imply about the relationship between value, literature and mimesis.

Foyster fills up three of *ASFR*'s large pages, ostensibly with the "question of whether there should be a market for writers who want to write about adult ways of thinking and, conversely, science fiction books for adult readers." Unfortunately, the analysis of these concepts (not to mention, indeed, the structure of the article) is confused to an extent that renders the argument near-incomprehensible. It appears to rely upon these baffling moves:

1. The late Terry Carr complained about the lack of sf books which are not "reworkings of basic ideas and plots" but which are, rather, "moving forward"—Carr saw the new Ace Specials as making up this lack.

2. A number of authors associated with the Ace Specials have been part of the cyberpunk group.

3. Therefore, in searching for adult science fiction, perhaps we had better look to the subgenre of "cyberpunk."

4. There is a kind of fiction (the novels of Jane Austen, Anthony Trollope and Barbara Pym are paradigms) for which Philip Larkin has mourned, saying that it now appears to lack a market. Larkin describes it like this:

> [It is about] people who have done nothing spectacular, who aren't beautiful and lucky, who try to behave well in the limited field of activity they command, but who can see, in the autumnal moments of vision, that the so-called "big" experiences of life are going to miss them, and I like to read about such things presented not with self-pity or despair or romanticism, but with realistic firmness and even humor. That is in fact what the critics call the moral tone of the book.

5. When we actually examine paradigm cyberpunk novels (such as *Neuromancer* and, supposedly, *Deserted Cities of the Heart*), they do not resemble the sort of fiction described by Larkin.

6. Therefore cyberpunk is not adult, and it is unlikely that much other science fiction is either.

Foyster's article *does* make these moves, but I find it difficult to see what relationship they are supposed to bear to each other. Unless we conflate "adult science fiction" with "science fiction that resembles the sort of stuff described by Larkin at point 4.," I don't see how the argument amounts to more than a series of unrelated points. And surely, when Terry Carr asserted that the Ace Specials (which *did* include some cyberpunk works) are not reworkings of basic ideas and plots, he was not therefore saying that they resemble texts such as Larkin had in mind (which, if they all matched Larkin's description, *would* be reworkings of the same basic idea!). It takes neither Foyster nor a ghost from the grave to foretell that we'd waste our time looking for skiffy that reads like Austen or Trollope. Any experienced science fiction reader, much less a critic of Foyster's sophistication, should know that much, so why pretend otherwise? Isn't the argument disingenuous? Maybe the article should have been called "*Critics* in Costume."

Back a step.

Larkin writes about the fiction he wants as being in the "tradition" of Austen and Trollope. Now Jane Austen was born in 1775 and died in 1817. Her first two novels, *Sense and Sensibility* and *Pride and Prejudice*, were begun in the late 1790s and published in 1811 and 1813 respectively. Her other four novels were published from 1814 to 1818 (the last two appeared posthumously, as did some stray bits and pieces). Anthony Trollope was born in 1815, when Jane Austen was still alive and writing, published his first novel in 1847, died in 1882. The "tradition" which Larkin identifies is an historically recent (and possibly ephemeral) phenomenon which reached its climax over a comparatively short period. Perhaps the last uncontroversially great novels squarely in this "tradition" were Henry James's *The Ambassadors* (1903) and *The Golden Bowl* (1904). We're talking about a form of narrative whose popularity and influence peaked for about a century, 93 years, in fact. Literary historians might, and do, speculate elaborately about the social conditions which gave rise to this period of rich, complex novels of a certain kind.

The "certain kind" is what Northrop Frye called the "low mimetic mode." In a sweeping historical analysis of the modes of fiction and their relationship to mimesis, Frye identified this mode in the very same way as Larkin: describing its distinctive character types—characters whose environments, attitudes, degrees of empowerment all resemble those of middle-class readers:

> If superior neither to other men nor to his environment, the hero is one of us: we respond to a sense of common humanity and demand from the poet [Frye's general term for creative writers] the same canons of probability that we find in our own experience. This gives us the hero of the *low mimetic* mode, of most comedy and realistic fiction. "High" and "low" have no connotations of comparative value, but are purely diagrammatic, as they are when they refer to Biblical critics or Anglicans.

Unlike Larkin and Foyster, Frye separates the low mimetic from other modes of narrative (marked, for example, by gods, wizards and heroes...or the surreal creatures of a Beckett play) in a diagrammatic description. He makes no culture-bound attempt to prescribe one form at the expense of others.

Frye's low mimetic, narrative which deals with the people and problems of everyday life, without attempting to heighten them as in tragedy, epic or melodrama, is the stuff whose passing Larkin mourns. Whether any of the novels of, say, Jane Austen would really match Larkin's more detailed and specific description of what he yearns for (all that stuff about bourgeois stoicism as the "moral tone") is not clear to me, but so be it. In any event, following Frye's lead, let's keep the argument in historical perspective.

There was a very long tradition of narrative before 1811. Many traditions. There is an ocean of narrative with a thousand currents produced since 1904. It seems extraordinary to assume that adults have not been engaged by narrative except over that period of 93 years, so I assume that other forms of narrative or fiction might be written for adults—at least adults *apart from* Larkin, Foyster, and maybe F. R. Leavis—or have adult concerns. In which case, why on earth assume that contemporary science fiction—even contemporary science fiction designed for a sophisticated readership—should resemble anything that Philip Larkin may have had in mind?

A sophisticated science fiction reader might *also* enjoy reading Jane Austen—whether as technical *tour de force*, historical documentation, or even on something like its original semiotic terms (if the reader is cluey about literary and social history). Some of us just might wish to see more works, and more sophisticated works, which revive or revise Austen's narrative mode. But that does not confer on us a right to prescribe that *any* science fiction books should do so, much less assume that Terry Carr was asserting that the Ace Specials were meant to.

II.

Foyster eventually considers some actual texts; so should we.

He picks out William Gibson's *Neuromancer*. Okay: no other '80s novel has been so loudly admired and debated by respectable skiffy critics. The choice of Lewis Shiner's *Deserted Cities of the Heart* is more surprising, since Foyster is purportedly investigating the cyberpunk "sub-genre."

Now: Lewis Shiner may a cyberpunk. Gibson thanks him (along with other, undoubted, cyberpunks) in *Neuromancer*. He is guiltily associated with Datlow, Dozois, *Science Fiction Eye*...and with other novelists who have the same associations in turn. But *Deserted Cities of the Heart* does not seem like a cyberpunk novel to me. Quintessentially, cyberpunk foregrounds the layers and textures of high-tech jungles. It depicts the adaptive mechanisms of men, women and corporations, records their hurried, amoral struggles to survive and prevail. Occasionally a bit of moral tone also endures. Unlike *Frontera*, Shiner's first novel, *Deserted Cities of the Heart* is not much like that. But let it pass; this doesn't necessarily affect Foyster's main argument. Anyway, *Neuromancer* is as cyberpunk they come—*the* paradigm. The classic.

To deal first with Foyster on *Neuromancer*: again, the moves are baffling. Thus:

1. The plot resembles one that was "endemic" in the 1940s and 1950s—a loner from the underclass who enjoys reasonable success with women, but also has reliable male buddies, takes on the most powerful entity in the world, the Tessier-Ashpool artificial intelligences.

2. Instead of being about psi or space-ships, the book is about another "major icon of male teenagers', the computer network.

3. The book's modern attitude to drugs and sexuality reflects rather than advances current values.

4. There is nothing adult (apparently in the sense of resembling Philip Larkin's wished-for mode of fiction) or progressive, in the sense of "fitting Terry Carr's goals" about *Neuromancer*.

For a start, Foyster seems to recognize here that the argument is confusing two quite separate accusation: maturity and originality. In fact, as we've seen, Larkin has a narrow view of what he wants from novels and any novels which fitted his concept would be at least as lacking in originality of ethos, tone and character types as *Neuromancer* on Foyster's (misleading) description of its "endemic" plot. The business about reflecting rather than advancing attitudes to drugs and sexuality is also completely unhelpful; it has nothing to do with either accusation. For the record, the book deals with these things with a swiftness of tempo and a fierce amorality that I find refreshing. I *don't* find that the most prevalent current values are reflected in this book at all, compare the pious claptrap politicians subject us to about how cocaine-users are ultimately giving financial support to evil mercenaries in Bolivia (forgetting that repressive laws breed violence and corruption, in which mercenaries, particularly evil ones, I suppose, are likely to find a handy environmental niche). If the values of *Neuromancer* are truly modern, or reflect one strand of true modernity, that is a point in the book's favor.

Moreover, Foyster's description of the book's plot is startlingly reductive; he conveys nothing of its tone and poetry; he does not seem to care that *Neuromancer* is one of the most rigorous depictions in our whole language of what a counter-factual world might *feel* like. *Neuromancer* has the signatures of a gritty Dashiell Hammett thriller, but written in prose which goes deeper into the textures and modifications of life *in a different reality from our own* than any detective-story prose could cope with. The Thomas Pynchon of *The Crying of Lot 49* seems to stand behind this book, with its obsessive poetry of electronic media, circuits, cybernetics, just as the Pynchon of *Gravity's Rainbow*, a book which *could* have been called *Life During Wartime*, stands behind Shepard's novel which *was*.

Gibson's protagonist, Case, *is* a loner, but has less than reasonable success with women (his first girlfriend, Linda Lee, runs out on him; his partner/lover, Molly, ultimately does likewise) and his male "buddies" are far from reliable—his partner/boss, Armitage, psychically disintegrates as the book goes on. He does not "take on" the Tessier-Ashpool artificial intelligences, though he does do some work for one of them, frustrated by the other, as well as by the international police agency called "Turing', the Tessier-Ashpool business house itself, and others. United as they ultimately become, the artificial intelligences perhaps do end up as the most powerful entity in the world, but they hardly begin so, and the transcendent state they reach is not one where they are interested in wielding anything resembling political power (if we read on, we find in *Count Zero* and *Mona Lisa Overdrive* that the Wintermute-*Neuromancer* amalgam, like its tool, Armitage, undergoes a kind of psychic disintegration, becoming a multiplicity of expressions of itself, behaving like Voodoo spirits).

Foyster's description is so simplistic and distorted that he and I seem to have read different books, and I wonder whether he read *Neuromancer* with any sympathy at all.

In any event, the critique of *Neuromancer* really comes down to two points: that the book is about people at the edge of major change, not merely about domestic relations *within* the society it depicts; and that it is dominated by powerful genre images such as the computer and cyberspace. Guilty on both counts, though, in passing, most commentators have praised Gibson's work not so much for the cyberspace concept as for its extraordinary vividness and ubiquity within his texts. In this way, *Neuromancer* was a step ahead of anything that had been written before, meeting Terry Carr's needs if not Philip Larkin's. To dismiss this book on these grounds, having read it through distorting lenses, *Foyster-shades*, without appreciation of its sparse, tough beauty, is just to miss the point.

With *Deserted Cities of the Heart*, Foyster's game moves are swifter, almost cyberpunk:

1. The novel is unoriginal to the extent that its separate sf elements involving all-in-the-mind time travel are not new, though, Foyster adds, "their combination may be (even though this does not interest me particularly)."

2. It contains a number "male teenage icons', viz: "the rock guitarist (who played with *Hendrix*!)", "the hip journalist (who writes for *Rolling Stone*!)"; and "the anthropologist Working for a Sound Ecological Future', likened by his publisher to Castaneda.

3. Though the characters are engaged with one another, these engagements are generally superficial.

I commented on *Deserted Cities of the Heart* in a previous issue of *ASFR* (Number 18). ["Lewis Shiner's *Deserted Cities of the Heart* [is] an almost-mainstream novel by an acknowledged cyberpunk [...and is] highly recommended [..]. The story is nowhere near as zany and absurdist as the blurb suggests. It's a pretty tough political thriller in which reality is just a little bit alternative to make some points about the morals and aesthetics of guerrilla war in Latin

America, about US political hypocrisy, the residue of Vietnam, about sex, drugs and mirrorshades. There's also rock 'n' roll. It's violent, slick, erotic and clever stuff, with firmly drawn but confused characters in morally complex situations. But maybe Shiner should be reading Broderick, Adams and Wolfe. The ending is nowhere near obscure enough. Sure, there's a touch of the Fantastic as defined by Todorov (were the climactic events governed by genuine magic or wild coincidences?), but the *deus ex machina* elements, and the heroine's ultimate fulfillment-through-pregnancy were so predictable (in terms of the movement of the book) and so *boring* as to make me want to puke. Pity, in what is otherwise such a very good novel."]

Foyster's description seems to me to be (again) reductive and largely asserted rather than argued. But, if only to save space, I'll concentrate on the areas where the novel is guilty as charged—that will enable me to contrast it with *Neuromancer*. The "crimes" of which *Neuromancer* is guilty came down to one: *it is a* (very good but) classic science fiction novel complete with genre icons and plot. By contrast, the real difficulties about *Deserted Cities of the Heart* relate to elements that are quite extraneous from its sf/fantasy tropes. It's plain self-indulgent in using a character from *Rolling Stone* and another character who played guitar with *Hendrix*, and with the whole anthropological set-up. Crude, over-direct, gratuitous. Why not an investigative reporter from almost anywhere else? Why not someone who's just a damned good guitarist? Yet the book could be rewritten with those elements changed. It would get tougher and leaner. Great. And the ending needs added toughness and darkness. There's just a tendency for this novel to be flabby and soft-edged. If I had the privilege of editing something this (otherwise) good, it would probably turn out more like *Neuromancer*, much to its detriment from Foyster's point of view.

But the genuine faults of *Deserted Cities of the Heart* have nothing to do with its science fiction connections. They are the faults endemic (dare I say) to someone like Tom Robbins, writing at the whimsical/magical end of the mainstream—nothing to do with skiffy at all. *Neuromancer*, as it happens, does *not* suffer those particular faults, and it only confuses the issue if we assume that something useful about science fiction is being said when Foyster discusses Shiner.

III.

George Turner's "Sci-Fi and Psi-Fi" begins on the page after "Cyberpunk and the Kids in Costume." Both articles attempt to deal with the relationship between social-individual reality and literary production: lurking behind Foyster's piece is a view that science fiction's development has been constrained by the tastes of a youthful commercial readership; Turner's article attempts to sort out how critical evaluation is shaped by the ideologies, experiences and aesthetic assumptions of particular reviewers.

Turner remarks that three points of difference between himself and John Foyster led to Foyster's reviewing Lucius Shepard's *Life During Wartime* favorably, while he, Turner, is far less impressed. Conveniently, he lists these:

1. Foyster (along with Shepard) lacks Turner's "firsthand experience of soldiers and warfare."
2. Foyster, unlike Turner, "accepts psi as legitimate science fiction."
3. Foyster has a more generous set of beliefs about human nature.

These points were addressed last issue by both Foyster and Shepard. When I had virtually finished this article, Turner's further rebuttal arrived. He is entitled to have his opinions published in this issue without being subverted by my commentary. And this article is a *Foyster* hunt. Accordingly I will add nothing to what I had written about Turner before his latest contribution to the debate. But let this also be said: I value *Life During Wartime* even more than Foyster—for me it is one the most powerful and important science fiction novels *ever*. I hope to find another opportunity to explain why. As for Turner's three points, only the second is relevant to my argument. So I turn to it.

Turner indicates his view of "telepathy and other psi manifestations" thus:

> It is that there are solid physical and psychological reasons militating against the propagation of psi forces, particularly telepathy, and the development of such talents would be an unmitigated disaster for the human race. Evolution usually knocks such anti-

survival factors on the head before they become endemic.

"Endemic," note, is a plague-word in this debate. Endemic to it.

I am skeptical as Turner about the existence of psi forces, despite having written some stories which postulate their existence as a metaphor. But, remember, writers who depict psi need an enabling device either to write an exotic adventure story, or to investigate a moral theme, or both (these are *not* mutually exclusive). Depiction does not entail credulity.

Turner appears to accept this in conceding that the writer "can introduce a fantasy element to describe or suggest a truth...but he may not, in my view, plaster it on to a background of savagely realistic narrative and expect it to be accepted as truth in itself." He proceeds to task Shepard with failing to make psi scientifically plausible (e.g. by describing what cerebral systems are stimulated by the psi drug, explaining why the drug is dangerous, or conceding and developing Turner's pet theory that projecting emotions would be something like method acting—laboriously working oneself into *the role* and then projecting it on the victim).

By implication, this critique of Shepard applies to virtually all science fiction which has used psi, or the many other conventional genre tropes that can't be given convincing scientific foundations. The trouble is that science fiction is not actually read—*decoded*—in this way by anybody much except George Turner. Northrop Frye (remember) writes that we demand from the low mimetic poet "the same canons of probability that we find in our own experience', but Lucius Shepard is no low mimetic poet. Reading any narrative involves the reader's construction of the text, based upon thousands of cumulative and mutually referential signs. These shape, *inter alia*, the acceptable boundaries and forms of empowerment available to characters in the narrative. Whether the narrative oversteps its own boundaries at some point and so loses its authority or "realism" will be a question for the reader which is answered, in practice, tacitly and subliminally. To the extent that it can be argued about, it takes some close and fancy analysis of language to debate what is *really* being promised and delivered. Turner writing on Shepard, like Foyster writing on Gibson, avoids this; his argument relies upon a global attempt to discredit entire subgenres, such as sword and sorcery, which, of course, contain texts that make perfectly good sense, read on their own terms (as well as texts that do not).

Shepard makes the same point more succinctly and colorfully: "To huff and puff about the legitimacy of conventions is worthless prattle." *Exactly*: you can't say anything worthwhile about a science fiction novel by quarrelling in advance with genre conventions that it adopts. You *can* ask, at the level of fine response, whether it uses the conventions in a confused and inconsistent manner, or with a density and reinforcement of purpose that gives rise to "some form of precision and principled statement" (Shepard's words again).

In fact, Shepard's novel establishes and meets its own canons of probability with spectacular success. The writing is not merely powerful and realistic: Shepard writes prose in the high American style of *Gravity's Rainbow*, sentences and paragraphs articulated like road trains, ramified like Morton Bay fig trees, *visionary*. Super-textured, hyperdense with sensoria, ultra-real to the point of hallucinogenesis. It's the textual equivalent of *Apocalypse Now* deepened, solidified, granulated by some brain-raving wired-up hippy's Bad Acid. His prose, his tropes and tactics are cyberpunk and magic realism combined, as someone said before me, *like* Pynchon (yes!) but with an unrelenting narrative design that keeps you reading and turning and reading where the diffuse structure of *Gravity's Rainbow* puts even my word-oriented deconstructor friends to sleep reading in the back of a car charging down the Hume Highway (this happens); and even I, with a Ph.D. on Frye and Pynchon and on and on, start turning pages hurriedly, wishing Slothrop would forget his name, get on with that narratalogy of *sparagmos*, mate.

His kind of writing, Shepard's, enables the fusion of modes. Descriptions of commonplace activities fuse with those of peculiar, anomalous events, with fables within the fable, overt drug fantasies...and the "true" phantasma of mind contacts. The whole never ravels, never relents, almost never shows its seams, and it achieves its formidable social/psychological purposes. *Life During Wartime* is an extraordinary and sinister portrayal of human identity, stripped of limitations, fast losing its claim to common humanity.

Perhaps surprisingly, Foyster makes a similar point, responding to Turner. Surprising, because he seems to apply different rules when attacking Gibson from those he wants to grab for in defense of Shepard. Foyster on Gibson:

> Earlier novels were built around rocket ships, blasters, inter-stellar (or inter-galactic) empires, psi powers, and so on....*Neuromancer* is built around a latter-day equivalent of psi and the rocket-ship com-

bined: the mind powers released by humans linked into computer networks. Psi and the rocket-ship were the glamor icons of lonely teenagers in the 1940s and 1050s, whereas in the 1980s the computer, and especially the computer in a network, has a similar iconic function.

The *same* Foyster (on Turner on Shepard):

> I therefore take it as a reasonable assumption that, except in the crudest pulp fiction, a serious writer uses psi as a social device, rather than a scientific (as George Turner seems to prefer it, a Gernsbackian) device. I don't assert that George Turner has to have my view, of course, but I note that if that scientific purism is maintained then one locks oneself out of a large amount of reading and interpretation. After all, there really aren't orcs, are there? Or dragons? Or spaceships? Or near-immortals?

Good! But why should the benefit of that same latitudinarian aesthetic be denied Gibson and Shiner in Foyster's reductive look at kids-in-costume and cyberpunks? After all, we could view orcs, dragons, spaceships and near-immortals through *Foyster-shades* rather than *Turner-shades*. We could list them out as the fantasy icons of teenage boys (and girls—especially in the horsey case of Anne McCaffrey). Now I don't see anything artful or dishonest, precisely, in the way Foyster slams the use of conventional genre images in one context (criticizing them as fantasy icons) but defends them in another (where someone else criticized them for being unscientific). No...but the discordancy shows how damn tough it will always be to write consistently about these things. I have to bite the apple, if not the bullet, and apply Foyster's words, point out that *of course* Gibson was seizing upon the computer network/cyberspace concept as a social device not as a Gernsbackian device or a mere teenage icon, and...but what the heck! I think the point is made.

In which case maybe we can all stop thrashing about futilely, blurry whirligigs berating the codes that breed us. We can drop back on the useful function of skiffy criticism, to deepen our understanding of (yes, and joy in) the literature which we choose and which still excites some of us. That means reading science fiction as if it were a legitimate mode of narrative in its own right. Which it is.

And *that* means reading it closely on its own terms, not on some slack set of terms appropriate to a college course in Bourgeois Representational Narrative 1811-1904. Reading without denying ourselves, reading as sophisticated science fiction readers (aren't we?).

Not critics in costume.

SUCH HEAT IN THE KITCHEN!

by George Turner

Shepard and Foyster assert that the title of my "Point of View" essay disguises a low motive. Shepard sees my objective as self-aggrandizement while Foyster finds it a display of obsession and neurosis. Each selects the reading which suits his point of view, which is what the essay was about. Between them, they support me!

Fay Weldon has noted that "Writing is like putting your head out of a trench to be shot at"; after thirty years of it I am used to the rattle of musketry and can even absorb the occasional well-aimed shot with only a sigh for my imperfections. Lucius Shepard will live to do likewise and to realize that one should never reply while shaking with rage.

Let me say at once that his complaint that I have misread the end of his novel may be justified. I have been wrong before this and admitted it in print (which is more than most critics will do) but must point out that this does not vitiate my basic premise, which is that the novel fails to command suspension of disbelief because its drama is rooted in an unreality which the author makes no attempt to justify. The powerful writing—and it is powerful—is expended on an ultimately meaningless subject.

Three points should be addressed. One is his claim that generals make disastrous errors and a novelist must be allowed to do likewise. Yes? But generals pay for their errors and so must the novelist when a little enquiry among suitable people could have put him right. Getting details right in an imagined environment can be difficult, but one has to try.

Picking on Norman Mailer's "fuggin" for "fucking" was a more excusable misjudgment in that Shepard would not be old enough to recall the literary scene of 1948 when *The Naked and the Dead* was published. The freedom of expression enjoyed by the modern writer did not exist then; it was being fought for by writers and publishers, fought against by the obscenity laws of most countries and the outcries of old ladies of all sexes. Some books got away with explicit language, some did not; the scene was chaotic but the trade pushed steadily at the barriers. Mailer (or perhaps his publisher) met the prohibition with the impertinent invention of "fuggin," which made plain exactly what it meant while remaining technically within the bounds of decent expression. In that day an odd "fucking" or two might have got by but not the couple of hundred repetitions in that novel. *The Naked and the Dead* did not win the obscenity war alone but it was a notable win from which today's writers derive the benefit. Yet as recently as 1982 the late lamented Terry Carr insisted that I find substitutes for "fucking" and "shit" lest ladies of the Legion of Decency (or whatever) tear copies of *Universe 12* from library shelves in the American mid-west.

My familiarity with GIs, which Shepard questions, covers some twenty years, both in and out of active service. I find Joe Haldeman's restrained portraits in *War Year* more recognizable than the superheated products of film and popular novel, also the very human trainee marines in Kubrick's *Full Metal Jacket,* but few in other major war films. I agree with Shepard that wars decades apart do not resemble each other—but the men who fight them change little. Save in extreme circumstances they remain decently human—which is true of peacetime history also. The circumstances of the soldiers in *Life During Wartime* were not extreme in any military definition.

The rest of his letter, when you look closely, turns out to be mostly angry and highly personal conjecture without much substance. Put it down to that bout of flu he mentions near the end.

I know how Lucius Shepard feels with his work under attack, having been there so often, but John Foyster has no such excuse for his tirade. It seems to have been concocted on some Zeus-throne of majestic rightness, with much hurling of thunderbolts, unaware of never hitting his target square on. He sets the tone with a paragraph of plodding satire (it needs a lighter touch) on a point so peripheral as to be unworthy of mention. Its purpose appears to be to prepare the reader for a display of magisterial opinion which will grind the freethinking apostate into the dust. This freethinker denies Zeus his worship and feels not at all ground.

First, what makes him think that I missed the fact that war is only a backdrop to the novel? The second paragraph in my article indicates otherwise. Did it have to be spelt out? My criticism remains valid whether it is backdrop or foreground; even a context has to be correctly observed. John doesn't really deal with disagreement; he swipes at it and passes on.

My mention of *The Naked and the Dead* excites further ire. That he wrote of an altogether other aspect escapes him rather than me. Things equal to different things are not equal to each other.

Then John tells how he has solved the "critical bias" problem. Alas, he has solved nothing; he has adopted a mode well known in reviewing and no doubt suited to his present thinking. Next year may be different. All methods have their pluses and minuses; none covers all the possibilities and personal bias remains, no matter how the reviewer may wriggle.

His next move is a resort to open insult ("obsession" and "neurotic"), self-demeaning from a man of his intellect and backed up with a shameless misstatement saying that this obsession "he devotes all his energy to arguing about." At the time of writing he had probably worked himself up to believing it (my opportunity here to offer a psychoanalytical slur, but I will mind my literary good manners); by now he may well have reconsidered. Of course I have argued about psi—when the occasion called for it. It makes scarcely a crotchet, let alone an obsession; to me it is just one of the fantasy elements that drain meaning from much modern science fiction. Shepard also takes this up in the spirit of: "If others do it, why shouldn't I?" A fair enough plea, I suppose, if you prefer assembly line props to creative thinking.

There follows at once an ersatz quotation (real con-man stuff, this one):

> "All others," he [Turner] has effectively said, "have gotten it wrong, and I alone (in several works) have dealt with psi in an honest, a *scientific* way."

I have never said, effectively or ineffectively, anything of the sort. (Nor do I ever use "gotten.") I certainly have written that I have indicated my opinion of psi by my treatment of it in several tales and novels but I have never used the words "honest" or "scientific" or "alone" in that fashion. John hides behind "effectively" because he has no genuine quotation or reference to offer. (He will need quite a few of them to justify the tone of his attack.) What I have always tried to demonstrate is that a little common sense and application of what we already know about the working of the mind makes psi at worst an obvious fairy tale and at best poses questions science fiction should seek answers to. I expect better of John than fabrication to drive home a non-existent nail.

His next bit is fascinating, on the "social" function of psi in science fiction: "its offering of salvation in a godless world threatened by nuclear destruction." I suggest that psi is mere whistling in the dark, promising nothing, unable even to demonstrate its existence. Prayer might do better—it sometimes puts a bit of backbone into believers—but most of us prefer to dodge the fairy floss and seek practical solutions, which are not impossible. Or did he mean it only in the fictional context? Then it means nothing because fiction is its only context.

The next paragraph is about the dreariness of scientific purism and how orcs and dragons and such are needed because in denying the use of them "one locks oneself out of a large amount of reading and interpretation." I don't want to lock them out. They have their place in fiction but can only rarely intrude into a serious work because it is difficult to make a valid point on a basis of fantasy. The premises are suspect and belief is withheld. Fantasy provides metaphors, which is not enough. Few fantasies in all the world's literature have persisted in print by reason of their practical or intellectual content; the mythologies covered the field before literature began and most of what remains is imitation. The real-plus-fantastic mixture can and does make acceptable entertainment; when it aspires to seriousness, the seams gape.

Another gem awaits us: "If George Turner wants to come to grips with real science fiction then he has to shake off his Gernsbackian science-fiction-as-prediction nonsense..." On this subject George Turner has in fact written: "Futurology is about as dependable as teacup reading," and has enlarged on that statement in the Postscript to *The Sea and Summer (Drowning Towers)* in the US). Is a refusal to fantasize the mark of the leper? I prefer dreams with meaning and John knows very well that does not mean "nuts and bolts." And what is this "real" science fiction? If John knows he may be alone in the world, guardian of the secret. One recalls the famous, "What I point at when I say it."

So Shepard writes about the relationship of science fiction to the real world? Good for him. And what he writes is gospel, is it? As an isolated fact, that news is no argument for anything.

John's response turns out to be an unprimed thunderbolt with no aiming system. There's certainly plenty of thunder but no lightning, much opinion which it seems the reader is expected instantly to recognize as truth writ in concrete, but not a fact to back it up. It is a personal viewpoint seeking to impose itself. and personal viewpoint is where the whole thing started.

Let the Rev. Richard Barham, a notable fantasist, have the last word:

> He cursed him in standing, in sitting, in lying;
> He cursed him in walking, in riding, in flying;
> He cursed him in living, he cursed him in dying!
> Never was heard such a terrible curse!
> But what gave rise
> To no little surprise,
> Nobody seemed one penny the worse!
>
> ("The Jackdaw of *Rheims*")

LETTER FROM GEORGE TURNER

Russell Blackford writes: "Shepard's novel establishes and meets its own canons of probability with spectacular success." My complaint was that Shepard's method *established* nothing. He offered a *statement* (about ESP and the power urge) on the understanding that the reader, brainwashed by some fifty years of the same, would accept it, and wrote his novel as though it had been established. (Shepard himself noted that he did only what others do, i.e., take advantage of a convention. I feel that conventions should be taken out and dusted every couple of years—with an eye to dumping.) No "probability" was at any stage proposed except on a fantasy basis.

Russell writes also: "That means reading science fiction as if it were a legitimate mode of narrative in its own right. Which it is. And *that* means reading it closely on its own terms [...]." The rest of the sentence seems to mean that anybody not agreeing with this is old-hat and incapable of reasoned criticism.

Well, I stand on my right to reject any novelist's or genre's terms if I find them unacceptable, and to criticize on that basis. Novelists, particularly in popular genres (romance, private eye, espionage, science fiction), have done more than enough to feed uncritical minds with garbage which insidiously, by repetition, takes on the air of truth. Terms should be questioned, particularly when, as in the case under consideration, an unprovable premise is used to make a statement about the human psyche. That I agree with the statement is irrelevant; what matters is that no justification is offered for the making of it. It results in the sort of product which, by reason of the extreme persuasiveness of the writing (one can't deny Shepard's literary talent) prompts the reader to react with *How right he is!* without considering the possibility of an opposite verdict. In this case, despite my personal view, I see that an opposite verdict is quite possible.

(If Shepard had wanted a relevant example of his thesis in action, he could have used Stalin, whose excesses—accomplished without ESP—make Mingolla's look like nursery games.)

Let us by all means read fantastic literature for pleasure and speculation but let us also not permit its fabulations to cloud the realities of logic and knowledge with which, willy-nilly, we must confront the world and the future. Historically, attempts to follow fantasy to its "logical" conclusion have plunged the world into bloodshed and misery. Its terms are suspect.

LETTER FROM LUCIUS SHEPARD

I've just finished reading George Turner's response to my letter, which in turn responded to his commentary on my novel, *Life During Wartime*. From my reading of his piece, I'm of the opinion that Mr. Turner did not pay very close attention to what I wrote, and I'm not at all surprised that he has tried to pass off my letter as a choleric outburst from someone who one day soon will learn to temper his reactions and accept the judgments of his betters: to say "tut, tut, young man" will sometimes disguise the fact that one has nothing of consequence to say. He suggests that I was "shaking with anger" when I responded to his article. While I will admit to annoyance—I am by nature intolerant of puffery—I was not shaking then, nor am I shaking now, other than with amusement, because Mr. Turner has misapprehended—or else has chosen to avoid confronting—almost every point that I have made.

For instance, in his original article he stated that the design of my artillery base, the Ant Farm, was strategically unsound and that this testified to my lack of experience with things martial and to the unrealistic nature of my scenario. I replied that I had found such unsoundness and incompetence to be characteristic of the modern military, and that the war upon which I modeled my fictive war was prone to unsoundness in almost every area—had I described a strategically perfect war, it would hardly have been realistic according to my experience. In his response to my letter, Mr. Turner seems to believe that I was putting forward the notion that because "generals make disastrous errors [...] a novelist must be allowed to do likewise." I do not consider a rendering in fiction of unsound practices in any way an error, and I am at a loss to understand how Mr. Turner's statement relates to what I have said. I can only wonder in what strange universe the logic that provoked this curious statement was fabricated.

In his original article Mr. Turner claimed that I had no knowledge of how soldiers spoke and pointed to *The Naked and the Dead* as a novel that embodied the honest-to-Jesus true-life vernacular of soldiers everywhere. I do not consider *The Naked and the Dead* a work of such biblical significance, nor do I feel that it has more than passing relevance to wars fought some thirty years later than the one it describes. In stating this, I mentioned the fact that Mailer had used the word "fuggin" for "fuckin", and now Mr. Turner has seized upon this in an attempt to defuse my argument that soldiers in wars separated by decades tend to have different speech mannerisms—an argument I would not have been forced to raise by anyone with a degree of common sense. Mr. Turner makes note of the fact that "fuggin" was used to avoid a censorship problem. While this, indeed, is true, it begs the issue, and is not in the least responsive to my point.

Mr. Turner then goes on to state:

> I agree with Shepard that wars fought decades apart do not resemble each other—but the men who fight them change little. Save in extreme circumstances they remain decently human—which is true of peacetime history also. The circumstances of the soldiers in *Life During Wartime* were not extreme in any military definition.

The first portion of this statement appears to be aimed at the comment in my letter that the men who fought in World War II were on the average some eight years older and represented far more of a cross-section of the American populace than did those who saw action in Vietnam—the American contingent who participated in that futile exercise consisted in large part of poor whites and minority groups, had an average age of nineteen, and had a much weaker motivation to fight than did the soldiers of World War II, who were doing battle against a madman who menaced all the civilized world. Mr. Turner's comments do no more than restate what he originally said, insisting that his impression of the behavior of men in World War II—an impression that, judging by his claims as to their nobility and decency, seems derived from a more innocent period of the cinema than he accuses me of imitating—be taken as a template for the behavior of men who were fighting against guerrillas, who were plagued by drugs, by a hapless chain of command, and whose morale was afflicted by strident vilification on the home front. Given the sum of these disparities, Mr. Turner's position is patently absurd, unless he is referring to the fact that all fighting men are governed by basic human drives, a simplistic point that has no bearing upon the matter at hand. As to the second portion of his statement, I will only say that "decency" is not a word I associate with the battlefield, and I must assume that Mr. Turner's definition of "extreme circumstances" is not mine. In this statement, he again avoids coming to grips with the issues I have raised.

Mr. Turner continues to chide me for using genre conventions, stating that using them is all right to do "if you prefer assembly-line props to creative thinking." What can I say more than I have already? I can't recall a single science fiction novel I have read that does not resort to this kind of usage to one degree or another. Such props are there *to be used,* they are the furnishings of our genre. FTL, psi, alternative worlds, and so forth are things we depend upon our readers to understand, just as a mainstream author depends upon his readers to understand the basic furnishings of a city street without having to describe them in minute detail and explain how they came to be. The subject of *Life During Wartime* was not psi—psi was merely part of the furniture, or more accurately—one of the colors I utilized in order to enhance the book's central considerations. Of course Mr. Turner's harping on this matter relates to his insistence that the Siamese twins of science fiction and fantasy be sundered at the hip and sent to their separate corners. I am unable to fathom why this seems of moment to him, but I much prefer to remain in the dark rather than having to listen to him explain it.

Mr. Turner gleefully interprets the fact that John Foyster and I have approached in different ways the refutation of the arguments put forward in his original article as validation of his childishly obvious point that one's critical judgments are affected by one's background (I hardly thought this matter was in doubt). That he chooses to ignore the larger fact that John Foyster and I are merely taking note of two huge holes in a leaky bucket lends support to my belief that his motives in having at my novel were self-aggrandizing, even if only to the end of puffing himself up. In his current piece, he salts his rhetoric with all manner of gentle remonstrance and talk of "literary manners" in an attempt to deflect attention from his failure to sound a single argument of substance. His dismissal of my letter as being the product of misguided anger strikes me as much the same thing—a cheap tactic of evasion, of dismissing salient arguments to which one is unable to respond by countenancing them as personal attacks, a tactic acceptable, perhaps, in the political arena, but one completely inappropriate to the rigors of critical debate. It's quite clear that he does not choose to debate, only to pontificate, and I am led to conclude that either Mr. Turner would be incapable of recognizing a substantial argument if it jumped up and bit him, or else that he has some particular axe to grind. In deference to Mr. Turner's skill as a writer and the mental acuity this implies, I have decided to believe that he is not so ingenuous as to be unaware of what he is doing and what he is failing to do.

> [...] I have received a number of bad reviews and unfavorable comments in my time, and until now I have quarreled with none of them. But I quarrel with Mr. Turner's because—as I stated—its tone is smug and condescending, its logic an utter sham, and its claim to scholarship entirely specious.

I freely admit that the tone of my responses to Mr. Turner has been somewhat more harsh than that usually found in critical journals, but I see no reason not to be direct—I don't wish to risk further misapprehensions on Mr. Turner's part, and I do not feel that his treatment of me deserves any better in the way of courtesy. As he himself mentions, when one essays a career in writing; one opens oneself up to the critics. Fair enough. But the same thing applies to those who criticize, and while I am willing to bear the whips and scorns of intelligent criticism, I draw the line at allowing whomever has a clot of mud handy to hurl it at me without a return volley. Mudslinging is something I take personally. Perhaps this is unmannered of me, perhaps it is boorish and something just not done, but frankly it seems far more unmannered and boorish to launch such a thoroughly unsupported attack as Mr. Turner's, and then to hide one's true intent—whatever it may be—behind a facade of effete, pseudoacademic posing and so-called "literary manners." I would have respected Mr. Turner a good deal more if he had said he hated my guts, burned my books in public, and called my mother a whore. That, at least, would have smacked of honest emotion.

If Mr. Turner cares to step down from his eminence, to drop his tone of lectoral pomp and engage me in a civilized dialogue with real arguments and real logic, I would be delighted to do so—on any subject he may choose. I would be especially interested in hearing his views on what is and is not fantasy; at the very least I suspect that there would be some clinical interest in the results of such a debate. Otherwise, I can find no purpose in continuing this exchange—though I'm almost certain that Mr. Turner will attempt to provide me with one, for it is evident from the two pieces I have read of his in *ASFR* that his usage of these pages is merely an exercise in vanity, and that his purposes are not those of intellectual truth, but involve the celebration of his own self-importance. I have no intention of providing him with a further platform.

A COMMENT FROM JOHN FOYSTER

The long-suffering readers of *ASFR* had to endure an overkill in the Summer 1989 issue, generated, alas, by some of my remarks: George Turner responding to my "Desperately Seeking Lucius" in Number 21, and Russell Blackford responding in part to an article of mine back in June of 1989.

Neither Blackford nor Turner has anything substantial to say, in my view, but they say it *differently*.

I'm not sure where George Turner got the idea that simply denying the truth of what I wrote, paragraph by paragraph, constituted any sort of argument. Perhaps it is a result of listening to too many politicians or spruikers for failed capitalist enterprises.

But whatever the reason for George's confusion of denial with refutation, the way he chose to reply will at least draw the reader's attention back to what I originally wrote. There the reader will be free to explore what was actually said and I am quite happy with what I wrote in "Desperately Seeking Lucius."

Russell Blackford's more extensive remarks require a lengthier response; not because they have any more content, but because the way they are framed will lead the unsuspecting reader to believe that Blackford is actually dealing with the argument I presented so long before. Such a reader, failing to make use of the published text, will mistakenly associate me with the peculiar views advanced by RB as being *mine*. Such a reader needs to be encouraged to go back to the original text, at which point it will become clear that RB is dealing with some strange fantasized version of my argument, perhaps as a result of an advanced case of FBS [Fannish Brown-nose Syndrome].

Furthermore, RB's avoidance of the point I was seeking to make is an example of just the phenomenon I was seeking to draw attention to, and the important point—well, the point which *I* think is important—is at risk of being lost once again, and I don't want that to happen.

Despite RB's advanced thinking, as demonstrated by his frequent appeals to Northrop Frye, he has unfortunately failed in his "Foyster hunt" in part because he does not read carefully enough what is really plain text; he appears to indicate, for example, that he has read "Desperately Seeking Lucius," and indeed quotes from it, but somehow RB has failed to note the passage in which I describe how I go about dealing with the writings of others.

That RB misreads me is evidenced immediately by what he presents as a summary of the argument made by me; six points are listed which purport to present the sequence of my argument, but you will not find in RB's list the center of the matter, an argument about an existence theorem.

After this central point is omitted RB invites the reader to assume that my writing floated in a contextless void, enabling the simple point my article made to be swept back under the carpet; even then RB is unable to resist the temptation to misrepresent, for within the unfocused model RB invents he ignores the key role played by one of the points he did note...But perhaps RB felt constrained by the tight self-imposed writing limit of four and a half pages he set for himself, for after all I had taken a whole three pages myself.

Readers who do not choose to go back to my original article may find the following summary useful.

1. Finding myself having to talk about "adult science fiction," I looked for some suggestion as to what characteristics it might have.

2. In an introduction to the new series of Ace Specials, Terry Carr said some things which seemed to be helpful.

3. Furthermore, there's been some concern expressed recently (by Silverberg and Spinrad, in particular) that the science fiction market has been turning into a teenaged-only market, making it difficult or impossible for writers who write for a non-teenaged market to sell their books.

4. Indeed, a similar phenomenon has been noticed outside of science fiction, for example by Philip Larkin (who actually refers specifically to "science fiction rubbish" and thus reminds us of how we are perceived by outsiders).

5. Maybe we can learn more about this by looking at whether at least some science fiction is meeting the criteria set down by Terry Carr.

6. If we do that, we find that a couple of sample cyberpunk novels, Gibson's *Neuromancer* and Shiner's *Deserted Cities of the*

Heart, don't seem to match up to Carr's definition, so cyberpunk at least isn't what Terry had in mind.

7. In fact, if you look at it closely, cyberpunk, as represented by these two novels, is indeed the kind of teen fiction about whose dominance of the world of science fiction Silverberg and Spinrad were expressing concern.

Not much like RB's description? But that's exactly what the flow of "The Role of the Science Fiction Reader: Cyberpunk and the Kids in Costume" is.

The key question addressed in my article is, plainly enough, is teenaged science fiction being squeezed out of a competitive market?

On the face of it, this is not the most profound question ever asked in the field of literature, yet it seems to present significant problems to at least some seemingly careful readers (my title bowed, of course, not only to the reader-response school, but also to the role of the teen reader in shaping the science fiction field identified by Silverberg and Spinrad and finally to the lack of response to my January 1987 editorial). Why is it that the dominance of the science fiction field by works targeted at young readers is not a subject which may be brought up in polite company?

It is really impossible to doubt their dominance; it is not merely the listings of books which appear endlessly in *Locus,* trumpeting more and more of the same, but even the encroachment of such works on the Nebula Awards at least, where a work which is (how shall I put this delicately?) urbanely unsophisticated can be judged the best novel of the year. Good luck to Ms. Bujold, one might sportingly say, but if that is the kind of fiction which her fellow members of the SFWA admire so intensely, then perhaps we ought to pack up our critical bags and retreat to that unfailing fawning upon which RB so generously relies.

My initial intention must be, however, set aside at least temporarily, since there appears to be so little interest in it. For not only does RB fail to take up the question posed: he heads off in a direction of his own, and from this he ought perhaps to be discouraged.

For example, when Terry Carr sets up as criteria elements such as plot and style (which he does) and I am plainly using that pattern, it is not easily open to RB to bring in other criteria without at least trying to make some sort of case in terms of relevance to the matter being argued. To assert baldly that I write nothing of *Neuromancer's* "tone and poetry" as RB does is to pronounce one's incapacity to carry an argument in a grave sense: it demonstrates that RB must clutch at elements not being considered; it demonstrates that RB believes that tone and poetry are not to be found in works for teenaged readers (for otherwise why would he advance the proposition?); it demonstrates the impact of an advanced case of FBS.

Such a situation is scarcely likely to aid one's understanding, unless one succeeds in penetrating the underlying reason for RB's dyspepsia; that he really and objectively has misunderstood the point of the argument. This is made clear with RB's words "To dismiss this book on these grounds"...

Who is dismissing what?

Neuromancer, I wrote, neither fitted Terry Carr's goal nor was "adult." To fail to meet Terry Carr's goals for the Ace series is not, it seems to me, fatal. RB appears to be advancing the case that when I argue that a particular work is targeted at teenagers I am dismissing the work or regarding it as inferior to "adult" fiction.

This is not the case. I am (laboriously) making the point that there is more to life than being a teenager. Unlike RB, I am constantly brought into contact with teenagers and their interests and disinterests. This helps to rid one of the notion that difference constitutes inferiority. But of course if the main point of my article has been missed, then I suppose RB must stumble about looking for some case to make.

Now the truth of the matter is that it is quite difficult to miss the point of my piece which I placed, perhaps too deviously for RB, in my final paragraph:

> ...the primary case being advocated here [...] is that there is decreasing room for science fiction which is not derived from the fantasies of teenagers, especially and generally male teenagers.

Now it may be that RB and other readers didn't get this far, because the few lines preceding this place the question of the other qualities of fiction in the appropriate context—had RB read them he would not have had to trouble himself for four and a half pages.

But RB goes a good deal further than this; as he demonstrates to a greater and greater extent the ravages of FBS ("I value *Life During Wartime* even more than Foyster does—for me, it is one of the most powerful and important science fiction novels ever") he also wanders jerkily through a mass of assertions about what may or may not legitimately be said about written works.

A fair chunk of this stuff is directed towards the legitimacy of my consideration of *Neuromancer* as peddling male teen icons. (Hm, I thought it a fair enough point, since it includes the two elements in the argument—the dominance of the teen market and the question of what kind of conventions are adopted in *Neuromancer.)*

This is not, RB pontificates, legit, and he calls upon Shepard in support. Two can play at that game, and I believe that in dealing with those conventions I was doing no more than has been advocated by at least one major literary critic, namely to examine a writer "in terms of the conventions he chose."

In this case it is appropriate to dwell extensively upon the nature of the conventions of a work, because for many readers these can make up the "essence" of science fiction—whence "techies" and so on.

All of these forms of science fiction have a legitimate place. But it does not follow that they should force out of existence science fiction written for adults—which is where we came in, or at least one of us did.

LETTER FROM PETER NICHOLLS

I wrote to you in January suggesting among other things that *ASFR* would be improved if it no longer published contributions by George Turner, John Foyster, and Norman Talbot. A bit later on I felt I'd been needlessly offensive, and telephoned you some weeks back, requesting that my letter be made retrospectively "Not for Publication."

It just goes to show that first thoughts are best, for now I've read the April issue, Number 23, I feel the same way even more strongly. Come on, fellers, enough is enough.

It's been suggested to me that *ASFR*'s policy of letting arguments ramble on endlessly is justifiable in that controversy gives the magazine pungency and juice. But it doesn't, honestly it doesn't. It would only do that if contestants were evenly matched.

What we have is ongoing tackiness, arguments *ad hominem*, and endlessly whining last words being allowed to the local lads. Turner, Foyster, and Talbot all have them this time. We're not talking about critical discourse here, for light is not being shed. We're talking about three old farts pompously and endlessly regurgitating pedestrian bees from their shrunken bonnets.

Even that wouldn't be so bad if they did it demurely, but their combination of malice and self-importance is degrading both to its producers, puffed up and squirting poison like toads, and its courteous and patient recipients. You really shouldn't be publishing this stuff.

It makes the five editors and the magazine itself look bad when you publish nominally critical material that is self-evidently fatuous. Where are your standards? Can Talbot, each of whose contributions to the Benford/Le Guin debate would certainly have been failed as first-year student offerings by me, really be a university teacher?

Let me draw breath and get down to cases. George Turner's medieval critical views are in themselves boring, because like John Foyster he confuses text with narrative. The reductive technique of both of them is first to make an extraordinarily simplistic synopsis of whatever it is they're purporting to discuss, and then to criticize the synopsis for being simplistic. It's a bit like an arsonist torching the Taj Mahal, and then saying with the smug air of one who knew it all the time, "What a pile of burned-out junk!"

But it goes further than this. Turner's discussion of Lucius Shepard's *Life During Wartime* was both savage and patently wrong. These insults are compounded by the appalling tone of lofty condescension that George assumes as a matter of course. I needn't go into this in detail, since Shepard's splendid letters say it all fairly politely and very devastatingly. George is like a spiteful footballer who gnashes someone's leg in the scrum, and then complains to the referee about an unprovoked attack on his teeth. The sour smell of wounded vanity is evident in most of what he writes, as it is with Foyster.

Foyster's most recent critical pieces assume that a novel can be discussed in terms of his own infantile précis, following which he gleefully points to its "adolescence." Russell Blackford points to some of William Gibson's many strengths; Foyster cries "Foul," saying his argument is restricted to "plot and style." One hardly knows where to start with stuff like this.

For one thing, John, if you restrict a discussion of a book to plot, you're talking baby-talk. The meaning of a book simply cannot be derived from plot analysis. Secondly, by admitting the word "style," your whole argument goes down the tubes, since it was precisely Gibson's style that Blackford rightly picked you up on, for what are "tone and poetry" if not the very heart of an author's style? Thirdly, plot and style can *not,* positively cannot, be separated as if they were philosophically distinct entities. The way a writer says a thing is part of what he's saying. Fourthly, fiction in part *about* adolescence, as Gibson's trilogy certainly is, is not the same thing as *being* adolescent. Fifthly, even if it were, what makes you suppose the deep human yearnings and miseries of nineteen-year-olds suddenly disappear when you're twenty-one? If you've never diagnosed the adolescent in the adult, you've never looked in a mirror.

But all this would make your unnecessary, self aggrandizing and enormously long letter merely boring, and it's worse than that. Is your control of your own voice so negligible that you cannot tell how wincingly out-of-place schoolboy abuse is in a literary journal, especially when it comes from an editor? How do you dare to respond to Blackford's lively but careful analysis with phrases like "fannish brown-nose syndrome" and "unfailing fawning"? Can't you hear the petulant malice in your own voice? Can't you see what it makes you look like?

It comes as no surprise that George Turner dedicated his most recent novel to John Foyster, for they have much in common. As critics, they discuss surfaces only; they seem wholly unaware of the function of metaphor even when talking about such essentially metaphorical sf as Gibson's and Shepard's; and they seem unable to recognize a sub-text even when it is effectively the heart of the text itself. This is fan criticism at its most definitively puerile. However George's last word, if it is his last word, though redundant, was a good deal more dignified than Foyster's.

Last and least, Norman Talbot. He is truly disgraceful. I have personally known both Ursula Le Guin and Gregory Benford for many years, and of course I've read their books. As they know, I would disagree with them (in different ways) on a variety of issues. But for many reasons they deserve a great deal of respect, Benford no less than Le Guin.

Ursula doesn't need groupies, Mr. Talbot. She's a tough lady who can look after herself. She certainly doesn't need the tone that you adopt towards her supposed detractors, the falsetto whining alternating with hysterical insult, which is quite astonishing coming from a supposedly reputable academic. You're like some ghastly Walter Raleigh falling fatly into the mud you were attempting to protect her from with your cloak.

And in your last word in *ASFR* 23, when you had an opportunity to apologize for your previous mistakes, what did you do? You feebly postured, pouting like some grubby schoolboy, and said "it wasn't my fault." "My anger was in defense of great literature, not for any selfish motive." Do you suppose the readers can't see through you? Patting yourself on the back won't mend things. Especially when you're still abusing Benford with terms like "incompetent," "worthless," "for the first time in his life...guilty of modesty." Really, I could despair. This is Australian literary criticism at its apogee? How do you tell the apogee from the nadir?

Benford is an experienced and stimulating literary critic, as well as a (sometimes) distinguished novelist; he is habitually generous even to writers who work in modes very different from his own hard sf. Le Guin's *The Dispossessed* is deeply interesting but certainly too flawed to be termed "great." The way one talks about these things is fairly to confront the issues on both sides. [...]

Now that the SF Collective has by implication allowed gratuitous personal insult into its pages as a valid part of critical discourse,

I feel no need to apologize for any of the above, which strikes me looking back as maturely moderate in comparison with the tone adopted by its targets

AN EDITORIAL COMMENT FROM RUSSELL BLACKFORD

Well, I don't know where to start with this. George Turner, John Foyster, and Norman Talbot seem to me to be dependable, rough-and-tumble controversialists whose writings I enjoy even when I disagree with them. Their approaches are, in fact, very different from each other's, which is why they're often at each other's throats. We welcome submissions from all three. Sorry Peter.

However, your letter has raised an important issue which was already troubling me and some other members of the *ASFR* Collective: namely, the tendency of the controversialists in our magazine to go, on occasion, beyond merely robust, lively and witty attacks on their targets—and to rely on *ad hominem* argument and personal abuse.

Take the example of Professor Talbot: he engages in the most comprehensive and intense possible counterattacks on other critics—all in defense of literature whose beauties he considers to be underappreciated. His critique of Brooke-Rose on Tolkien [published in *ASFR* 13, and reprinted in *Chained to the Alien*] was a *tour de force* example of this. Good on him. We're proud of publishing such contributions. And two of us (Janeen Webb and myself) owe a lot to Norman Talbot. We learnt much of what we know about literature, literary and cultural criticism, and literary theory from him; he supervised both of our Ph.D. dissertations, and with great skill and generosity.

But in this case I believe that Talbot went over the top in his critique of Benford on Le Guin (and I'm pretty sure that Janeen would agree).

To elaborate: the beauties of Le Guin's text can look after themselves; *The Dispossessed* has become one of the few true canonical works of sf, and rightly so. Even Greg Benford acknowledged this state of affairs, and that it was justified. But that does not, in its turn, justify the thread of savagely personal attack running through Talbot's piece on Benford (at least one of whose books—*Timescape*—also belongs in the sf canon).

I won't comment on the merits of Foyster's piece replying to my "Skiffy and Mimesis" article. But I do say this: "Skiffy and Mimesis" was fairly aggressive at times in its defense of Gibson etc.—but it was also careful, as Nicholls says, and good-humored, even when sending up its targets (it was a Foyster hunt, yes). I tried to pay close attention to the literary qualities of texts and the logical structures of arguments, and I tried to avoid mere abuse.

I'm unhappy with Foyster's response only for this reason: it undermines the credibility and reputation of the magazine, when Foyster resorts to accusing an antagonist of something called "fannish brown-nose syndrome," apparently for defending the literary qualities of William Gibson and Lucius Shepard. This rather begs the question as to whether those writers could only be admired by sycophants with long, dun-colored noses, or whether some of us admire them because of the qualities and quality of their fiction. I don't mind the insult personally, as it happens, but I feel a bit ashamed really to see this sort of schoolboy abuse, appearing in the course of an article published in a magazine I co-edit.

LETTER FROM DOUGLAS BARBOUR

[...] the sheer narrative drive as well as the high adventure of the Foyster/Turner/Shepard/Blackford row. Whew!

They have had at each other now so well and completely that it would be a foolish angel indeed who sought to tread where they have rampaged, but I have to confess to acknowledging the partial truths in all of their contributions to the exchange. Certainly, I don't find *Neuromancer* simply adolescent, if only because I'm too old to be one and I really like the book. Yet [...] there are criticisms which can be made of all three books (and, horrors of horror (since it is an example of dreaded academic response) I have a student writing a Master's Thesis on Gynergy in the trilogy, in which he both acknowledges the brilliance of some of the writing and shows how Gibson, like many other male writers today, still can't quite figure out how to textually "place" that Other which is woman). But that's all right, isn't it? Are there any books we find absolutely perfect?

So I wonder why Turner is so *angry* about Shepard's very powerful novel. He admits the writing is worthy; yet he lambastes it for being an sf novel. I use only the initials there because I tend to side with Shepard in the matter of purity: I like what I wish to consider "good" fantasy and "good" science fiction both, and I have no problem when a book is something of a hybrid. But then I've always thought of all the "science" in sf as essentially tropic, anyway. Thus, reading psi or whatever as metaphor makes it as easy for me to believe in "magic" in fantasy novels. Perhaps I am simply too willing to suspend my disbelief, but otherwise why read the stuff? I have no doubt, for example, that David Zindell, whose *Neverness* is a large and fascinating exploration of a far future worthy to be at least put on the same shelf as Gene Wolfe's *New Sun* quincunx, knows a lot about mathematics. I don't, and although I believe those who do when they say that math has a beauty of its own, I can only take their word for it. But Zindell makes a poetry out of the fact of mathematics, and he makes mathematics the very basis of both his

FTL travel and the lives of the pilots who fly between the stars. That he then also makes these people intriguingly human even in their ranging beyond "our" "humanity" as we understand the term "normally" today is why the book exerts such a strange and powerful hold over this reader at least.

At any rate, the whole grand argument does support that part of Turner's original diatribe in which he was suggesting that all readers are different and therefore each reader's novel will differ somewhat from every other's. But, but, there must be some overlap? So magazines like *ASFR* can continue to carry interesting reviews and articles which other readers (of both the books critiqued *and ASFR*) can argue with to everyone's mutual pleasure? I certainly believe so. I read quite a bit of sf (both fantasy and science fiction), much of it for "mere" pleasure, some of it for much more than that, and when I find high literary values in it I am glad, but even we academics need a rest sometimes, and a good mystery or a good sf book can provide it.

Mind you, when the ordinary pleasure suddenly becomes something much more deeply moving, I am happy. As in reading Ursula K. Le Guin's magnificent overturning of so many high fantasy tropes (or, in the hands of lesser writers, clichés): *Tehanu: The Last Book of Earthsea*. But why do we all read differently? That's a big question, and as Russell Blackford knows no one has managed to answer it fully yet. But I love some pop music, much pop culture, as well as jazz and classical music; I am very interested in modern painting; I am a student and lover of modern and postmodern poetry, and of Canadian writing of the twentieth century as well as—in the past few years, and as a result of trips Down Under—a lot of Australian and New Zealand poetry and some of their prose. A case in point, for me it's a very small jump from [Peter Carey's] *Illywhacker* or [Murray Bail's] *Homesickness* or [Jean Bedford's] *Sister Kate* to, say, Gibson's or Shepard's books, or Delany's Neveryona books, or *Always Coming Home*. Certainly there are a lot of pleasures that I get from both supposedly different kinds of writing, as well as all the pleasant differences which make a world worthwhile. But then, the writing which really gets to me, finally, whether in sf or out, is a writing in which language and style are central, and of course, or so I think, that's why I read and write poetry too.

DIRECTIONS

NEW DIRECTIONS IN SCIENCE FICTION

by George Turner

[This paper was delivered at the Nova Mob meeting on 5 October 1988.]

In "The Real Science Fiction" [reprinted in *Chained to the Alien* (2009)] I spoke of "fringe sf" in general terms, holding that some of the sf that has entered the world's permanent thinking has been written by non-sf practitioners and that fandom has always been far behind the general public in realizing that something worth preserving has appeared.

That essay was devoted to writers working outside the sf ambience, attempting to show that writers unhampered by the conventional uses of sf are producing more creative work than the genre practitioners. If you look to sf purely for entertainment my selections may not interest you. If you look to have your imagination steered in new directions and your interest fired by writers who don't give a damn for the mass readership, they may interest you deeply.

Few genre writers ever steer their chosen form out of its inbuilt mediocrity; it takes the stroppy outsider to drag it, screaming, in new directions.

To demonstrate this, I propose to discuss three groups of novels.

The first group consists of three recent works by genre sf writers trying and failing to give stature to the genre form.

The second group is of four novels—one old and three new where the attempt has been made to use basic ideas for fresh purposes and to produce work directly related to contemporary issues.

Finally, there is a single work which uses science, real science, in a breathtaking fashion to relate it to our daily lives.

§

The first of the works trying to give intellectual and literary stature to genre conceptions is *Ancient of Days* by Michael Bishop, published in 1985. Its theme is as old as Conan Doyle's *Lost World* (1912), the persistence of a group of pre-humans—in this case *Homo habilis*—into the present day. The story, briefly, is of a black, dwarfish apeman found, by a woman painter, lurking in the US state of Georgia. As part of her effort to preserve him from scientists as well as from local prejudice, she marries him and they fall genuinely in love. But the curious world, both scientific and secular, moves in on them, and they flee to Haiti where the rest of Adam's primitive tribe is located. Here the wife, Ruth, discovers the culture of *Homo habilis*, finding it, in philosophic terms, richer and more advanced than ours.

The novel is deliberately written in defiance of sf conventions, with some artistry expended on minor characters, dialogue, discussion and the minutiae of daily life. No attempt is made to force the plot, which moves naturally from each situation to a sensible solution. The author's concern is with the question of what is or is not human and with the reactions of those who think that only they are human while in fact they behave like animals. The implicit intention is to force us readers to question what we are.

For me the book is a brave failure. I found the love affair between the modern woman and the furry apeman hard to swallow but was prepared to go along with it. I balked, however, at the Haitian scenes wherein *Homo habilis* is depicted as having an intellectual and spiritual life far advanced over that of *Homo sapiens*. In terms of evolutionary persistence the extinction of such intellects, barring one small tribe, makes no sense and the hyped-up conclusion left me feeling that Bishop had lost control of his plot and settled for pseudo-sf spectacle.

Nevertheless, *Ancient of Days* is a pointer to where sf can go if a writer concentrates on his theme to the exclusion of genre expectations. David Brin spoiled *The Postman* by the same inability to think as a novelist when in the climax he settled for genre manipulation. *Ancient of Days*, given its weaknesses, is a promising attempt to link the themes of sf to the concerns of everyday life.

The second novel in this group, Stanislaw Lem's *Fiasco* (1987), must be counted a failure in purely novelistic terms but must also be counted an extraordinary attempt to link super-science with present-day concerns. It is probably the adamantine hardest of all "hard sf" works, 130,000 words of scientific overkill in pursuit of a sardonic commentary on human intelligence.

An interstellar expedition finds the planet Quinta and discovers it to be in a condition of total war, one half of the planet versus the other half. The Terrestrian Commander feels it his duty, as the possessor of superior armaments, to intervene and impose peace. The outcome is, of course, the fiasco of the title, with the Earth-folk slaughtering the people they proposed to help.

There is more complication than this. The central character is an old friend, Pirx the Pilot—or is he? Two pilots have been discovered dead but in suitable condition for resuscitation, but only one has been restored and nobody, including the memoryless restoree, knows which he is. Nor does Lem tell us. I think he represents, in this very diagrammatic work, the primal innocent observing the behavior of his own race.

There is little action in this novel but by God there is talk—rivers, rockfalls, avalanches of talk. Nobody blinks without a discussion of the philosophic implications of blinking. The book is, in fact, a series of arguments about the rights and wrongs of every fresh situation, the point being to demonstrate—at least to Lem's satisfaction—that the human animal will always find a valid reason for doing what pleases it and calling it logical. The result, as he points out in a quite beguiling final chapter, is inevitably catastrophic.

These arguments, taken separately, are a joy in their subtle demonstration of how intelligence tricks itself, but there are too many of them; the story is forever halting to go into argumentative mode for a dozen pages or so. There is, in the end, a feeling that Lem is fighting from a tunnel-view position and not admitting that other conclusions are possible. My feeling is that any intelligent Commander happening on this total war set-up would observe, shake his head and go elsewhere, but Lem argues him out of a common-sense decision.

There are also extensive lectures on faster-than-light travel, black holes, machines wired directly to the nervous system, conditions on Sol's satellites, the possible unrecognizability of a non-carboniferous life form, attack tactics in space, alien technology and everything else that puts the opera into space opera. *Fiasco* is just about the ultimate space opera. Lem has taken hard sf about as far as it can go without discarding the fiction element altogether and at the same time linked it to the literary function of discussing humanity in operation.

The problem here is method overkill, more hard science than the story-line can stand—a collection of scientific and philosophic articles linked by brief spats of activity. You will be fascinated or bored stiff, according to taste. Lem has pushed a method to its limit and produced a monster.

The third book in this group is the absolute antithesis of *Fiasco*. Where Lem tried to bring philosophy to sf, Iain M. Banks tried, in *Consider Phlebas*, to grace space opera with all the embellishments of highbrow literature. Not surprisingly, his novel suffers from the same disability as *Fiasco*, overkill, but in the opposite direction. *Consider Phlebas* may be, from the obscure title (from T. S. Eliot's *The Waste Land*), the most pretentious sf novel yet written.

It has literally everything: two star systems with opposing philosophies battle for supremacy, allowing much inconclusive philosophic discussion. (Lem does this bit rather better.) The hero is a shape-changer working through a group of interstellar pirates who are committed to neither side. There are gorgeous pirate girls who fuck in the cabin and kill in the fight. There is a monstrous artificial world where mad gambling games flourish and an equally monstrous space ship which conceals a whole fleet in its belly. There are battles and captures, escapes and philanderings, with all the usual special effects twice as big and gaudy—and all of it, wrapped in self-consciously literary prose, is utterly pointless.

Of course it has its moments. I admit to being fascinated by some of the extended dramatic scenes and also to skipping pages of rumination wherein nothing happened and the author played with words while advancing neither plot nor understanding. At the end I felt a sort of dubious admiration for a brilliantly executed thimble-and-pea trick. The thimbles covered nothing and the pea vanished somewhere in the shuffling.

Banks, like Lem, has pushed a particular form to its limit and produced a monster. On the whole I prefer Lem, who at least had some provocative argument to offer.

These three novels fail in their attempts to glorify bread-and-butter concepts by dressing them in glittering disguises. It won't work on genre fiction; it never has worked. They have imposed literary approaches on the concepts instead of re-examining the concepts to find what new thing was to be said and a better way of saying it. So they have produced artifice instead of art, snow jobs that melt away on a second reading.

So, let us see what other approaches may achieve.

§

There are quite a few examples available, of which a novel by Anthony Burgess forms a strange but useful sport. *The End of the World News* (1982) is a three-in-one novel about our happy progress to cultural suicide. One strand is a story of Sigmund Freud becoming a symbol of the genius who outruns his own perceptions and eventually leaves us a legacy of psychological confusion claiming to be understanding. A second strand tells of the life of Trotsky being turned into a Broadway musical—a life's struggle seen as razzmatazz entertainment. The third strand tells of the launching of a starship. It is a launching fraught with precisely the selfishness and wrongheadedness that has made the trip necessary. In the Epilogue, some generations in space later, the descendants of the pioneers are contemptuous of the tales of old Earth, which to them are myths. They are true descendants of their fleeing parents, totally unwilling to accept ideas which do not tally with their own preconceptions. With them the end of the world becomes a continuing serial.

It is not one of Burgess's best novels but is full of humor, ingenuity and food for thought. He has used this part-sf insertion in at least two other works. One is *The Clockwork Testament.* Here, in an Epilogue, the author has a group of future children doing a guided tour of present-day New York, described as a "vicious but beautiful city, totally representative of the human condition." You may gather that Burgess has little respect for the human condition. The third is the Epilogue to *Enderby's Dark Lady,* last of a series of novels about an outrageous, egocentric poet; here he uses time travel to introduce Shakespeare at a production of one of his own plays.

Using the future to comment on the past is not new in sf but Burgess's handling is not only new but startling in effect. He writes a fairly straightforward comedy of the present day, leading the reader to some more or less convenient conclusions, then brings him hard up against a final section asking: how will this seem in a hundred or a thousand years' time? And all your comfortable assurances begin to look uneasy and ill-founded.

It may be a one-off effect that only Burgess can manage and it does not allow the books to be classified as sf, but it certainly uses sf to make observations and ask questions from oblique and unexpected points of view. He edges sf ideas into the reading of the larger general audience and uses them for intelligent purposes.

My next writer is a Russian, Vasily Aksyonov, who has turned the good old alternative history into a devastating political weapon.

In *The Island of Crimea* (1985) he postulates a Crimea saved from the revolution of 1917 and grown rich as part of the Western world, a sort of Russian Hong Kong, doing better in capitalist insouciance than Russia in all its communist seriousness. The story tells in great detail just how the Kremlin goes about drawing the Crimea back into mother Russia with every dirty trick in the political trade, and how the Crimea succumbs through being too silly to recognize its own vulnerability. The lesson is addressed to the Western world and you can be sure that even *glasnost* has not yet [in 1988] allowed Aksyonov publication in Russia.

This is a science fictional conception, alternative history, applied directly to the present day, not as fantasy or wish fulfillment but as straight talk about what we are and why we are so.

This application to real life, with no holds barred by the sugary intrusion of fantasy for fantasy's sake, is foreshadowed in Bishop's *Ancient of Days* and was in fact attempted as far back as 1974 in Thomas Disch's guided tour of the big city of the twenty-first century. It was called *334*, which is a house number in future New York, a tenement where ordinary people (whom sf tends to ignore) live out their private comedies and dramas in a world of new parameters. If you have not read it, seek it out. It is one of the few great sf achievements.

To view the present day in sf terms it is usually necessary to gain perspective by planting your action a few years into tomorrow and looking around at what has happened because of what we are and what we have done. This is what Rodney Hall has done in *Kisses of the Enemy* (1988). Hall took up the question of Australia as a Republic and allied it to the influx of overseas money. When the dust of becoming a Republic in the 1990s has died down it becomes apparent that American finance has literally bought the country from under us and that the Australian Presidency is a puppet of American big business. The result in misery and misfortune is foreseeable and so, unfortunately, is the reach-me-down plot, wherein a few brave men led by a brilliant old woman free the country. Except in one fine sea action towards the end of the novel, poet Rodney Hall displays no feeling for action drama and his gutsier scenes fall soggily flat. Also he seems uncertain whether he is writing a melodrama, a comedy of errors or a symbolic parable, and the parts fight against each other.

Kisses of the Enemy must be praised for its brave intention rather than for its effectiveness, but it is a move in what seems to me a right direction. If it fails as a novel, it remains rich in entertainment; if there are times when you feel inclined to mutter, "For God's sake, Rodney, get on with It!" there are also dozens of passages to be wallowed in for sheer brilliance of presentation. One that I and the other judges of the Victorian Premier's Awards will not soon forget is poet-and-word-magician Rodney's 800-word description of the monstrously obese President on pages 232-4; it is almost worth the price of the book. Read it for its intermittent brilliance and because it is another attempt to link the sf mode with present reality. Hall has moved sf in the direction in which Tom Disch in America and Vasily Aksyonov in his exile from Russia—and, incidentally, I myself—feel is most productive, most useful in a world of problems and an increasingly uncertain future. We need more of them.

§

There remains *Roger's Version* (1986), by John Updike, possibly the most extraordinary example of the use of science—and I mean science in huge, multi-page slabs—in a novel about faith in God and about self-understanding. It is easily obtainable and has been happily ignored by sf fandom the world over—possibly because it manages its drama with only a single act of violence, and that off-stage.

The Roger of the title is a minister of the church who no longer preaches but holds a Divinity chair in a church-run university. He does not think about faith, taking it for granted. To him comes Dale, a young computer technologist, seeking a grant to search for evidence of the physical existence of God. His argument is detailed and convincing. He argues the Big Bang down to its moment of the emergence of something from nothing (a quite remarkable exposition of modern cosmology, readable and up-to-date at his time of writing) to point out that the question of origin still is unanswered. Can the computer grind the evidence smaller still, pushing back through creation until the hand of God appears?

Hypothetical? Of course. So Dale turns to the various theories of evolution with their gaps and inconsistencies and failure to come to terms with the question of origin. Again the argument is fully up-to-date, encapsulating and pointing schisms commonly at work in the scientific community. Can the computer resolve them and locate the primal cause?

Finally, he treats of mathematics, explicating the universe as a single primal function (an idea familiar to modern philosophy). If this is true, the computer should be able to trace the originating formula and the mathematician behind it—God.

These arguments are not new but the practical application of them is Updike's own. He uses them to question all basic philosophies and make us ask ourselves what we in fact believe— whether the cosmos is the work of God or the outcome of blind forces we cannot penetrate.

There is nothing dull about the plot he weaves round this uncompromisingly abstract theme. He works it out in terms of anger, jealousy, love, viciousness and some very steamy sex—all of which contribute to stripping down the scientist and the divine to the reality of their beliefs—which I leave you to discover for yourselves. The book is worth your attention.

The reason Updike has been able to create this collision of the material and the abstract lies in a matter so obvious but so difficult to handle that genre sf could not begin to attempt it, and in the mainstream only Huxley, Wells and Stapledon have made the trial, albeit rather timidly. It is this: that science has become so much of a commonplace of our daily lives that it can no longer be set apart as something special for eggheads and boffins. Its blunt intrusion questions the very existence of the assumptions of mystery we have carried with us from the caves. We must come to terms with it but we will not do so while literature coyly avoids noticing its existence. Updike has made a challenging beginning.

Please do not brush Updike off as peripheral or merely superstitious. One of the commonest statements in modern cosmology is that more and more as the universe is probed, it begins to take on the characteristics of a vast thought.

Rosaleen Love has pointed out that *Roger's Version* is a theological novel, not to be confused with sf. This is true. The science is used purely to penetrate to the heart of the argument. My point is that the new use of science in mainstream fiction shows that genre sf is being increasingly relegated to a readership ghetto. There will always be a genre sf but the valuable work will come from the mainstream writers who see science as just another area of cultural experience with specific social impacts.

To underline writerly recognition that science is one of the commonplaces of our lives, there is playing in London at the moment a drama called *Hapgood* which I hope will find its way to Australia. It is by that intriguing manipulator, Tom Stoppard, and it deals with spies and politics as exemplified by quantum physics. It even includes a lecture in quantum mechanics which scientists report to be spot accurate.

It begins to sound as though genre sf is to become as dated as the classic detective story or the Cartland bodice-ripper—still active but read only by the very young, the very old and the very devoted. The new look is science *in* fiction, with science regarded sensibly and familiarly and not as a springboard for fantasy.

And, if I be permitted to intrude myself, that is one of the half-dozen or so things that *The Sea and Summer* is about. I include myself among those who have consciously tried, successfully or otherwise, to break the mould.

SELECTED BIBLIOGRAPHY

Aksyonov, Vasily, *The Island of Crimea*, New York, Vintage, 1984.
Atwood, Margaret, *The Handmaid's Tale*, London, 1985; Virago Press, 1987.
Banks, Iain M., *Consider Phoebus*, London, Macmillan, 1987.
Bishop, Michael, *Ancient of Days*, New York, Arbor House, 1985.
Broderick, Damien, ed., *Chained to the Alien: The Best of Australian Science Fiction Review (Second Series)*, San Bernardino, Calif., Borgo/Wildside Press, 2009.
Burgess, Anthony, *The End of the World News*, London, Hutchinson, 1982.
Charney, Maurice, *Comedy High and Low*, New York, Oxford University Press, 1978.
Delany, Samuel R., *The Jewel-Hinged Jaw*, Elizabethtown, N.Y., Dragon Press, 1977; New York, Berkley Windhover Books, 1978.
Derleth, August, ed. *Time to Come*, New York, Farrar Straus & Young, 1954.
Dick, Philip K., *Beyond Lies the Wub*, Volume One of *The Collected Stories of Philip K. Dick*, London, Gollancz, 1989.
—— *Second Variety*, Volume Two of *The Collected Stories of Philip K. Dick*, London, Gollancz, 1989.
Fish, Stanley, "Critical Legal Studies (I) Unger and Milton," *Raritan* 7 (2), Fall 1987, 1-21; 15-16.
Gibson, William, *Neuromancer*, New York, Ace Special, 1984.
Hall, Rodney, *Kisses of the Enemy*, Ringwood, Australia, Penguin, 1988.
Herbert, Frank, *Dune*, Philadelphia, Chilton, 1965.
—— *Dune Messiah*, New York, Putnam, 1969.
—— *Children of Dune*, New York, Berkley/Putnam, 1976.
—— *God-Emperor of Dune*, New York, Putnam, 1981.
—— *Heretics of Dune*, New York, Putnam, 1984.
—— *Chapterhouse: Dune*, New York, Putnam, 1985.

Holdstock, Robert, *Earthwind,* London, Faber and Faber, 1977.
—— *Mythago Wood,* London, Gollancz, 1984.
Hume, Kathryn, *Fantasy and Mimesis: Responses to Reality in Western Literature,* New York and London, Methuen, 1984.
Jameson, Fredric, *The Political Unconscious,* Ithaca, Cornell University Press, 1981.
Kingsley, Charles, *The Water Babies,* New York, F.A. Stokes, 1891.
Le Guin, Ursula K., *The Left Hand of Darkness,* New York, Ace, 1969.
—— *The Dispossessed,* New York, Harper & Row, 1974.
—— *Always Coming Home* (with composer Todd Barton, artist Margaret Chodos, geomancer George Hersh) (with cassette tape), New York, Harper & Row, 1985; London, Gollancz, 1986.
—— "Buffalo Gals, Won't You Come Out Tonight," in *Buffalo Gals and Other Animal Presences,* Santa Barbara, Capra Press, 1987.
Lem, Stanislaw, *Fiasco,* New York, Harcourt Brace Jovanovich, 1987.
Lowes, John Livingston, *The Road to Xanadu,* 2nd ed., London, Constable, 1951.
Margolis, Maxine L., in *Mothers and Such: Views of American Women and Why They Changed,* University of California Press, Berkeley, 1984.
Moore, Alan (writer) and Dave Gibbons (artist) aided by John Higgins (colorist), *Watchmen,* DC Comics, 1986-87.
Rickman, Gregg, *To the High Castle Philip K. Dick: A Life 1928-1962,* Long Beach, California, Fragments West / The Valentine Press, 1989.
Robinson, Kim Stanley, *The Planet on the Table,* New York, Tor, 1987.
Rybczynski, Witold, *Home: A Short History of an Idea,* New York, Viking Penguin, 1986.
Shepard, Lucius, *Life During Wartime,* New York, Bantam, 1987.
Shiner, Lewis, *Deserted Cities of the Heart,* New York, Spectra, 1989.
Smith, Cordwainer, *The Instrumentality of Mankind*, London, VGSF Classics, Gollancz, 1988.
—— *Norstrilia,* London, VGSF Classics, Gollancz, 1988.
Spence, Catherine Helen, *Handfasted,* ed. Helen Thomson, Penguin Australia, Ringwood, 1984.
—— *A Week in the Future,* intro. Lesley Durrell Ljungdahl, Hale & Iremonger, Sydney, 1987.

Turner, George, *The Sea and Summer,* London, Faber, 1987; as *Drowning Towers,* New York, Tor, 1987.
Unger, Roberto Mangabeira, *Knowledge & Politics,* New York, The Free Press, 1975.
Updike, John, *Roger's Version,* New York, Knopf, 1986.
Wolk, Anthony, "The Sunstruck Forest: A Guide to the Short Fiction of Philip K. Dick," *Foundation*, No. 18, Jan. 1980.
Wright, Austin Tappan, *Islandia*, intro. Sylvia Wright, New American Library, New York, 1966.

ABOUT THE AUTHORS

DOUGLAS BARBOUR, poet, critic, and reviewer, is Professor Emeritus of English at the University of Alberta, where he has taught creative writing, poetry, Canadian literature, twentieth century poetry and poetics, and science fiction and fantasy. *Visible Visions: The Selected Poems of Douglas Barbour* (NeWest Press 1984) won Alberta's Stephan G. Stephannson Award for poetry.

ZORAN BEKRIC, trained in drama, is a longtime Role Play Gamer and a convenor of the sf study group Critical Mass. He lives in Adelaide, South Australia.

GREGORY BENFORD, a winner of the United Nations Medal for Literature, is a professor of physics at the University of California, Irvine. A Woodrow Wilson Fellow, he received the Lord Prize for contributions to science, the Japan Seiun Award, and the Nebula Award for his landmark novel *Timescape*. He is a founder and Chairman of the Board of Genescient Corporation, dedicated to finding cures to aging.

JENNY BLACKFORD, classicist and former computer networking specialist, recently published her first novel, *The Priestess and the Slave*, set in ancient Greece. A reviewer for *The New York Review of Science Fiction*, she was one of the five judges for the World Fantasy Awards 2009. Otherwise, she devotes her life to Mystical Prince Felix, a truly enormous Ragdoll cat.

RUSSELL BLACKFORD is a philosopher and critic. He is known especially as an outspoken defender of secularism and individual rights. He has published three novels set in the Terminator universe, among others, and holds a law degree and a pair of Ph.D.'s. He and Jenny Blackford recently moved to Newcastle, New South Wales.

DAMIEN BRODERICK has only one Ph.D., but has published more than forty novels, scholarly tomes, and popular science books on the paranormal, the technological singularity, the prospect of radical life extension, and the very far future. These days he lives in San Antonio, Texas, but remains a senior fellow in the School of Culture and Communication at the University of Melbourne.

JOHN FOYSTER was a polymathic force of nature: educator, critic, statistician, and creator of famous fanzines known only to the elite, with titles such as *exploding madonna*, *The Journal of Omphalistic Epistemology*, and *Chunder*. He died in 2003.

PETER NICHOLLS was the first Administrator of the Science Fiction Foundation between 1971 and 1977, and edited its journal, *Foundation*. He is creator and co-editor, with John Clute, of the most important resource in science fiction studies, *The Encyclopedia of Science Fiction*, which won the Hugo Award for both its editions (1980, 1994). After many years in the UK, he returned to Australia and now lives in Melbourne, Victoria.

YVONNE ROUSSEAU lives quietly in Adelaide, South Australia in the large equally book-crammed house she shared with husband John Foyster, reading prodigiously and writing wittily but publishing far too little.

LUCIUS SHEPARD, perhaps the most distinguished newcomer to the genre during the 1980s, won the 1985 John W. Campbell Award for best new writer, wrote little in the following decade but returned with strong work in the last decade or so. He has won the Hugo, Nebula, Locus and Rhysling awards.

NORMAN TALBOT, an ebullient, well-regarded poet and scholar of the life and work of William Morris, was Associate Professor in the English Department of the University of Newcastle. He died in 2004.

MICHAEL J. TOLLEY, Ph.D., an expert in crime fiction as well as utopian and science fiction, taught English at the University of Adelaide. With Dr. Kirpal Singh, he edited *The Stellar Gauge* in 1980.

GEORGE TURNER remains perhaps Australia's most highly regarded if contentious science fiction author and critic. He shared the 1962 Miles Franklin literary award for *The Cupboard Under the Stairs*. His sf novels include Beloved Son, *The Sea and Summer* (*Drowning Towers*), *Brainchild* and *Genetic Soldier*. He died in 1997.

JANEEN WEBB holds a Ph.D. from the University of Newcastle, and until recently was Associate Professor and Reader in Literature at ACU, Melbourne, Victoria. She has published two novels and a number of nonfiction books. With Jack Dann she co-edited *Dreaming Down-Under*, a milestone anthology that won the World Fantasy Award in 1999.

INDEX

334, 263
Ace Science Fiction Special series, 194
Ackerman, Forrest J., 12
Adams, Douglas, 81
"Adjustment Team," 68, 77-9, 80
Aksyonov, Vasily, 262, 264
Aldiss, Brian W., 123, 215
"Alpha Ralpha Boulevard," 26
Always Coming Home, 33-6, 256
Ambassadors, The, 221
anarchism, 180
Ancient of Days, 259
And Then There Were None, 69, 130
Andrews, Edward Deaming, 166
Animal Farm, 183
Ant Farm, the, 211, 239
Apted, Michael, 169
Archimedes, 97
Aristotle, 100, 101
Atwood, Margaret, 109
Austen, Jane, 134, 139, 197, 220-23
Bach, J. S., 55
Bacon, Leonard, 130
Bail, Murray, 256
Banks, Iain M., 261
Barbour, Douglas, 118, 255
Barham, Rev. Richard, 236
Barnard Eldershaw, M., 130
Barnard, Marjorie, 129
Bateau Ivre, Le, 29
Bedford, Jean, 256
Bellamy, Edward, 145, 165, 174
Beloved Son, 204
Benford, Gregory, 143-92, 249-54
Best of Philip K. Dick, The, 69
Bester, Alfred, 14
"Beyond Lies the Wub," 44, 47, 56, 60, 77
"Beyond the Door," 82
Beyond This Horizon, 152
Bible, 74, 86, 111
Bishop, Michael, 259
"Black Air," 20
Blackford, Jenny, 15, 18, 37, 154
Blackford, Russell, 12, 14-5, 219, 237, 244, 250, 253, 256
Blade Runner, 57

Blake, William, 49, 66, 85, 87, 105-07
Blish, James, 204
bonnets, shrunken, 249
Book of the New Sun, The, 121
Boucher, Anthony, 51
Bradbury, Ray, 93
Brave New World, 115, 145, 165, 175
"Breakfast at Twilight," 73, 78-9
Brin, David, 259
Brooke-Rose, Christine, 253
Bug Jack Barron, 152
"Builder, The," 56
Bulletin of the Atomic Scientists, 87
Burgess, Anthony, 262
butterfly effect, 93-100
Cage, John, 121-22
Calvinism, 138
Campbell, John W., 48
Capp, Al, 45
Carey, Peter, 256
Carr, Terry, 13, 195, 199, 220-25, 233, 245-47
Catherine Helen Spence, 140
Chained to the Alien, 14-5, 215-16, 253, 258
chaos theory, 93
Chapterhouse: Dune, 121-26
Charnas, Suzy McKee, 151, 174
Charney, Maurice, 41-2, 54, 82
Children of Dune, 119
Christie, Agatha, 69
Circe, 44, 46, 56
Clockwork Testament, The, 262
Cold War, 29, 52, 57-8
Collected Stories of Philip K. Dick, 41 et seq.
"Colonel Came Back from Nothing-at-All, The," 29
"Colony," 48
Comedy, 41-3
Comedy High and Low, 41
"Commuter, The," 77, 80
Conan Doyle, Arthur, 259
Conquest of America, The, 124
Consider Phlebas, 261
contraception, 113, 115, 132, 134, 138
"Cookie Lady, The," 60
"Cosmic Poachers, The," 81
Count Zero, 225
Counter-Clock World, 80

Critical Mass, 194-95, 200
"Crystal Crypt, The," 57, 77
cyberpunk, 12, 198-201, 220-25, 229, 245-46
Dance of the Intellect, The, 121
Dangerous Visions, 80
Datlow, Ellen, 198-99, 223
David Copperfield, 137
DC Comics, 84
"Dead Lady of Clown Town, The," 26, 28
Dean Drive, 204
"Defenders, The," 52, 63
Delany, Samuel R., 18, 145, 147-48, 150, 153, 155-57, 161-64, 173, 185, 256
Deserted Cities of the Heart, 199, 200, 219, 220, 223-26, 246
Dianetics, 204
Dick, Philip K., 12, 41-82
Dinner at Deviant's Palace, 174
Disch, Thomas, 263
"Disguise, The," 20
Dispossessed, The, 145-90, 251-53
Ditko, Steve, 88, 103
Do Androids Dream of Electric Sheep?, 57, 72
Dozois, Gardner, 198-99, 223
"Drunkboat," 29-30
Dubliners, 19, 20
Dune, 118-26
Earthwind, 37, 38
ecology, 119
Einstein, Albert, 86
Eliot, T.S., 261
Ellison, Harlan, 156
End of the World News, The, 262
Enderby's Dark Lady, 262
Expendable, 51
Eye of the Heron, The, 148-49, 181-82
"Faith of Our Fathers," 80
Fantasy and Mimesis, 176
Farmer, Philip José, 199
"Father of Stones, The," 218
FBS (Fannish Brown-nose Syndrome), 244, 247, 250, 254
Female Man, The, 151, 188
feminism, 112
Fiasco, 259
filmatic effects, 87
Finch-Reyner, Sheila, 153
Finney, Jack, 199

Fish, Stanley, 158
Ford, Gerald, 99
Forerunner, 138
Forgotten Life, 215
Fowles, John, 166
Foyster, John, 154, 194, 202-07, 215, 219-33, 241, 245-55
Frame, Janet, 141
"From Gustible's Planet," 29
Frontera, 223
Frye, Northrop, 221-22, 228-29, 245
fugging, 212
Full Metal Jacket, 203, 233
Fuller, R. Buckminster, 55
Gakov, M., 148
Galactic Pot Healer, 54
Garnett, Constance, 156
Gass, William, 156
Gathered In, 136
Gell-Mann, Murray, 94
Gibbons, Dave, 84
Gibson, William, 198, 219-30, 245, 250-56
Gilman, Charlotte Perkins, 138
God Emperor of Dune, 120-24
Golden Bowl, The, 221
Golden Man, The, 76
Gravity's Rainbow, 210, 224, 229
"Great C, The," 56, 59
Green Eyes, 215
Greenland, Colin, 143
"Gun, The," 52
Haldeman, Joe, 203, 233
Hall, Rodney, 263
Hammett, Dashiell, 224
Handfasted, 128-41
Handmaid's Tale, The, 109-17
Hapgood, 265
Hayden Elgin, Suzanne, 112
hedonism, 132
Heinlein, Robert A., 67, 152, 159
Heraclitus, 53
Herbert, Frank, 77, 118-26
Heretics of Dune, 118-23
Herland, 138
Higgins, John, 84
History of American Socialisms, 167
Holdstock, Robert, 37-8

Home, 33, 35, 197
Homer, 86
Homesickness, 256
homosexuality, 132, 186
"Hood Maker, The," 67
"Houston, Houston, Do You Read?, " 151, 189
"Human Is, " 70-1
Human Universe, 124
Hume, Kathryn, 176
Huxley, Aldous, 37, 145, 165, 173, 175, 265
Icehenge, 19
Iliad, 86
Illywhacker, 256
"Impossible Planet, The," 82
"Impostor," 71
In the Drift, 194
"Indefatigable Frog, The," 56
"Infinites, The," 48
Instrumentality of Mankind, The, 22, 26, 29
"Is Gender Necessary?", 34
Island, 145, 165, 175
Island of Crimea, The, 263
Islandia, 128-41
Jack of Eagles, 204
Jackdaw of *Rheims*, The, 236
"James P. Crow," 58, 74
James, Henry, 131, 134, 221
Jameson, Fredric, 157
Jewel-Hinged Jaw, The, 153, 155, 163, 185
"Jon's World," 58, 72, 74
Joyce, James, 19, 94
Judas Rose, The, 112
junk food, sf as, 219
Juvenal, 87
Kael, Pauline, 216
Kalila and Dimna, 24
Kaveney, Roz, 149, 164
kemmer, 187
KGB, 192
kids in costume, 196
Kigmy, 45-6
"King of the Elves, The," 50
King, David, 219
Kisses of the Enemy, 263
Kissinger, Henry, 99
Knowledge & Politics, 158

Kropotkin, Prince, 148
Lamb, Charles, 29
Larkin, Philip, 196-98, 220-25, 245
Last Word, A, 129
Laziness, Stupidity, and Malice, 160
Le Guin, Ursula K., 12, 33-6, 129-31, 137, 143-50, 154-57, 162-63, 167, 170-88, 192, 249, 251, 253-56
Leavis, F. R., 222
Left Hand of Darkness, The, 130-31, 187
Lem, Stanislaw, 195, 259
Lenin, 148, 167, 183
Lévi-Strauss, Claude, 125
libertarianism, 157
Liddy, Gordon, 99
Life During Wartime, 202-03, 208-10, 215-19, 224, 227, 229, 233, 239-41, 247, 250
Linebarger, Paul Myron Anthony, 25
"Little Movement, The," 44, 50
Locus, 196, 246
Looking Backward, 145, 150, 165, 174
Lost World, 259
Love, Rosaleen, 265
Lowes, John Livingston, 162
"Lucky Strike, The," 19
Maggot, A, 166
Mailer, Norman, 203, 212, 232
Malafrena, 149, 181
Malzberg, Barry, 156
Man in the High Castle, The, 73, 80
Margolis, Maxine L., 169
"Mark Elf," 29
Martian Time-Slip, 62
"Martians Come in Clouds," 60, 63, 71
Matheson, Richard, 56
McCaffrey, Anne, 230
McCarthyism, 46, 58
"Meddler, "53
"Mercurial," 19
Merril, Judith, 52
Merwin, Sam, 199
Metropolis, 56
Miller, P. Schuyler, 216
mimesis, 11-14, 24, 220-21
Mirrorshades, 198
Mona Lisa Overdrive, 225
Monastery, The, 136

Moore, Alan, 84-107
More, Sir Thomas, 172
Morris, William, 145, 165, 175
"Mother Hitton's Littul Kittons," 26
Motherlines, 151, 188
Mothers and Such, 169
Mr. Hogarth's Will, 136
"Mr. Spaceship," 49
Mythago Wood, 37, 38
Naked and the Dead, The, 203, 212, 215, 232-34, 239-40
"Nanny," 57, 58
Native Tongue, 112
Nebula Awards, 246
Neuromancer, 198-200, 219-26, 229, 245-48, 255
Neverness, 255
Nevèrÿon series (Delany), 173
New Atlantis, The, 150
New York Times Book Review, 197
News from Nowhere, 145, 165, 175
Nicholls, Peter, 12, 249
Niven, Larry, 152
Nixon, Richard M., 98-9
"No, No, Not Rogov!", 29
Norstrilia, 22-8, 44
Norstrilia Press, 22
Northanger Abbey, 139
Nova Mob, 258
Noyes, John Humphrey, 167
Oath of Fealty, 152
Odysseus, 44, 46, 48
"Of Withered Apples," 60
Old North Australia, 24, 27
Old Testament themes, 146, 178
Olson, Charles, 124
Oresteia, 115
Orwell, George, 173
"Out in the Garden," 57
Palmer, Jane, 189
paradigm, dominant, subvert the, 13
Partial Payments, 197
"Paycheck," 54
Penultimate Truth, The, 52, 63
People Called Shakers, The, 166
Perloff, Marjorie, 121
Piercy, Marge, 151
"Piper in the Woods," 48-9

Planet Buyer, The, 23
Planet Dwellers, The, 189
"Planet for Transients," 58-9
Planet on the Table, The, 18
Planet Stories, 44, 48, 52, 57, 74
Platoon, 203
Pohl, Frederik, 152
Political Unconscious, The, 157
Portrait of a Lady, 182
posing, pseudoacademic, effete, 242
Postman, The, 259
poststructuralism, 13, 125
Pournelle, Jerry, 152
Powers, Tim, 174
"Present for Pat, A," 75, 80-1
"Preserving Machine, The," 55
"Prize Ship, " 49, 73
"Profession of Science Fiction, The," 168
"Progeny," 59, 74
"Project: Earth," 66-7, 77-8
"Prominent Author," 73, 77
psi, 198, 202-06, 212, 215-18, 223, 227-30, 234, 235, 241, 255
Psi-Fi, 217, 219, 227
"Pursuit of Miracles, A," 204
Pym, Barbara, 197, 220
Pynchon, Thomas, 210, 224, 229
Quatermass Experiment, The, 48
"Queen of the Afternoon, The," 29
Queer Theory, 13
"R & R," 211
Rabkin, Eric, 143
RB (Russell Blackford), 244-48
reactionary, 112, 144-48, 150, 151-52, 164, 171-75, 183, 186-89
"Real Science Fiction, The," 258
Realism, 93, 100-05, 108
Rediscovery of Man, The, 26
Rickman, Gregg, 44, 59, 60
Riddley Walker, 173
"Ridge Running," 19
Rimbaud, Arthur, 29
Road to Xanadu, The, 162
Robinson, Kim Stanley, 12, 18, 19
Robinson, Spider, 115
robots, 27, 31, 34, 59, 74-5, 78, 81
Roger's Version, 264
"Roog," 44, 52, 57, 79

Rorschach Blot Tests, 95
Rottensteiner, Franz, 195
Rousseau, Yvonne, 15, 33, 128, 160, 202, 215
Russ, Joanna, 130, 151, 153, 174, 189
Russell, Eric Frank, 130, 217
Rybczynski, Witold, 197
Satanic Verses, The, 205
Savage Mind, The, 125
Scanner Darkly, A, 41
Schmoo, 45-6
Science Fiction Chronicle, 196
"Science Fiction in the 1970s," 164
Scientific Meliorism and the Evolution of Happiness, 141
sci-fi, 12, 13, 217, 219, 227
Scott, Sir Walter, 136
Sea and Summer, The, 218, 266
"Second Variety," 48, 52, 57-8, 68-9, 72-4
sercon, 12
Serling, Rod, 73
SFWA, 246
Shakers, 166
Shepard, Lucius, 12, 200-09, 215, 217-20, 224, 227-40, 248, 250-56
Shiner, Lewis, 199, 200, 219, 223, 225
"Short Happy Life of the Brown Oxford, The," 56
Shrinking Man, The, 56
Silverberg, Robert, 156, 195-96, 245-46
Singh, Kirpal, 44
Sister Kate, 256
skiffy, 11-4, 221, 223, 226, 230
"Skull, The," 52, 73
Slusser, George, 143
"Small Town," 76-7
Smith, Cordwainer, 22-32
Snyder, Gary, 131
Solar Lottery, 82
"Some Kinds of Life," 58, 78
Songs from the Stars, 145
"Sound of Thunder, A," 93
South Australia, 135, 139
Spence, Catherine Helen, 72, 128-41
Spinrad, Norman, 58, 145, 152, 195-6, 245-6
"Stability," 44, 56-7, 77
Stapledon, Olaf, 265
Star of the Unborn, 145
Star Trek, 195
Star Wars, 195

Stars My Destination, The, 14
static in time, utopias as, 144, 172
Stellar Gauge, The, 44
Stone, Robert, 156, 200
Stoppard, Tom, 265
Storm Warnings, 143, 160
"String of Days, A," 168
stroon, 24, 27
Sun Yat Sen, 25
"Sunstruck Forest, The," 60
"Surface Raid, A," 63-6, 70, 74
"Survey Team," 63
Swanwick, Michael, 194, 198
Swastika Night, 115
synergy, 55
Talbot, Norman, 22, 171, 249, 251, 253
teenager, more to life than being a, 247
Tehanu, 137, 256
Telzey Amberdon, 204
Ten Little Niggers, 69
Thing (from Another World), The, 48
"Think Blue, Count Two," 29-30
Thomson, Helen, 129, 135, 140
"Those Who Walk Away from Omelas" [erroneous title], 146
"Those Who Walk Away from Omelets," 146, 178
Tighe, Margaret, 114
time travel, 53-4, 72, 199, 225, 262
Timescape, 164, 254
Tiptree, Jr., James (Alice Sheldon), 151, 189
"To Read *The Dispossessed*," 147
To the High Castle, 60
To the Is-land, 141
Todorov, Tzvetan, 124, 226
Tolkien, J.R.R., 253
Tolley, Michael J., 41, 44
Tolstoy, 147-48, 166, 183
Tomorrow and Tomorrow and Tomorrow, 130, 141
Trollope, Anthony, 197, 220, 221
"Trouble with Bubbles, The," 77, 79
Turner, George, 171, 202, 209-19, 227-35, 239, 244, 249-53, 258
Twilight Zone, 73
Ubik, 54, 60, 79, 80
Underpeople, The, 23, 26-8
Unger, Roberto Mangabeira, 158
Updike, John, 264, 265
USA, 13, 166, 169, 180, 184, 188

USSR, 29, 180, 183-85, 192
utopia, 33, 56, 74, 128-89
utopia, ambiguous, 161
utopias, feminist, 150, 151, 166, 170
utopias, socialist, 166
van Vogt, A. E., 68, 118
Vaneglory, 204
"Variable Man, The," 49, 53
Varley, John, 114
"Venice Drowned," 19
Vietnam war, 98-9, 203, 210-11, 226, 240
Wagner, Richard, 55
Wakefield, Edward Gibbon, 139
Walk to the End of the World, 188
"War No. 81-Q*," 29
War of Jenkins' Ear, 210
War Year, 203, 233
Waste Land, The, 261
Watchmen, 12, 84-108
Webb, Janeen, 12, 109, 253
Week in the Future, A, 128-29, 141
Weldon, Fay, 232
Wells, H. G., 64, 265
Werfel, Franz, 145
"Who Goes There?", 48
Wild Shore, The, 18
Williams, Paul, 44
Wizard, 114
Wolfe, Gary K., 23
Wolfe, Gene, 121, 255
Wolk, Anthony, 60
Woman on the Edge of Time, 151, 188
Wood, Susan, 13
World Conference on the Changing Atmosphere, The, 124
"World She Wanted, The," 77
Wright, Austin Tappan, 128-35, 141
Wright, Sylvia, 128, 141
Years of the City, The, 152
Yes, Minister, 137
Zamyatin, Yevgeny, 173
Zebrowski, George, 55
Zindell, David, 255
Zweig, George, 94

www.ingramcontent.com/pod-product-compliance
Lightning Source LLC
Chambersburg PA
CBHW032103090426
42743CB00007B/215